THEN CAME BRAIN DAMAGE

THEN CAME

Life (?) **BRAIN**

after **DAMAGE**

Pro

Football

Alex Hawkins

LONGSTREET PRESS
Atlanta, Georgia

Published by
LONGSTREET PRESS, INC.
2150 Newmarket Parkway
Suite 102
Marietta, Georgia 30067

Copyright © 1991 by Alex Hawkins

All rights reserved. No part of this book may be reproduced in any form or by any means without the prior written permission of the Publisher, excepting brief quotes used in connection with reviews, written specifically for inclusion in a magazine or newspaper.

Printed in the United States of America

1st printing, 1991

Library of Congress Catalog Number 91-91941

ISBN: 1-56352-013-3

This book was printed by R. R. Donnelley & Sons, Harrisonburg, Virginia. The text was set in Clearface by Typo-Repro Service, Inc., Atlanta, Georgia.

Design by Jill Dible.
Jacket photo copyright © 1991 by Tommy Thompson

DEDICATION

I have written this book with the hope of sustaining myself and immortalizing some of my friends for the truly unique characters they are.

What would life be like without friends? They are the reason this journey is worthwhile, because life is for sharing and your friends are the ones you share it with.

I've been extremely lucky. I've got more good friends than anyone I know. So I dedicate this book to good friends, and they know who they are . . . those who stood by me and never said no when I needed them, those who helped me help myself.

And a special thanks to Louis Rubin for allowing me the opportunity to be read. God bless you all.

INTRODUCTION

Let me tell you a story. It's about a young boy who grew up in West Virginia. His name is Alex Hawkins, but everyone called him "Iron Head." He was mule-headed and proud. He wouldn't listen to anyone. He had to do everything his way.

There were but three things he enjoyed in life: sports, girls, and movies. Every Saturday he went to the theater and watched a double feature. But every other day he was in somebody's yard playing whatever sport was in season.

People took an interest in him because he was so little, yet so competitive. He cried every time he lost. He was too small to ever have a future in athletics, but you couldn't tell him that. It was football in the fall, basketball in the winter, and baseball in the spring and summer. All he wanted to do was play. He was a dreamer, an incurable romantic, but everybody liked him because he could laugh about anything.

His was a separate reality. The only way he could feature himself was being a famous actor or football player. It was sports in the daytime and girls at night. Girls always liked him. They all seemed to want to mother him as if he were a child.

He was a pretty fair student until his junior year in high school when he finally started to grow. After that, it was all sports. And he got pretty good at them. He started thinking like a jock and acting like a jock.

And being a jock isn't all bad. For one thing, you get immediate acceptance from your peers. No one expects much from you, so when you claim you can't do something, someone is always willing to do it for you. There is always a cheerleader or majorette who will take your exam or write your term paper. And if all else fails, your teacher will grade you leniently or just give you a C so you'll be eligible for the homecoming game.

Secondly, people just naturally admire your physical prowess. You generally get your pick of the ladies, and nobody calls you a dumb jock to your face for fear of being hit.

And if you're a good enough jock, the rules that others abide by don't apply to you.

And you don't have to be dumb to be a jock; you just have to act dumb. So you can let your mind get lazy, and, like water, you can follow the path of least resistance.

1

And you're an automatic member of the most exclusive fraternity in school: the Letterman's Club.

People are, by nature, pretty kind to the poor dumb jocks and want to help them. So the poor dumb jocks let them and it makes both parties happy.

In his senior year, Alex was an outstanding, happy-go-lucky jock. Good enough, in fact, for a football scholarship to the University of South Carolina. There he fell in line with a lot of other slap-happy jocks from several other states and rose to the top of the ranks. Many will tell you he was about as goofy as anyone who ever attended that school. But he played football well enough that they kept him eligible until after the final game of his senior year. Then he was thrown off campus for not attending classes. This glimpse into the reality of the world did not even phase him.

Instead, he was rewarded by being the Green Bay Packers' second-round pick in the 1959 draft, the thirteenth player selected overall. Since the average salary in the NFL back then was $9,000, his $11,000 contract made him the second-highest-paid player on the Packer team. This was more money than he had ever dreamed of. He was rich. So he married the cheerleader and homecoming queen and went on with his charmed life.

Vince Lombardi didn't find him that talented or charming and traded him to the Baltimore Colts. The Colts were World Champions that year and he pocketed an additional $8,000.

At twenty-one years old he had already realized his richest dreams. He was a professional jock! Less than two percent of college players ever made it in the pros and he was one of them.

Back then, players were cautioned that football was a means to an end, not an end in itself. About half of the veteran players were working in the off-season preparing themselves for life after football. They sold beer, whiskey, insurance, whatever, and some even started their own businesses. Not Alex; he was doing exactly what he wanted, playing football in the fall and just playing in the off season.

Over the next six years, he played for the Colts, first under Weeb Ewbank and then Don Shula. Football was his vocation and avocation. Colt owner Carroll Rosenbloom was concerned about his future and offered to finance him in the business of his choice. "No, sir," he replied, "Football is my business and when I'm through with that, I'll throw myself into something else with the same enthusiasm."

And while he was rarely a starting player, he was a student of the game. He played five different positions for the Colts and was a team captain.

But in 1966 the over-achiever in him won out and he asked to be sent to the expansion Atlanta Falcons so he could be a starter. His wishes were granted and he moved his family of three to Atlanta.

In his entire athletic career, he had never played on a losing team. He was miserable with the Falcons and had numerous run-ins with the management. He was traded back to the Colts and played his last two years there.

In the ten years he played pro football, he had never taken a job or looked into a business. But he never had a worry or a doubt about his future. Although his top salary had been $23,000, he had always gotten by. Football was the only thing he knew, cared about, or ever made a dime at.

So at age thirty-two with a jock mentality and a future that was grim but certain, he retired from football and took a job as color man for the Falcon football network. The job paid only $3,500 a year. The outlook for this career was as dark as the inside of a wolf's stomach and . . .

"Wait a minute, wait a minute, I don't like the way you're telling this! I'm Alex Hawkins. It's my story. Let me tell it.

"Most of what that narrator told you is true, but I'm a new guy now. I'm a big boy and I'm ready to tackle the real world. I took the radio job with WQXI because I'm a little bit leery of life without football. I love the game and I know a lot about it. I don't know a lot about broadcasting, but it can't be that difficult. Frank Gifford does it and so does Pat Summerall.

"Besides, Norm Van Brocklin is coaching the Falcons, and I've always enjoyed him. Some say he's nuts, but he sure is colorful, and he damn well speaks his mind. He and I are a lot alike, and it's going to be fun traveling with him."

3

1

I made it through my first Falcon game well enough. I interrupted the play-by-play man, Jack Hurst, a few times, talked into a commercial, coughed into the microphone, but nothing worse than that.

Our second game was in Boston against the Patriots. I, now in the real world, was reading something besides the sports page. Two minutes remained in the second quarter when I announced that my half-time guest would be Ted Kennedy. This was just one month after his accident with Mary Jo Kopechne at Chappaquiddick.

At halftime I apologized for Kennedy's delay in arriving. I explained that he was having problems getting across "some" bridge.

This was cruel and insensitive, but try to understand — I didn't think; I just talked. I hadn't been out of my jock strap but a month and a half.

Our next game was in Washington. Vince Lombardi was now head coach of the Redskins. During a break in the action, Lombardi had asked to speak to one of the officials. Jack turned to me and asked what they might be discussing. I told him that the referee was probably asking the "little dago" what he should do.

Again, horrible taste *and* poor judgement, but I had grown up ... make that ... was reared in West Virginia in the 1940s and early 1950s. West Virginia was a melting pot of ethnic groups and nationalities. During that period, it was common to tease people about their origins. People were just not sensitive or thin-skinned about those matters back then. The same was true in

Baltimore during the 1960s, but probably even more so. I did not have a clue that the world was changing.

The following week in New Orleans, I thought it would be cute to tell a few Polish jokes. Later, I compounded matters by referring to Colonel Sanders as a bearded Man from Glad. I added that his hands were probably greasy. God help me, without knowing it, I featured myself a stand-up comedian. Colonel Sanders was one of our major sponsors.

The last preseason game was in Canton, Ohio. There was no space in the press box for our radio team, so they had built a small wooden structure in the grandstands. It couldn't accommodate chairs, so we had to stand up for four hours to do the game.

My halftime guest was Artie Donovan. Artie was an old teammate of mine who had been inducted into the Hall of Fame the year before.

If you've seen Artie on "The David Letterman Show," you know how funny he is. You may also know he is one of the most wonderful, but irreverent Irishmen ever to come out of the Bronx.

Artie is a storyteller supreme, but many of his stories are "locker room" or ethnic. Well, Artie went on for almost thirty minutes with his "wops, spicks, spades, and kikes," sprinkling in several GD's or "Christ as my Witness."

Monday in Atlanta, I received a call from WQXI station manager Jerry Blum. Jerry very calmly asked me if I could stop by the station and chat for awhile.

When I walked into his office, he handed me a list of five topics he wanted to go over with me. First was the Ted Kennedy thing followed by the Vince Lombardi bit. He explained to me that there were some things that were better left unsaid and other things that were *never* said.

Then he handed me a letter from the mother of a Polish child in Atlanta. In it she described how her son had come home from school crying because some kids had teased him with the *exact* Polish jokes I had told on the air. As for Colonel Sanders, Jerry explained—with considerable disgust—that of all the sins in broadcasting, you *never*, but *never* make fun of a sponsor. Jerry didn't hold me responsible for Donovan's monologue, but he did caution me about being more careful in the future.

My relationship with the Falcons, which at one time had been strained, was going smoothly. Owner Rankin Smith was going out of his way to be nice to me. He was trying to like me and I was starting to like him. By hiring the Dutchman, he had proven to me that he wanted to win, and he was staying out of the Dutchman's way. Everyone was!

Socially, Rankin and I were mixing well. His friends had become my friends and I fished with him and his oldest son. Returning from Kansas City, Rankin and I had flown on to Bimini in his new private Falcon jet and stayed a couple of days at his house there, and he took the opportunity to introduce me to bone fishing.

I was a little surprised that I didn't miss playing. For the past eighteen years that was all I had ever done on fall weekends, and somehow being close to the game made me still feel a part of it. I had played with and against most of these Falcons just the year before. I was considered by coaches and players around the league as a peer. They didn't look at me as a media person or an old man. I was still one of them . . . nothing had changed in my life.

The Falcons had a fantastic draft that year. Norm Van Brocklin, never timid, had taken complete control of the organization. He made all decisions and was the final word in all departments. Drafting, travel, scheduling, whatever, no one questioned his judgement. He was much feared and rightly so. His very presence put white caps on an aquarium. Why? Let me take a minute to tell you.

On March 15, 1926, Norm Van Brocklin was born in Eagle Butte, South Dakota. His father, a watchmaker by trade, would never again see a clock with a stranger tick.

Three years after his birth, the New York Stock Exchange collapsed and sent our nation into the Great Depression. By the time Norm started school, the Dust Bowl had ravaged our central plains. In 1941 the Japanese bombed Pearl Harbor and we were at war. Norm Van Brocklin, just fifteen years old, would be blamed for all three of these national calamities by someone or another.

When Norm was just a child, his father moved his family of ten to Walnut Grove, California. When asked why they had not gone on to Oakland or San Francisco, Norm replied, "That's where we ran out of gas."

Norm played high school ball, but was expelled in his senior year for striking a teacher. The school came up with a plan whereby he could be reinstated. Norm refused the plan because it included an apology. Instead, he joined the Navy and spent two years in the South Pacific.

After his discharge from the service, he enrolled at the University of Oregon where he made All-American, married his biology teacher, finished four years of academic work in three, and signed a contract with the Los Angeles Rams.

That was Norm Van Brocklin. The Dutchman, he was called, for his stubborn ways. He was hardheaded, talented, strong-willed, and abrasive. Norm Van Brocklin had no idols; he was his own hero.

There was no middle ground with the Dutchman. Everything was black or white. You were either solidly behind him or you were against him. You were his devoted friend or his hated enemy, sometimes both in the same day. His moods were volatile, his patience thin, and his tongue was quick and barbed. His hatred for the press was legendary. When asked what he would do when he retired, he shot back, "Become a sportswriter like you idiots." If Dutch had been ambassador to Switzerland, they would no longer be neutral. He loved to argue and would take either side.

But as a player, he could only be described as a winner. Sharing the quarterbacking with Bob Waterfield, he won conference championships with the Rams in 1949 and 1950 and the World Championship in 1951.

His throwing skills were unsurpassed. He could hit a helmet six out of ten times from sixty yards. He once put forty-one points on the scoreboard in a single quarter. His 554 passing yards in one game is still a record.

Norm was traded to the Eagles in 1958 and took them to a World Championship in 1960. He is the only man to ever beat Vince Lombardi in a Championship game. But that is where it seemed to stop.

In 1961, he became the first head coach of the Minnesota Vikings. In six years as coach of the Vikings, he managed but one winning season. He was fired after the 1966 campaign.

Out of work and too proud to accept an assistant coaching job, Norm signed on with CBS as a color analyst for the 1967 season.

That was doomed to failure as Norm had long ago declared war with the media. His one-year broadcasting career came to a climax when he threw league commissioner Pete Rozelle head first into a trash barrel in New York.

Three games into the 1968 season, Norb Hecker was fired in Atlanta. The Dutchman was called in to take charge of the Falcons. By this time, Norm was a known quantity. The smart people knew that the Dutchman would not only bark . . . he would bite.

It was not like Idi Amin had arrived in town, but it was not altogether unlike it either. "It's my way or the highway" was his motto, and he meant it. In Minnesota, he had gone through more personnel than the manager of a car wash.

The Dutchman had always considered himself a winner. He knew the game and fancied himself a brilliant strategist. The problem was, he could no longer play and he had failed to find a quarterback with *his* particular skills and talents. He could not find a body that would house his brain. He longed for an extension of himself on the field. Fran Tarkenton had not been that man, for in most ways Fran was a total opposite. It's useless to explain any further.

The Dutchman managed to win two games that year. By the summer of 1969, he was ready to start putting his mark on the poor old Atlanta Falcons.

From top to bottom, things were changing. New coaches, new trainers, secretaries and players. Only five original Falcons remained. Dutch was fashioning this team in his own image. His players would be tough, disciplined, clean cut young men whose respect for the game would be equal to his.

The Dutchman and I were getting along fine. I had been *his* kind of a player. Tough, hard hitting, two fisted, and stand up. I played hurt.

9

He invited me to watch films with him and I did. He invited me to drink with him, and I did . . . and did . . . and did. Our likes and dislikes were similar. Neither of us liked communists, orientals, homosexuals, unions, change, long hair, earrings, bell bottoms, Democrats, Volkswagens, quarterbacks who scramble, and most of all, *losing*.

Dutch hated Russians because not only were they Communists, they were stupid. While serving in the South Pacific, he traded them his peanuts for their vodka.

He disliked Volkswagens and *hated* the people who drove them.

Dutch said if you wanted to wear bell bottoms, "go join the Navy." If you liked long hair, "go work in the league office." If you wanted to wear earrings, "have a sex change."

We only differed on two major issues. I liked sportswriters and he didn't. I thought Johnny Unitas was the greatest quarterback who ever lived. Dutch had somebody else in mind.

The 1969 season rocked along well for both of us. WQXI was delighted with my work. We were picking up new stations, and the number of listeners had increased. New sponsors were signing on and the price was going up. I, personally, was developing a following. People started bringing radios to the games to hear what Jack and I had to say. This light, candid, whimsical new style was refreshing, and it was catching on. People watching the games on television were turning off the network audio and listening to us on the radio. Sponsors were filling our broadcast booth for home games. The four salesmen at the station and I were having drinks a couple of times a week. I had been pretty well celebrated as a player but my popularity now far exceeded that.

Van Brocklin seemed to be turning things around. He wound up winning six games that year. That matched the number of wins recorded by the Falcons for the three previous years. Even better, they had won the last three games.

Two weeks later, Rankin promoted Van Brocklin to general manager and moved his accountant, Frank Wall, in as president. Rankin became chairman of the board.

2

There are only two seasons to an athlete. There is The Playing Season and The Off-Season. It was clear that I could not live on the $3,500 I was being paid for the Falcon games, so in the off-season of 1970 I went commercial.

Jerry Blum had become something of a father figure to me, so I went to him for career counseling. He suggested I concentrate on my commercial value. I immediately asked him for a raise.

I had been paid $175 a game and I asked that my salary be increased to $500. We settled on $250, but he agreed to employ me at the station doing one-minute sports vignettes for an additional $125. WQXI was the hottest station in town, and he explained the exposure would be good for both of us. I had a free hand as to subject matter and content, and I could tape all five shows in the same day. He then steered me over to a local television station and I did the same for them. The TV job paid $150 and gave me even more exposure.

I found a producer and we put together a Falcon highlight show for a Monday night review of the previous game. Falcon players were to be guests on my show. I personally sold the show to BP Oil Company and would make $200 a week hosting it that fall. It would be hard to count all this money as fast as it was going to be rolling in. I did commercials for a local car dealer, and he furnished me a car.

I started representing a brick company and took on a line of sliding-glass doors. I was becoming a virtual conglomerate.

Sports Illustrated featured me in a two-part article . . . . I was upset that I wasn't on the cover. I signed with an agent to further promote myself. I was fast becoming the most talked about man on Peachtree Street.

It wasn't long before Jerry Blum called me into his office. "Alex, I want to talk to you about something, and I hope you'll take it as it is intended. I may be wrong but I'm afraid you're starting to believe your own bullshit. It's okay to tell people that you're the last word in sports, but for God's sake, don't you start believing it."

"What do you mean by that?" I struck back.

"Alex, if you don't know what I'm talking about, I can't explain it. I have nothing more to say on the subject, but I hope you'll give it some thought."

I had just been given the best advice I could ever receive in journalism and I didn't even know what Jerry was saying.

I loved being a celebrity in the football world. I could not envision it ever ending. I had no fear that it would.

An athlete learns to deal with many kinds of fear. Fear of injury is one kind you simply cannot afford. You accept and dismiss it at the same time. You never even discuss it. Fear of failure or letting your teammates down is always with you. Only the superstars avoid that. People like John Unitas, Jim Brown, or Dick Butkus didn't seem to fear failure. I wonder if they did? I sure did. Fear of failure was so pronounced in me that, God as my witness, I used to tag every team prayer with "Lord, don't let me get hurt, and please Lord, don't let me fuck up."

But, at this point at least, I had no fear of life after football. I was having a hell of a time in the "real" world. During the season I was traveling to all the major cities in the country. I was staying in the finest hotels, and dining at the best restaurants. I was more celebrated than ever before, and I had no bed check.

In the off-season I was enjoying the company of my wealthy Buckhead friends. Buckhead is an area in northwest Atlanta that is home to the rich and social—the old, established families who were socially and politically prominent. I had access to the Piedmont Driving Club and, as I was not a member, could not pay for a thing. The Buckhead Boys and I were touring three or four states playing golf on the weekends. It was all I could do to keep up with them financially, but they were my closest friends and, damn, they were fun. Now, fun is something that I've never run away from, and sooner or later some of their money was bound to rub off on me.

Sure enough, one day that spring I got a call from Bubba Mason. Bubba was in the idea business. By that, I mean he was in the premium promotions business. He developed giveaway games as traffic builders for oil companies.

While Bubba was not a football fan, he was intrigued by the growth and popularity of pro ball. He reasoned that if we could develop a comprehensive football game cheap enough to allow oil companies to give it away, they would be fighting for the rights to it.

In 1969, the oil business was very competitive, and the only inducements to fill up with brand X were coffee mugs and drinking glasses. There were only two or three football games on the market, and they were far above the prescribed price of twelve cents.

Bubba showed me the numbers on what a game could potentially generate in dollars, and the payout was staggering. It was a slick concept, clearly worth my valuable time. His job was to produce the game for under twelve cents. My job was to: a) get Johnny Unitas to endorse it; b) sophisticate the game and make it authentic; and c) to sell it.

Bubba knew the oil business and was brilliant with numbers, but he was shy and uncertain of his sales ability. He stuttered when he was nervous. He didn't exactly stutter; he stammered. His mouth couldn't keep up with his mind. He liked me, but I made him real nervous. He trusted me, but he could not overlook my somewhat erratic work habits. My flip attitude and flaky demeanor added to his anxieties.

I told him he had a partner. I picked up the phone and called Unitas. I told John what I needed and explained that we couldn't promise him anything but as a favor I needed his name and pictures. I also added that I might need him for a commercial and to make a sales call with me in Chicago. I was asking the biggest name in the history of the game to do all this for me as a favor, *for nothing*. Do you know what he said?

"Sure, Whitey, whatever you need. It's better than having you move in with me."

I put Bubba on the phone with John for confirmation.

Bubba couldn't believe it. He hung up the phone and said, "I . . . I . . . we've . . . we've . . . look . . . I've got to . . . have . . . you know . . . something . . . something . . . in writing. I . . . I . . . mean . . . you know . . . to . . . to . . . make it legal."

I just sat there laughing. Bubba was in total shock.

Seizing the moment, I phoned Don Shula, who had just joined the Dolphins. I told him the same story and asked the same favor. This time I said that we needed it in writing.

"Sure, Hawk," he replied, "anything to help you." We received his permission on a stained cocktail napkin a couple of days later.

Bubba was dumbfounded, completely paralyzed. He just sat in his chair, staring at the floor, shaking his head.

"Don't you people do things like that for each other in the real world?" I asked.

He stared at the floor for a moment and then answered, "Well . . . well . . . no, no we don't."

I wonder if players and coaches still help each other today? I hope so. They've missed a lot if they don't.

We were on a tight budget and we couldn't afford a prototype so we had to sell the idea, not the actual game. We sold 310,000 games to Murphy Oil, Gulf, and Crown Petroleum on a test basis.

The promotion didn't do as well as we had hoped, so we missed the big payday. It seems that, back then, women bought most of the gas and women preferred glasses and coffee mugs over football games.

Also, the sad truth is that my only sale of bricks netted me just $800. And it is an even sadder truth that I had been completely shut out as a sliding-glass door salesman but, honestly, there was not much glamour in the building business. Once again, I was looking forward to the start of another football season.

My first Falcon highlight show was pretty ragged, but nobody panicked. I was told that was to be expected. The next two shows were no better. Fortunately, the show was new to the Atlanta market so they had nothing to compare it with. Besides, I owned the show so they couldn't fire me. I had always used a teleprompter on TV, but you couldn't teleprompt a half-hour show. It never occurred to me that I wouldn't improve. I never suspected that hosting a show of this kind required *talent*.

My biggest concern was the sports vignettes. Ten shows a week was putting a strain on me. I was running out of topics. I had long since been writing about things I was ignorant of, but I had my opinion. That, in itself, created controversy, and controversy carries an audience. Damn, man, I was in show business.

In October, former heavyweight champion Muhammad Ali came to Atlanta to fight Jerry Quarry. Ali had been stripped of his title for refusing induction into the armed services. He had not been allowed to fight in the ring for three years. A fight of this magnitude was big news in Atlanta. Ali was news all over the world.

Blind patriotism was still very much in vogue in 1969, and *most* of America still supported the war in Vietnam. The very idea of allowing Ali to fight in the ring when he would not fight for his country had me up in arms.

I considered myself a color analyst when working the Falcon games, but now that I was on television and writing my own scripts, I featured myself a full-blown journalist. Of course, I had no notion of what journalism implied. I was ignorant of the Moslem faith, knew little of Ali, and the war in Vietnam was just that . . . war was war and a draft dodger was a draft dodger. In addition, people didn't go around changing their names. It was just that simple to me. I denounced the fight and Ali with great passion and enthusiasm.

The day after my piece had run on TV, I was ringside at Ali's gym along with my "fellow reporters" and media people. One of Ali's people had mentioned that Ali was not happy with me.

Ali was standing in the ring looking down on the assemblage and holding court as only Ali could do. Suddenly his eyes fixed on mine and stayed there as he fielded questions for fifteen or twenty minutes. His eyes never left mine as I tried to play the game of stare-down. It was a mismatch. I had never felt the presence and power of a man like that. I felt like a child. What unbelievable confidence. What an incredible man! As a football player I always felt pretty macho, but as an opponent of Ali's, I was a total fool. I was relieved when the press conference ended. I could now let *him* go!

The Dutchman was making fair but not great progress with his young team. Then suddenly in November, the wheels came off. Up until then he had been fun to be around. He hadn't made friends with the press, make no mistake about that, but he didn't treat *me* like the rest of the media.

Each week I would go to him and ask about his game plan. He would state his intention openly and honestly. Sometimes I would question the sanity of his decisions, but always in a light-hearted fashion — like, "Do you think that's smart?" He would good-naturedly but resolutely answer with, "By God, we'll find out."

Sometimes the Dutchman was so stubborn he would overlook the subtleties of tactics to prove an unprovable point. One day in November, after he had called the same play nine times in a row, without success, I made the mistake of laughing about it over the air. That was the wrong thing to do.

The following Tuesday I was approached by a Falcon player who informed me that he could no longer be seen talking to me. Neither could any other Falcon. In a team meeting, Dutch announced that "Every city has a former player who whores himself by joining the media." In Atlanta that whore was me. It was a $500 fine for being seen with me. Five hundred dollars was a price greater than they cared to pay.

No one escaped the fury of the Dutchman for long. I had seen it before and it was my turn now. I was the newest member of his "hate" club. Norm Van Brocklin gave a new meaning to the word *hate*. In a sense it was an honor because you knew you were being hated by the best. It was useless to try to out-hate the Dutchman. He hated with beauty, passion, and great originality.

I rode on Rankin's private plane to avoid that cold, venomous look in the Dutchman's eyes, and since the Falcons lost five of their last six games, I was doubly relieved. I continued to speak to Norm when we happened upon each other, but he never spoke back.

Even though the Falcons were losing, it did not diminish my

popularity or listening audience. I was more popular and talked about than ever. But the same could not be said for my other work. The Falcon highlight show, which never improved, was cancelled for lack of public interest.

I tired, ran out of bullshit, and quit doing my sports vignettes on both radio and television.

My agent resigned over a conflict of interest.

The car dealer cancelled and recalled the car after my second wreck. It was my first peek at the real world, and I still couldn't see it.

3

New Year's Eve of 1971 was no different than any other night. Every day was the 4th of July and every night was New Year's Eve to me.

I was thirty-four years old and still looking for my niche in life. Most people my age had already established themselves in a business and had ten or twelve years experience in their field. I figured I had one advantage over all of them. I was Alex Hawkins. I was still a hot property. My phone number was unlisted.

We had bought a home in a nice neighborhood in 1967. My wife, Libby, had done a great job raising our two children, Steele, eleven, and Elizabeth, nine. I gave her full responsibility. Both children attended private schools, as did most of the neighbors' children.

Libby is from Manning, South Carolina, a small town of 4,000, sixty-three miles southeast of Columbia. It would be wise for any man looking for a wife to give this area serious consideration. Women from this part of the country are . . . well . . . tolerant.

Libby and I first met while in school at the University of South Carolina. She had been an honor student, beauty queen, cheerleader and Homecoming Queen. At five feet, ninety-two pounds, she was the nicest, sweetest, cutest, most popular and sought-after girl on campus. She talked me into marriage in our fourth year of school.

Libby was one of those rare people who had no enemies. She was a threat to no one. She was friendly and warm, honest and loyal, faithful and devoted, polite and intelligent, understanding and kind. She had a strong moral code and religious conviction that she kept to herself. A good cook and an impeccable house-keeper, she dotted all i's and crossed all t's. She had her act together long before I met her.

Libby was naturally popular with the neighbors. It was a nice neighborhood of doctors, lawyers, dentists, accountants and an assortment of white collar salesmen and businessmen. These were settled, responsible, law-abiding citizens, too tame for me to run around with. It was rumored that Libby had a husband, but few ever saw me. Our hours simply did not coincide. I was coming home when they were going to work.

My transition from the football field to the real world was admittedly poor. This disturbed Libby, but she neither nagged nor complained. She knew she had married a child to begin with and figured that sooner or later I would come around to maturity just as the children had.

It was hard not to make money in this city. Every friend I had was rich or well on his way to being so. There was no rush to grow up or take life seriously. The adage was, "It doesn't matter what you do until you're thirty, because you'll probably screw it up anyway."

Jimmy Orr's restaurant was our hangout. We gathered there every day for lunch. This was home for the Buckhead Boys as well as the new movers and shakers who were molding this city. Syndications were big at that time. A group of investors at one table would put together a deal, add on some profit and sell it to another group at the next table. They, in turn, would tack on additional profit and sell it to another group across the room. Banking practices were liberal at the time, so financing was rarely a problem. It was a great time in Atlanta; everyone was making money . . . and spending it!

One afternoon a friend of mine came bouncing into the restaurant, slapped me on the back, and sat down. His name was Peek Garlington and, technically, he was in the insurance business. Peek was in about a dozen businesses, but was always looking for a new opportunity. Peek could sell sand to the Saudis.

"Hawk," he said, "you and I are going into the heating and air conditioning business."

"What? I don't know anything about the air conditioning business, and you don't either."

"That doesn't matter," he said. "It's simple. Look around you. This restaurant is filled with the biggest builders in the Southeast. And we know them all. I just talked to a guy in New Jersey who's a genius. He's developed a new heating and cooling system that's going to revolutionize the industry. Here's the deal. We get the specs and plans and send them to New Jersey. His people lay it out, cost it out and we get the commission. It's a cinch; don't worry about nothing. We're going up to see him tomorrow. I've already got the building specs on some new apartments."

The next day we landed in Newark, rented a car, and drove over to see this "genius." He was a strange little man, capable of genius, I suppose. He walked us through his plant and showed us his operation. We had no idea what he was talking about, so it made perfect sense to us. We thought BTU stood for British Thermal Underwear.

His system had something to do with convection and radiation. Cold or hot water was forced through these copper tubes at the baseboard and ceiling of the room, thus creating the desired room temperature. This was about all I remembered or understood. We handed him the building plans and went to dinner.

During dinner the genius explained that he had just recently developed this system and was looking for sales representation in the southeast. Peek quickly took over and reeled off about forty reasons why we were *his* boys, and the deal was cut. This little man said he had just finished installing his system in a hotel in Jacksonville and if we wanted we could go down and see the finished job.

The next day we strolled boldly up to the desk at the hotel in Jacksonville and asked to see the manager. We proudly announced that we were the new sales reps for the company that installed their new heating and cooling system.

Well sir, you would have thought we had kidnapped his children. The manager started ranting and raving, his face went red, his eyes bulged, and the veins in his neck almost exploded. He started around the desk at us, screaming so loud you could have heard him in Orlando. He cursed us for six solid minutes without repeating himself. We finally got him calmed down enough to explain that this was our first day on the job, so he took us upstairs to one of the rooms and showed us what the new system had done. The walls were peeling, and plaster was all over the floor. There was so much water on the floor, you could have grown rice in the room. The place was a wreck and the building was literally falling apart.

The problem was the system could not handle the amount of condensation created by the hot and cold water running through the tubes. We were out of the heating and cooling business that afternoon.

4

Tactically and from a business standpoint, I could not have made a wiser decision than to move to Atlanta when I did. I was almost thirty years old when I came here and nearing the close of a mediocre career. I had already played six years of pro ball, and, nearing my retirement, it was the perfect city to establish myself in business.

Since its incorporation in 1847, Atlanta had been competing with Birmingham and Charlotte for the title of "The Jewel of the South."

Atlanta had long since been the center of railway and airline transportation, and in the early sixties she stormed out in front, leaving the rest of the Southern cities in her wake. While the rest of the South was "brown bagging," Atlanta legalized alcohol, thereby attracting tourism and convention business. Then with the attention of the nation and the world focused on Martin Luther King and the forced integration in the 1960's, Atlanta had the imagination to coin herself the "City Too Busy to Hate." Shortly thereafter, the first blacks since Reconstruction were elected to public office.

By 1965, Atlanta, with a population of close to a million people, was no longer regarded as a Southern city. It was cosmopolitan. The Great Southwest Corporation expanded its operation into Georgia and opened the Six Flags industrial complex and amusement park, and the following year the Milwaukee Braves became the Atlanta Braves and the NFL awarded the Falcons a franchise. "Hotlanta" was "poppin'."

The old Atlanta power machine, no longer content with moderate but steady growth, started flexing its muscles. Corporations opened regional offices, and Atlanta became the New York of the South. Movers and shakers from all over the country were flocking here. It was a boom town, the Klondike of the South. And, like all boom towns, she got her share of legitimates, grifters, soldiers of fortune, and other speculators who follow the ebb and flow of business opportunity. It was an exciting time to live here. In addition to the native Atlantans who were making money faster than they could spend it, there was an influx of high-rolling out-of-towners who had come to take advantage of these backward southerners.

And that is precisely when I made the acquaintance of Mr. Hunt and Mr. Davees (Dah-vees) and formed such a wonderful and lasting relationship. While we never legally or formally had business dealings, we, nevertheless, referred to ourselves as the old firm of Hunt, Hawkins and Davees.

Generally speaking, the three of us got along quite well. We were not without our differences, but somehow or another we always worked out our problems. Our problems were always the same ... *dominance*. Who was the best leader? Who was the real cock of the roost? All three of us had definite but differing opinions on the subject, so let's go further.

In the animal world there is a definite order of dominance. In a community of chickens, for example, there is what is known as a "pecking order." The rooster pecks anyone he chooses and is never pecked back. Then the number-two chicken pecks the number-three and so on *down* the line. Nobody ever pecks *up*.

Now, as we discuss the members of the old firm, please bear in mind that the only way you can describe human beings is by describing their imperfections. So, if I at any time appear critical, it is only because I want you to know them *intimately.*

First, there is Mr. Hunt, the senior member of the firm. Senior by almost twenty years. He is an enigma, a contradiction in terms. On one hand, he is selfish, offensive, arrogant, pompous, vain, scattered, noncommittal, messy, and crude. He is totally insensitive to other people, but painfully sensitive toward himself. He will go out of his way to tell a dwarf he is short.

He has the patience of a hummingbird. "Knock-knock" jokes

are too long for him. "Let's move right along, Hawkins," he has often said; "we ain't got time to look up a dead horse's ass."

He has the social graces of a terrorist. He will command a nice little seventy-year-old lady with poor posture to "Put those shoulders back and show off those little titties." He also pinches "budding" little girls in training bras to remind them of their growth. Little children he refers to as little bastards or little shits. He dated a one-eyed woman with a patch on her eye and introduced her as "Single-eye." Nothing is sacred with this man, and he will not overlook or fail to point out your most obvious flaws. He is an elderly Fonz and a white Fred Sanford.

On the other hand, he is handsome, talented, stately, witty, charming, wise, crafty, and tenaciously competitive. He is the kind of man who will bet on himself and lose and then bet on himself again, and then again.

And despite what I have told you of his unsocial graces, he is adored by both men, women, and most of all, children. He is the life of every party and brings with him enormous energy and humor. He is a one-of-a-kind, once-in-a-lifetime experience.

Although Freudian by inclination, he is a brilliant conversationalist who can talk on any subject. He eliminates duplicity by getting directly to the point.

Mr. Hunt is not a romantic; he is a realist in the strictest sense of the word. He knows about life because he has experienced so much of it. After enduring the Great Depression in a small Texas town and having fought in World War II, he found it difficult to take life too seriously. He understood and accepted the harsh realities of life. He learned to rely on one person, himself. And he sees things as they are, not as he might like to see them.

He says many things he probably shouldn't say because he is so brutally honest, but he teases out of humor rather than cruelty, and while he appears crude and coarse, he is really very caring. He has a laser wit and a wealth of knowledge. He is a father figure to some and a lovable scoundrel to others. Men admire his honesty and confidence, and women pursue him in numbers. Children delight in his put-on gruffness and see him as a "teddy bear," a child much like themselves.

How dull it would be if we were all alike. How bland and

uneventful each day would be. Mr. Hunt will not harbor the notion of sameness. He views himself the cock of *any* roost. He finds it impossible to play a subordinate role. He constantly pecks everyone around him, but refuses to be pecked. You see, Mr. Hunt loves the person he is and cannot understand why others don't feel that way about themselves. He knows he's not perfect, but he is quite comfortable being the best John Hunt he cares to be. He loves himself, as is, and wants others to love him, as is. It's hard not to love a man who doesn't look down on the person he is.

Mr. Hunt was born in Bowie, Texas. His father was a car dealer until the depression, and then he was forced into doing the very best he could.

John was a middle child. He was a pretty fair athlete for awhile, but two double promotions in school destroyed his chances since he was always smaller than the rest of his class. He graduated from high school at fifteen.

He spent two years in a junior college where he grew tall and handsome and played end on the football team. He enrolled at the University of Texas, but made the mistake of visiting Dallas. In Dallas John discovered women and never returned to Austin. He went home for Christmas and left shortly thereafter for Seattle, hitchhiking with five dollars in his pocket. When he enrolled at the University of Washington, his grandfather wired him $350, which he promptly lost in a poker game the first night on campus.

This fast-talking Texan had no problem getting by. He worked his way through school. His first job was with J.C. Penney's, where he was the leading salesman for the first *half-day* he worked there. At lunch he met a man with Boeing Aircraft and talked his way onto the night shift. Commitment was never one of Mr. Hunt's long suits. He'd rather go to hell with a broken back than make a commitment. Had he been invited, he would not have RSVP'd The Last Supper.

Upon graduating from Washington at the age of nineteen, Mr. Hunt was commissioned as a lieutenant in the Air Force where he served in the South Pacific during World War II. Mr. Hunt was in charge of maintenance of airplanes at the first air base recaptured in the Philippines. Varying reports have surfaced over the years as to catastrophies or near catastrophies suffered at the base under his not so watchful eye. These malicious rumors have all been soundly dispelled by Mr. Hunt.

There is, however, one report confirmed by Mr. Hunt concerning his negligence in regards to burial procedures. It seems he came upon six dead Japanese soldiers lying near his runway. Mr. Hunt has no patience with his friends and even less with the enemy. He ordered a bulldozer to cover them over on the spot. When this was brought to the attention of his superiors, Mr. Hunt was asked, rather rudely, to exhume them immediately.

After his honorable discharge in 1945, Mr. Hunt enrolled in graduate school at the University of Southern California. He attended school on the GI Bill but supplemented his income by working part time at the nearby movie studios as a stand-in actor. He was never awarded a speaking part.

While in California, Mr. Hunt found time to get married, but the union was short-lived. The marriage produced one child but little else. It ended on a Christmas Day. Mr. Hunt woke up that morning under the Christmas tree. The problem was, it was the wrong tree.

After graduation, he went to work for Rheem Manufacturing as sales manager where he tripled his salary in three short years. Now in his late-twenties, he had a firm philosophy of life which was and is ... there are only two things important in life, money and sex, and they are only important when you *don't* have them.

Mr. Hunt was now on his way up and changing companies like shirts. As sales manager with Kraft Container Company in Dallas, John was drawing a high five-figure salary, a lucrative expense account, but perhaps even more significant, he had access to the company airplane, a hundred-foot yacht with a crew of six, a townhouse bachelor pad, and a position of power and dominance over his sales staff.

Mr. Hunt has many mottos, one of which is, "You're not going to get anything if you don't ask for it, and don't take no for an answer." Since Kraft Container was a newly formed company, John reasoned that experienced salesmen might well be intimidated by the larger accounts. The one thing John understood was intimidation, so he hired no salesmen with previous experience in the container business. Instead, he hired nothing but the brashest, most abrasive, young men he could find — men who would not be intimidated.

This included a friend of his from Los Angeles whom we will refer to as "Stumpy." Stumpy had a wife and three girlfriends he was trying to keep up with, along with his sales duties and running around socially with Mr. Hunt. Few men could keep pace with Mr. Hunt and Stumpy was not one of them. Stumpy was burning the candle at both ends, or all "four ends," if you'd rather, and he finally died of a heart attack. Mr. Hunt graciously took care of the funeral arrangements.

Mr. Hunt is not sentimental in regard to death, as evidenced by the Japanese soldiers incident. While John was selecting a proper coffin for Stumpy's funeral, he discovered that an oversized coffin was three hundred dollars more than a regular one. Stumpy was too tall for the regular size coffin, so Mr. Hunt had his feet chopped off at the ankles. I swear to God, his rationale was that since no one would be viewing the lower half of the body, no one would be the wiser, and that the wife needed the money more than Stumpy needed his feet.

All went well with Kraft for awhile. Mr. Hunt was flying all over the country keeping check on his salesmen and giving orders and advice. There is nothing Mr. Hunt would rather do than give orders and advice. The yacht and its crew were getting a pretty good workout, too. The little company was indeed growing, growing so fast, in fact, that the stockholders sold it and fired all of the employees, including Mr. Hunt.

Mr. Hunt was not long in finding work, this time with the W. R. Grace Company. His new position was Vice President of Sales for their San Juan Paper Mills. His territory was worldwide. He commuted back to Dallas on weekends.

Back in Dallas, Mr. Hunt tried his hand at marriage again, this time to a wealthy north Dallas divorcee with three children. She had both money and social status. This marriage, of course, had no chance as Mr. Hunt was no social butterfly and is not fond of children of any description. John is just not the marrying kind. Being a child himself, he wanted the whole stage and the spotlight. The responsibility, routine, and commitment of a weekend marriage soon soured, and it ended around Christmas

Day in 1964. Once again, Mr. Hunt ended up under the wrong tree.

Out of work and short on money, he went to work for The Great Southwest Corporation. The amazing thing about John was that he always managed to secure a position of authority which entailed little or no responsibility. He was given the title of Vice President of Land Acquisition.

He moved to Atlanta with the secret mission of putting together three thousand acres of land for the development of an Industrial and Amusement Park. This was a top secret project and it was accomplished, *almost* without a hitch.

I first met Mr. Hunt at a bar late one night in 1966. You will not find John in a bar early in the evening as he never leaves home until after 10:00 p.m. His strategy is that by arriving late, the bar customers will all be pretty close to drunk when he gets there and he will appear smarter, more polished, and infinitely more clever. He will have to buy fewer drinks for the ladies and also avoid the nuisance of dinner checks.

I had just moved to Atlanta as a member of the Atlanta Falcons. This made me a pretty hot item, but not in the eyes of Mr. Hunt. He recognized me and sauntered over to my bar stool.

"Hawkins, get me a drink," he demanded. "I'm John Hunt, President of Six Flags."

"Hey, John, nice to know you."

"It's Mr. Hunt to you, boy," he smiled.

He was a big, blustering man, six feet three inches tall, about 250 pounds. His pants, not expensive, were plaid. His coat was fashionable, in years gone by. His summer shoes were white but not clean, and he wore no socks. He had a sock stuffed in his coat pocket where a handkerchief should have been. His thinning hair was well combed and his Santa Claus eyebrows shaded his bright blue eyes. He had a beautiful and radiant smile, a firm handshake, and a confident and cocky manner. He was a prominent and imposing figure. He looked as though he was *somebody*. He stood out in the crowd. He had a title, an apartment, a chauffeur, an expense account and a large car, which all Texans seem to drive. While his salary was only $35,000, he acted the part of a millionaire Texan, and he neither admitted nor denied being one of "those" Texas Hunts.

He was forty-nine years old when I met him. Most men that age are mellowing out and settling in to middle age. Not Mr. Hunt. He had the energy and enthusiasm of a seventeen-year-old. He was the eternal teenager.

He had no trepidation about his age. Longevity ran in his genes. His grandfather lived to be ninety-eight, his mother eighty-five.

His Father was seventy-five when he died, and John was at his bedside when he passed away. He had prostate cancer and they had just removed his testicles, but it was his false teeth he was cursing when John entered the room.

"Sit down, boy, I'm glad you could make it. I don't have much time on this earth and I want to talk. Son, I don't have much and I'm leaving the little bit I've got to your mother. All you're getting from me, you've already got, a sense of humor, low cholesterol and a big dick. I wish somehow I could have done more for you, but things just never worked out. Still, I'd like to give you something that you can draw on when things look dark 'cause it ain't always easy in this world. Boy, life ain't always fair. A man should be able to keep his teeth all of his natural life, and his balls should automatically fall off when he reaches the age of seventy-five." With that, he rolled over, went into a coma and never recovered.

5

The third member of the firm is Don Davis, or Mr. Davees, as he is called. Don was born in Atlanta in 1935. He was the only child of a Buckhead dentist. His mother and father were kind, understanding parents. They let Don live his own life. Don was a precocious child. He was bright, strong-willed, and self-motivated. His parents allowed him to make his own decisions. He was a born leader.

Like his father, Don became interested in medicine at an early age. He was visiting the home of a classmate, a girl of seven, when he was discovered under a bed examining her. Don was unaware that their feet were sticking out from under the bed when the patient's mother dragged him out and beat him for practicing without a license. Don never understood why he had been punished for doing something so harmless that felt so good.

This in no way suggests that sex was Don's *only* motivator, but it would have been, in the absence of money. Those were the two things that drove him. He did not covet money as some people do; it was simply a fact that everything that pleased Don was expensive. Happiness drove Don, and women and money put him in bliss.

His was a normal childhood for a Buckhead boy in the 1950s. He was a good student and Boy Scout. He lettered in football and wrestling in high school. He was a lifeguard at the local pool. In those times, the lifeguard usually got his pick of the ladies. All Don wanted was a lifeguard's share of the women.

Upon graduating, Don enrolled at Emory University. Emory

had an excellent medical school, and where there are doctors, there are nurses. Doctors were all "good guys" back then, and everyone knows that nurses help doctors, so Don majored in pre-med and pre-dental and joined the Kappa Alpha Fraternity. He was smart, gregarious, and charming. He had no trouble moving to the front. By his junior year, he had lettered in both football and wrestling and changed his major to political science.

In his senior year, Don was elected president of the student body. He had an office of his own, a room in the dorm, another in the fraternity house and an apartment off campus. He was president of the Athletic Society and sports editor. He worked directly with the deans of the various schools and the president of the university. He had risen to a position of power, and he knew how to use it. He was autonomous.

Upon graduation, he was the obvious number-one draft choice of the major companies but turned them all down. He became disenchanted with them when they talked of health insurance benefits and retirement programs. His health was excellent and retirement was the furthest thing from his mind. Having just turned twenty-one, he was thinking more in terms of building an empire.

He shunned all offers, married a Sweetbriar graduate, and entered law school. While in law school, he supported his wife by selling cars and clothes. He excelled at both. He could take both of your eyes out of your head and convince you that you looked better without them.

He next turned his attention to real estate, having been licensed in his sophomore year. In 1960, with only two years of experience, he won the Cates Award, which was awarded by the Georgia Association of Realtors to the Outstanding Realtor in the state. At age twenty-three, he was the youngest man to have ever won it.

Two years later, the boy wonder figured out that if he was making five percent someone else was making ninety-five. So without further ado, "Little Big Man" formed the D. Davis Company.

Like Mr. Hunt, D. Davis had many mottos, but unlike Mr. Hunt, his were sound and well thought out. His theory on real estate was that if you could reduce your problems to cash, then you had *no* problems. Venture capital was always available to a clever person. OPM, or Other People's Money, was Don's idea of finance. After one year, he was well on his way to that empire.

He built shopping centers and warehouses, office buildings and apartments. Everything he touched turned to gold. OPM was readily available. He was now able to speculate in raw land, which he did, including thirty-six acres west of Atlanta. And that is how he came to meet Mr. Hunt.

One night Don was watching television and they were officially announcing that the Great Southwest Corporation was expanding to Atlanta. The three-thousand acre tract they had purchased was the largest land deal in the history of the city. Crow, Pope and Land had actually put the deal together under the auspices of Mr. Hunt. All the big-wigs of the Great Southwest Corporation had flown in from Dallas to make the official announcement that Six Flags was coming to Georgia.

Don was in bed propped up on a pillow, watching Mr. Hunt going over a map where three thousand acres were blackened, designating the exact location of the Industrial and Amusement Park.

Giving Mr. Hunt a pointer was like giving Cyrano a sword. To begin with, Mr. Hunt is at his best when he is the center of attention. This pointer, as a prop, added to his demeanor, and he was strutting around like a peacock. He loved being interviewed and he handled it well. He was impressing everyone . . . except D. Davis.

Don was lying there quietly grinning. Those dark, darting, beady little eyes were all aglow. Don knew something that John did not yet know. Thirty-six of those three thousand acres blacked out on the map did not belong to Six Flags. Those thirty-six acres in the exact center of what would be the Industrial Park belonged to D. Davis. He had purchased them for a thousand dollars an acre, but the price of land was about to go up!

There is more to the story, it seems. Don Davis did not care for Texans. To his credit, Don was indignant that Atlantans were not developing their own city. And it was true that Atlanta was being developed by Texans. The "real" Hunt boys from the Lone Star State had just finished the Twin Towers office across from

Lenox Square. The bulk of the new apartments was being built by Texans. Don was a proud Buckhead native who strongly resented these interlopers. He was set on testing these Texas blowhards.

Nobody holds a grudge like D. Davis. The next day, he called Mr. Hunt's office and notified them that the thirty-six acres was for sale. Two days later, his call had not been returned. He called again, but when Mr. Hunt was not available, he left word that the price of the land was $79,500 and *non-negotiable*.

The next day, a signed check for $72,500 was couriered over to D. Davis's office. Don sent it back with instructions that the land was now valued at $97,500, and once again it was *non-negotiable*. Mr. Hunt made a grievous mistake. He unwisely countered with an offer of $92,500.

This inflamed "Little Caesar," who when angered or insulted turned into a monster. Don, not always a gracious winner, intended to let these Texans know that a Buckhead boy could also "paint with a wide brush."

Having neither met nor talked with Mr. Hunt, he set a final figure of $109,500 or $30,000 more than his first demand. He then added boldly, "And, by God, this is *non-negotiable*."

When Don received the check from Mr. Hunt, the figure of $109,500 was obscured by the sprawled signature of John C. Hunt. It was signed in both haste and anger, in letters that were about twice the size of John Hancock's.

A week or so later, Don was at a piano bar when he overheard this loud-talking Texan relating this story about how he had been screwed by some no-good little shit named Don Davis. Don sat there with that innocent, naive expression that he assumes when he has mischief on his mind and waited for him to conclude. He then approached Mr. Hunt and extended his hand.

"Mr. Hunt, I'd like to introduce myself. My name is Don Davis."

"So you're the little shit who screwed me out of $30,000?"

"Yes, sir, Mr. Hunt, I certainly am."

They had a Dutch lunch together the next day and have been close friends ever since.

I first met Don at a party at the Peachtree Town Apartments (P.T.A.) in 1966. Don had completed the apartments the year before. They were the first singles-only apartments in the world and were featured in *Time* magazine. I was playing with the Falcons at the time and several of my teammates were living there. They assured me it was *the* place to be, as a party was always in progress. Don Davis saw to that.

Don was just thirty-one at the time and at the top of his game. He was a daring and imaginative businessman and a brilliant promoter. He understood human nature better than anyone I had ever known. He was known by his tenants as Mr. Davees, and I have never inquired as to why, but there must have been a reason. There was always a well-formulated, cleverly conceived reason for anything Don ever did.

We hit it off from the start and talked well into the night. He understood young people and the boy-girl relationship. Petting was carried on in cars in the fifties, so he sold cars. But as we entered the mid-sixties, the pill made America more serious about sex, so Mr. Davees built singles-only apartments.

"Mr. Hawkins," he began, "Atlanta is the greatest city in the world. Every year in May there is a graduating class from every school in the Southeast. A large percentage of these graduates will have the compelling desire to look for a more exciting life. These will be the most thrilling, adventurous, aggressive young men and women of their areas. They will be coming here from Tennessee, Kentucky, North and South Carolina, Alabama, Mississippi, and Florida. They will be coming from every nook and cranny in Georgia looking for fun and excitement.

"I know how to have fun, and I know how to lead. I have to lead because I cannot follow. Most people do not want to lead. It takes too much time and is far too much trouble, and they don't want the responsibility. I personally feel responsible for taking the time to have fun. I am better at it than most.

"Mr. Hawkins, women rule the world, and they have since life began. The secret of life is understanding women. As you see, I am short and balding and have never been confused with Clark Gable. Nevertheless, I have always had my fair share of the pie. I know something about women that is often overlooked. Women love to laugh and they love to have fun.

"Having fun can be expensive, but I *invest* in fun. I am sometimes ashamed that this is so, but never for long. If having fun is my plight in life, then it seems I am saddled with that awesome responsibility. It is the cross I must bear. I am not always proud of myself, but sometimes we just have to 'turn Mother's picture to the wall.'

"Mr. Hawkins, attitude pulls appearance by the nose, and from what I can gather, your attitude is excellent. You must visit us more often. This party you are witnessing goes on every night."

And it did. And predictably, I was not a stranger to the P.T.A. There was never a vacancy at the 118-unit complex, and it was a fact that it cost $100 just to be on the waiting list.

Don had a loyal following of about fifty young people who he referred to as "Davees' Raiders." Without hesitation they would execute his every whim. At any hour of the day or night, they would answer his call. Boredom is something that Don could not abide. If he felt this horrible condition setting in, he would pick up the phone and call the Raiders. They, in turn, would call a friend, and in the space of an hour a party was going. Now, seventy-five to one hundred people is a small crowd, but if you start with that, it can only grow. He was the Bob Crane of "Hogan's Heroes."

During the course of the year, my visits brought me in closer contact with Mr. Davees and Mr. Hunt. Mr. Davees was unselfish with his praise of Mr. Hunt. He promoted John as he did his apartments. Mr. Hunt, sometimes tired of the blue-haired ladies, would come calling. Don knew that the only way John, twenty years our senior, could be made attractive to the young people was through status. John had to be viewed as rich and impor- tant. He became "Mr. Hunt." Occasionally, I would overhear Don alluding to Mr. Hunt's net worth with phrases like, "Can you imagine what it would be like to own Six Flags?" Mr. Davees never considered this misleading, as all he had done was pose a question. When he wanted John to appear cute, he would address him as "Johnnykins."

Don was as extravagant as Mr. Hunt was cheap. He added a Lear jet to his list of "toys" to expand his playground. Don enjoyed being a millionaire. Mr. Hunt kept insisting that sooner or later Don would go belly up. I couldn't imagine this ever happening. He was inventive and creative and his observations keen. This little man with the mongoose mind had the charisma and leadership of Charles Manson. He could hypnotize "his people" like James Jones, but unlike Jones, he always brought them back. Small in stature and large on brains, he side-stepped all direct confrontations. He was the artful little dodger.

I have always had a lot of everything in life except money. I loved Don's flamboyant style. He liked the finer things in life, and he knew what they were. His was the house of plenty.

How did three people so different in age, background, and intellect come together, coexist, or seek out each other's company to begin with? The answer is *serotonin*. Serotonin is the chemical the brain manufactures that determines dominance.

In studies conducted in forty-five separate monkey colonies, it was discovered that each colony had a dominant or "head" monkey. In all forty-five colonies the head monkey had a higher serotonin count than the others. But when the head monkey was removed from the colony and put in isolation, his serotonin level dropped to that of the remainder of the monkeys.

Meanwhile, with the leader removed from the colony, the serotonin level of *one* of the remaining monkeys began to rise until it reached the level of the exiled leader. When the former leader was returned to his colony, the serotonin level of his replacement dropped to the level of the rest of the monkeys. This held true in all forty-five studies.

So what we're talking about, once again, is *dominance*. Neither of the three of us would submit to being dominated for any length of time. While our respective serotonin levels have never been measured, it is a foregone conclusion that each of us considers our level higher than the other two. And that was, and is, the problem with the old firm of Hunt, Hawkins and Davees.

The fact that we differ so is of little or no consequence. The one thing that holds us together is a common gluttonous, libertine self-indulgence, a love of self-gratification. Irrespective of our ages, all three of us are nothing more than selfish, spoiled adolescents, hedonistically devouring life.

6

All was going well for Mr. Hunt. The Industrial Complex was moving along on schedule, and the Amusement Park was attracting large crowds. As long as John stayed away from things, they ran themselves rather smoothly. Occasionally, I would visit him for lunch and play gin rummy in his office. Even though I never won at gin, I refused to stop playing him. I just stopped paying him. I have never conceded to Mr. Hunt, and he has never conceded to me, not to this day.

Suddenly John resigned from Six Flags. He had been having some small differences with the parent company in Dallas, but that wasn't why he left. The company had ordered John to sell off some land adjacent to the Amusement Park in order to show a quarterly profit. John had advised them against it, saying they couldn't get what the property was worth. So John resigned, they sold the property, and John later acquired it himself.

For nearly thirty years, Mr. Hunt had worked within the corporate structure. This was his first venture as an entrepreneur. There is much speculation as to the actual reason Mr. Hunt purchased this property, but I cling solidly to one: John thought he could embarrass Six Flags into buying the land back. That is the only suitable explanation for the bizarre occurrences that took place thereafter.

Mr. Hunt opened an Elephant Walk. He actually opened an Elephant Walk. He took about five acres of land across from the main entrance to Six Flags and turned it into an Elephant Walk. Not one elephant, but two. A large one and a small one and an elephant trainer named Slim who was so lazy he pissed in his pants. That's correct—he actually, intentionally, and willfully pissed in his pants. Now if an elephant doesn't smell bad enough by himself, throw in a trainer who pisses in his pants in the hot summer sun and you've pretty much got the picture.

Mr. Hunt had read somewhere that elephant rides in California were becoming both popular and profitable. He intended to beat everyone to the punch, so he opened the first Elephant Walk in the East.

Directly across the street, he constructed an all-terrain vehicle course. He took about three acres and built this muddy track, lined it with used automobile tires, and hired a straw boss named Dawson. Dawson was John's managerial equivalent but far less assertive. He was to manage and maintain the track while Slim herded the elephants.

Well, John had done everything wrong. He committed Slim and the elephants for the entire summer, paid cash for these twenty all-terrain vehicles, painted the tires white, and believed this idiotic scheme would work!

Mothers were dragging their children up to the elephants, begging them to ride so they could get pictures of them. The children hated the elephants. I mean they despised them! There was not one picture taken of a child on an elephant in which the child wasn't crying.

Slim wasn't helping things either sitting there in his lawn chair pissing in his faded blue jeans. When the situation was brought to Mr. Hunt's attention, he snapped, "Slim ain't worth a pinch of owl shit, and those little bastards don't know *what* they want."

Across the street, Dawson was running around in a frenzy. Mothers looked on in shocked horror. The vehicles were breaking down in the mud, and kids were crying and getting run into by the ones that were working. The white-painted tires were now covered with red Georgia clay.

Mr. Hunt was running back and forth in his sportiest hat, cigar in the corner of his mouth, ranting and raving, screaming orders at Dawson, who was rushing around painting tires, dodging vehicles, rescuing stranded children, and trying to repair the stalled engines. John had been raised on a farm and could probably have fixed them, but that, of course, was beneath him.

Well, that was the standard scene of this Keystone Comedy for weeks until Mr. Hunt swallowed his pride and closed both places. But that was when the *real* trouble started. A couple of days later I received an urgent call from Mr. Hunt.

"Hawkins, you and Davees get your asses out here. I need help. *We're* going to build an outdoor country and western bar on that hill I own. We're going to call it Nashville Hill." Mr. Hunt had the imagination of a mirror, so I picked up Mr. Davees and we rushed on out to Nashville Hill.

When we arrived, we could see Mr. Hunt meant business. He had already graded about fifteen acres of this thirty-foot mound that overlooked Six Flags Road. I could just envision a very large, loud country and western band blaring out to an overflowing crowd of drunken, rowdy rednecks while the mothers paraded their children out of the entrance of Six Flags. This should be enough to embarrass management.

The instant we reached John, he began barking orders. Whenever Mr. Hunt gives orders, which is frequently, his pace quickens, his voice rises, he stammers and begins waving his hands and arms in the air.

"Davees," he commanded, "you're in charge of building a country and western bar on top of this fucking hill. You ain't got much money to work with but do it now. I'm leaving it all up to you. You know how to do all this shit so get started."

"Hawkins," he continued, "you're in charge of publicity. You know all those weirdos in radio and television and those people with the newspapers. Get them all out here to cover this place." At that, he pointed to a place on the hill that didn't yet exist.

"How much is my advertising budget?" I inquired.

"Not a fucking nickel," he announced. "I lost my hat, ass, and raincoat on those elephants. People owe you favors; go start collecting them."

"Yes sir, Mr. Hunt," and away we flew, Mr. Davees doing his thing and me doing mine. Mr. Hunt kept bellowing orders in both directions. He too was doing *his* thing.

It was incredible how that place took shape in just three days. Mr. Davees located five large funeral tents, placed them perfectly together, put down plywood floors, covered them with sawdust, used hay bales as seats, scattered two or three dozen live chickens around for effect, built a bandstand, iced down the beer, hired a band and we were in business. The place was absolutely adorable.

Meanwhile, I was doing my thing. I got nearly every radio and television station in the city behind us. Both newspapers gave us free coverage, and the word was out. Mr. Hunt rewarded our efforts by buying each of us an inexpensive western shirt, a pair of blue jeans, and a cheap pair of cowboy boots so we could look authentic for opening night.

On July 1, 1969, there was only one place to be—Nashville Hill. That afternoon we scurried about with our last-minute duties. I took Mr. Davees aside and asked, "I hate to bring this up, but what is going to happen if it rains?" "Mr. Hawkins," he immediately replied, "that means we're going to have a captive crowd."

It was unusually hot. About seven o'clock that evening it started to rain. The opening night traffic was heavy, but so was the rain. By eight o'clock the rain was coming down in sheets. The newly graded hill was a quagmire. People were rushing up the hill to get under the tents, but they were losing their shoes in ankle-deep mud. Parked cars were sliding down the hillside parking lot onto Six Flags Road. Wreckers were hauling away cars that had slid down and blocked traffic. Underneath the tents, Mr. Davees and his Raiders were having a wonderful time.

You would think that this sort of evening could only happen once. Not so. It rained every evening for twenty-eight of the thirty nights Mr. Hunt kept Nashville Hill open. Every night was the same.

"God" was never more "damned" than He was that month. Mr. Hunt was certain that the Big Guy had directed all of His wrath against Nashville Hill. Why hadn't Davees and I told him that God was opposed to country and western music played outdoors? Mr. Davees, God, and Mr. Hawkins received equal blame for the failure.

It had been a very expensive summer for Mr. Hunt. It seemed that embarrassing Six Flags was getting costly.

7

I'd like to confess to only two things. One, I have never been known for my good judgement. Secondly, Mr. Hunt is not *always* wrong. Just as he had predicted, things took a turn for the worse for Mr. Davees. Suddenly Don could do nothing right. He was divorced in 1967 and sold the P.T.A. shortly thereafter.

He devoted his energies and resources into the development of his new project—the Atlanta Town Towers, or the AT&T Building, as he referred to it. His new dream was to build a high-rise, singles-only apartment building on Peachtree Street.

For the first time in his life, money became a problem. O.P.M. was nowhere to be found. His business track record, unblemished, was ignored. His concept of a high-rise building for "mixed use" was way ahead of its time. No one believed you could blend apartments, offices, and commercial space in the same building. No one would back his new project. Mr. Davees does not give up on things easily, particularly when they are his ideas. Having never suffered a business defeat, he held on to *his* dream tenaciously. He held on too long and too tightly. Life teaches us that when you hold on to one thing too long, it will usually end up breaking your heart. The AT&T building was never built.

Don's lifestyle hadn't changed, but his financial position had. He went right on through 1967 and 1968 living off of the sale of the P.T.A. By 1969, he was broke. Gone were his Lear jet, his wife and two children, his house, his cars, and his credit. The "I told you so" people were wagging their tongues. All he had left were his Raiders. Now broke and divorced, he was living a day-to-day existence. His divorce had been friendly but costly. He thought very highly of his family and despite his lifestyle was a good father. Then again, he had his Raiders to entertain. They were his hole card. At a time like this, he couldn't lose them.

He made an agreement with an apartment owner to promote his complex. Don moved in, his Raiders quickly followed and the apartments started filling up. The party went on.

No longer owner of Peachtree Town, he needed a place to entertain. He agreed to promote a restaurant and bar. He turned it from a loser into a winner virtually overnight. For over a year it was the hottest bar in the city. The owner was coining money, and although Don was not paid a dime, he was running up some enormous checks of his own. Finally the owner, with a full house every evening, felt he could do without Don. He couldn't have been more wrong. Egos clashed and Mr. Davees took his crowd down the street to the Belaire Hotel.

Presto, like that, it was an instant success. That lasted a year, and then a similar disagreement moved him further down Peachtree Street to Jimmy Orr's End Zone.

Orr's quickly duplicated the two previous successes. You could not get into the place. It was uncanny how this little man could manipulate people. Don told me his secret: "Mr. Hawkins, people want to go where they can't get in. Crowds of people create even larger crowds. My Raiders constitute the nucleus of a crowd. The rest just follow. Young people are fickle, and the secret, as always, is knowing when to move on.

Predictably, after six months or so, he opened a place of his own called Uncle Sam's. It was located in an alley off Peachtree Street, not a hundred yards behind the Belaire Hotel. As always, Don was using other people's money because he was still broke. He prefers the term *broke* to *poor* because it has connotations of a more temporary condition.

He formed a partnership with three other men. One had operational experience in the bar business. The second was an architect, and the third was a psychologist. The architect was to transform a large, old garage into a functional bar. The operations man was to operate it. The psychologist was for no apparent reason that comes to mind. Don's job was, of course, to promote it.

Uncle Sam's was a huge success. During the weekdays over a thousand people entered the doors. On weekends, it was over two thousand. They used plastic cups instead of glasses. A red, white, and blue picture of Uncle Sam was on each of the one million cups used in the first year. The place was a gold mine.

Mr. Davees' financial position had been quickly reversed. He could see daylight, and the good times were flowing like never before.

Business was so good that Mr. Davees decided to entertain at Super Bowl V in Miami. The architect could not get away. The operations man had to stay and operate, so Mr. Davees and the psychologist flew to Miami. The psychologist was along to see that Mr. Davees used good judgement as to his expenditures.

They first rented the largest boat in Miami for a week. They rented docking space at the Palm Bay Club, which was *the* place in Miami at that time. They stocked it with enough food and beverage to cater the entire Super Bowl.

On Friday, Pete Rozelle hosted a party for about five thousand of his closest friends. Mr. Davees, never to be outdone, put Pete's to shame on Saturday. He rented the Run Away Bay Club on Biscayne Bay and flew an airplane over the city inviting Miami to a cocktail party. He invited the entire city . . . and most of it came. It started at noon and went on until game time the next day. It may well have been the largest cocktail party ever thrown. It *had* to have been the most expensive. The "guardian" psychologist was about to need one.

Mr. Hunt and I were in attendance, but not speaking. We had an argument on the plane going down and I hurt his feelings. Mr. Hunt was pouting. We went to the party without talking. We sat together at the game without talking. We checked out of the hotel together without talking. We cabbed it to the airport without talking and we boarded the airplane without talking. Sitting on the plane, Mr. Hunt finally bellowed, "Enough of this shit. I'll never fly with you again, but I'm bored. Let's play gin rummy."

Mr. Davees returned to Atlanta a few days later. After the bills arrived from Miami, he had a business meeting with his partners at which he sold his interest in Uncle Sam's. With his seed money in tow, he moved to Houston, Texas, in search of his fortune.

Mr. Hunt, failing to unload his Six Flags property, soon closed his downtown office and assumed a lower and less expensive profile.

8

One afternoon in New York I had stumbled onto a deal. After a long drinking lunch, I went down to Orchard Street in the garment district. Keep in mind, I take no credit for this; this was pure luck. I went into one of these stores and found some great prices on Alpaca sweaters. In the golf shops and department stores, a good Alpaca sweater would cost you sixty to eighty dollars. I felt like I was stealing from this poor dumb peddler. He had them priced at eighteen dollars and I could buy as many as I wanted.

I picked out a half-dozen for myself and then got to thinking. In Baltimore, there were lots of guys who sold clothes out of the trunks of their cars. All of my friends were golfers, and I could do them a favor by selling them sweaters for forty bucks. I would be helping them and at the same time pocket a handsome profit of twenty-two dollars. I had a large trunk in my car, and I figured I could carry several dozen at a time to the customers in Orr's Restaurant. I hated to take advantage of a New Yorker's innocence, but what the hell, this was business.

The longer I talked with this merchant, the more I liked him. He told me he could ship them to me, no problem. "What about your wife?" he added. "I've got them in women's sizes."

"Well, of course," I responded. "Why didn't I think of that?"

He was so nice that I felt guilty about it and told him my plans. He said he didn't mind being a broker and started showing me turtlenecks, mock turtlenecks, shirts, dresses, and women's lingerie. He had some great buys on ladies' panties, and I couldn't turn that down. He started advising me on colors and sizes, and before it was over I knew as much about his business as he did!

Frankly, I was a little surprised when he wouldn't take my out-of-town check, but this was New York. I called my bank, and they wired me $2,800. I left him my address, and he said I should have my goods in less than a week. I wasn't a dummy; I got a receipt.

About a week later, I was having lunch in Orr's when Libby called. She said a truck was in the carport with about a dozen large boxes, which had been unloaded. The driver needed $180 for delivery. I told her to pay him and I was on the way home.

When I got home and started opening these boxes, everything was there. I went over each item and everything was accounted for. There were, however, some unusual colors and sizes in the lot. Most of the men's wear I received was in small and medium sizes. My ladies' wear apparel arrived in a strange assortment of colors. I had a few male friends who could wear a medium, but only a jockey wears a small. And have you ever tried to sell navy blue, dark purple, or chocolate brown panties to a Buckhead woman? I called my merchant "friend" in New York and pointed this out. I was shocked at his rudeness when he announced that all sales were final and hung up.

The next day, I loaded my garments into the trunk of my car and went to work. I arrived at Orr's early so I could get the closest parking space in front of his restaurant. Inside of two weeks, I had recovered my initial investment plus a small profit. Unfortunately, most of my large and extra-large sweaters were sold. The women's sweaters in red, yellow, and blue were fast movers too. The ladies' underwear was slow even when I discounted the prices. No business is without its problems, and I started having mine. It seems that red is a very delicate color. This was brought to my attention by two disgruntled wives who informed me that the red sweaters I had sold them had faded and ruined some very expensive blouses. I also had some complaints from men in regard to shrinkage in some of my turtlenecks. One man told me that the entire neck had separated from the shirt as he was taking it off. I apologized, but informed him that all sales were final.

Then one afternoon as I was showing my goods, an officer of

the law strolled up and asked to see my business license. When I failed to produce one, he arrested me. He put me in his car, drove me around the block and explained that a merchant in the same shopping center had registered a complaint. He was both jealous and mad that I was doing more business out of my trunk than he was in his store. I was told to go indoors and to get a business license.

I knew by then the garment business was not my calling, so I had a dollar sale and closed shop.

On that same trip to Tall Town, I happened by Toots Shor's Saloon. Toots Shor's was "the place" in New York for sports people, media, and celebrities from all walks of life. No place for amateurs or light drinkers, Toots' was reserved for industrial-strength boozers. This was home for the world-class imbibers.

As the afternoon and evening wore on, I found myself at the bar with some serious drinkers. While I didn't consider myself in over my head, I was most certainly well challenged. A liar's poker game developed, and after awhile I fell in with the local migration that moved throughout the East Side. From Toots Shor's to Pear Trees, Play Street, Mr. Laugh's, and finally, P. J. Clarke's. On foot or in cabs, the poker game continued. I don't recall it ending. The next morning, I woke up in a hotel room staring at a man in the next bed who was staring at me. "Is this your room or mine?" I asked.

"It must be yours," he answered; "I live in Connecticut. Let's get some breakfast."

We introduced ourselves, showered, and went downstairs. During breakfast we tried to piece together the evening. From what we could jointly assemble, we had made a full night of it. His name was Chuck Melton, and he was a producer for CBS Sports.

I told him about doing color work for the Falcons. He had casually asked me to send him a tape of our games. I hadn't, of course, and in September, he called to remind me. It slipped my mind again, but in November, he called again. I phoned the station and asked them to please mail a tape to CBS Sports in New York. In February, Chuck called and told me I was hired.

9

On September 3, 1971, I was in the television booth in Baltimore for the preseason clash between the Cowboys and Colts. CBS had asked me to observe the style of Pat Summerall, their number-one color man. Usually Pat worked with Ray Scott, but this night he was paired with Don Criqui. I was seated right behind Pat with headsets on. This was my training for network sports.

Before the game, I asked Pat what to do. He held up what's called a "speed card" which contains names, numbers, heights, and weights of all the players on both teams. He told me to watch the game and comment on whatever I saw of interest. I had no idea how the replay worked, or anything else for that matter. I listened, watched and tried to figure it out for myself.

It seemed easy enough. The broadcast was smooth and professional. Pat used an economy of words, got his points across quickly, casually, and with little effort. I noticed that before each replay the voice from the director would come through the headset: "It's coming up." Pat would then say very calmly, "As we watch the rerun of that last play," and by that time the replay would appear on the monitor in front of him. That was simple; I could do that.

My first game was two weeks later in Atlanta. My partner in the booth was Jack Buck. CBS paired Jack and me for the season. Chuck Melton, the man responsible for hiring me, was producing. Tony Verna, the inventor of instant replay, was directing.

About a half-hour before game time, we rehearsed the on-camera opening. Five-four-three-two-one, you're on, and that little red light went on. Then came the voice of Jack: "Good afternoon, ladies and gentlemen, I'm Jack Buck. Alongside me is Alex Hawkins, a ten-year veteran of the Baltimore Colts, now working his first telecast with CBS." I gave Jack a nervous smile, made an awkward glance at the camera while he went on about where we were, who was playing, the weather conditions, and the fact that it was the start of another exciting season of NFL football on CBS. He then turned it over to me for my comments.

I cannot tell you the fear that swept through me when I looked at that tiny red light. I had been asked a question by Jack, but I had to answer to a little red light. It just wasn't natural. I stuttered, stammered, repeated myself, and spoke in broken sentences. I could not look into the camera and talk at the same time. Everybody laughed; they knew it would happen. They assured me that it happened all the time on the first take. They told me I would get better.

After a half-dozen repeats of the same, I suggested to Chuck that we do away with the opening. He told me not to worry, that I'd be fine by game time. I wasn't!

It was a horrible experience. It was a lot tougher than radio. I apologized to Jack and the crew and swore that next week I would get better. I didn't. Each week was the same. Five- four-three- two- one, you're on, and that damn menacing red light would send me into sheer terror.

Jack was patient with me, but less certain. Working each week with a man like myself could cost him a career. Then on the fourth week of the season, I outdid myself. Back then, the play-by-play man had a seventeen-inch color monitor directly in front of him. It was referred to as the line monitor. The color man had only a small, eight-inch black-and-white monitor in front of him, and it was snowy. The viewers at home had a much better picture than I did.

That day, CBS was experimenting. They had installed two small monitors in front of me. Before the game, the director had explained that one of the two monitors was an isolation shot and was not to be confused with the line monitor, which is the picture you see at home. I was nervous, as usual, about the on-camera opening but pretended to understand everything.

I had learned over the past three weeks that the announcers are to back up the director's choice of pictures and to support them with facts or comments. After another agonizing opening, we settled into the game. I was ready for this game between the Falcons and Cardinals. I knew everything about both teams.

I doubt that the viewing audience has ever experienced anything like what they saw and heard that day.

I kept getting the monitors confused. I spent most of the afternoon explaining replays that were not being shown on the screen at home. The director was showing a close-up of a coach on the sidelines, and I was explaining the success of the trapping guard; "Number 65, as you see him right there, is opening a large hole for Number 33, Cannonball Butler, who moves forward for a gain of seven."

I was brilliant, precise, perceptive. My timing was perfect. I was correct on every name and number. But while the cameras would be on the cheerleaders, I would be explaining the move that had gotten wide receiver Paul Flately open for a gain of twelve.

The director was trying to stop me and Jack was staring at me strangely. It was a very pathetic look, as I recall. The audience at home must have thought they were watching the wrong game. Finally, at halftime they sent someone up to the booth and jerked the isolation monitor out.

The following week I was working with Don Criqui. Criqui is a tall, handsome man who had played basketball at Notre Dame. He had a solid sports background and a keen wit and mind. He had not been with CBS long, and they were grooming him for big things.

Don was friendly, confident, and relaxed and told me that he would improve me. He did and it was fun working with Criqui. We had a good rapport and a similar sense of humor. The most striking thing about Don was his involvement in the game. We were anything but the toast of CBS and therefore were assigned to the poorer teams, but you couldn't have guessed it from the enthusiasm of Criqui. He was always up. He enjoyed football; not all announcers do.

I, frankly, was contemptuous of the losing teams and poorer

organizations. My comments were often critical, my humor, caustic. Don was crafty enough not to join in, but neither would he discredit me. Our frankness and candor were starting to be noticed in cities like New York, Philadelphia, Baltimore and Dallas. We began to get favorable mail.

Meanwhile, ABC was dominating the ratings with their telecast of Monday Night Football, an experiment they had started the year before. The networks were so certain of its failure that neither NBC nor CBS bothered to bid on it.

Initially, the broadcasting team consisted of Keith Jackson, Don Meredith and Howard Cosell. Early in the year they were drawing heavy criticism, but as the season wore on, public opinion shifted in their favor. As the rating points grew, the critics quieted. By season's end, it was the most controversial and talked-about show in the history of sports.

It was a bold experiment for ABC, but it had worked. The ratings continued to climb, even skyrocketed. They were the envy of the industry. Roone Arledge and his crew were making unprecedented innovations and boldly venturing into areas never entered into by television. Meredith and Cosell were the perfect match-ups as protagonist and antagonist. It was the unity of opposites, and it created a unique chemistry.

With his West Texas drawl, Dandy Don, as he was now called, blended just the right amount of humor and insight. Cosell, with his offensive, nasal Bronx accent, was constantly agitating and berating heretofore untouchables. He was stomping on hallowed ground. Nothing was sacred. Howard, with his eloquent verbiage, was forcing journalism into sports broadcasting.

Howard Cosell was both a producer and director in the booth. He was after numbers, big numbers, and he was serving notice to the pro football world that it was no longer a game. It had officially entered the realm of entertainment.

Their openings were exciting and inventive. The halftime show was fresh, upbeat, and insightful. The replays were clearly superior to those of CBS or NBC. They had turned the Monday night game into an *event*. Regardless of the match-ups or their relative positions in the standings, this game was a *happening*.

It is impossible to determine how much impact Monday Night

Football had on the broadcasting community. The old guard, set in its ways, was outraged. Men with less tenure were skeptical. But newcomers, like myself, were excited and challenged. ABC was the new standard-bearer. In just one year, Monday Night Football had become the measuring stick for sports excellence.

Criqui and I finished the season together. My last four games were not as good as my first four had been bad. I cannot speak for other broadcasters at that time, but the Monday night telecasts had influenced me.

I believed that the teams' performances on these Monday night games was superior to that of the Sunday games. I honestly felt that players were more motivated, knowing that they were being scrutinized by their peers. I also suspicioned that they were intimidated by the possibility of being criticized by Cosell or laughed at by Dandy Don. In any event, I was positive that the best game of the week came on Monday nights. It was a weekday Super Bowl.

And while I admired their telecasts, I was nevertheless envious of both Meredith and Cosell. I was being paid the unlikely figure of twelve hundred and seventy dollars a week, but it was rumored that Meredith was making over a hundred thousand dollars.

Then, too, I had played the game, and if anyone should be critical of the players, coaches, or owners, it should be me. I promised myself in the coming year I would be more comical than Dandy Don and more critical than Cosell.

10

My fame, such as it was, had now spread to other parts of the country. Several flattering articles had been forwarded to me from newspapers in Washington, Dallas, Philadelphia, Los Angeles, and yes, New York City. I figured that I was a shade flashier than Halley's Comet.

In early January, I got a call from Mr. Davees. He sounded prosperous and suggested that perhaps we might consider attending Super Bowl VI in New Orleans. He added that business was great in Houston; he was "heavy on the hip," and while he had no intentions of outdoing his extravaganza at the Run Away Bay Club, he could well afford to entertain Mr. Hunt and me comfortably.

I ran the idea by Mr. Hunt, and he was agreeable as long as we flew on separate planes. He added that he was not going to be responsible for rooms, tickets, badges, or large dinner checks generated by Mr. Davees. All this was mutually agreed upon, so on Wednesday prior to the game, the old firm of Hunt, Hawkins and Davees was reunited in "The City Care Forgot."

Five days with Mr. Hunt is like the month of February with anyone else, so I was not hurt when he chose to leave on an early flight and booked me on a late afternoon one. Our responsibilities were as follows: I was in charge of securing rooms, tickets, and badges to the game, all social functions, and the introduction to celebrities and other higher-ups. Mr. Davees was to "host" and, as such, was to handle all dinner and drink checks and to arrange transportation. Mr. Hunt was in charge of zero. He brought nothing to the party but chaos and confusion. His job was to make sure we did ours, which you can never do to the satisfaction of Mr. Hunt.

Before we proceed further, let me admit that this was not my finest hour. I had called for reservations at the Fairmont Hotel. They had requested an advance deposit which I had forgotten to send. I had not bothered to line up tickets because I knew everyone in football and CBS was televising the game. There was a possibility once we arrived we would sit in the press box.

A coach had once told me that "poor planning and preparation leads to poor performance," and this just happened to prove accurate in my case. When I arrived at the Fairmont, there were no rooms available. Instead, there was a message from Mr. Davees directing me to a hotel in the French Quarter. The hotel was nice enough, I suppose, but not good enough for a nationally known color man. I knew my friends with CBS would have room for me and I would be seeing them that night. I left my luggage in Mr. Hunt's room, and we went out for the evening.

I did run into some friends much later, but there didn't seem to be a vacant room in the city. Tickets were a little scarce, too. My friends with CBS could not locate a single one. Corporate America was starting to adopt the Super Bowl as "their" event. It was made clear to me that the "old firm" would not be in the press box with Rozelle.

I was surprised but not alarmed when old teammates and coaches were unable to help with tickets or badges. There was no need to panic; it was my first day in town, and I would have the entire next day to take care of my assignment. I spent the night on the sofa in Mr. Hunt's room.

Thursday was no better. I spent the day and night calling friends, players, coaches, general managers, and owners. They were nice enough, and many vowed had they known sooner, they could have helped me.

Tickets and badges had never been a problem for me in the past. It didn't seem fair. The Super Bowl was for the players in the league. It was where you came together after you retired. It was for *us*. Each denial brought on more frustration and then downright anger. This was no way to treat a veteran of ten years. This was certainly no way to behave to a network announcer. I was embarrassed and angry. I took to strong drink and, frankly, remember little else of Super Bowl VI.

11

I was nearly thirty-five years old and still looking for permanent employment. I was not the least bit concerned. I was looking forward to the fall and my second year of television. Then, too, I had a chance for a part in a movie. I've always been interested in the movies, and when Burt Reynolds contacted me about "co-starring" in *Deliverance,* which he was filming in the mountains of North Georgia, I just had to try it.

I went up to Clayton, met director John Boorman, and auditioned for the part of a local mountain mechanic. My one scene was with Burt. He and I were to angrily exchange words. Then came the stare-down. Burt, as the star, was to prevail, of course, but only after an undetermined amount of time.

I couldn't do the scene. Every time the stare-down started, I broke up laughing. Burt, needing a playmate in the mountains, insisted I could. Finally, after about a dozen unsuccessful takes, John Boorman broke in: "He can't do the scene." "Why not," asked Burt. "Because he wants your lines," said Boorman. That was the truth, and my movie career was on the back burner for the time being.

Later that spring, I was approached by a friend of mine, Dave Black, about going in the garbage business. He had been in waste removal for the past ten years, representing two or three different companies in a sales capacity. Every time he would help build a small company, the owners would sell it to a large company and Dave would be left with nothing. He too wanted his piece of the pie.

Dave was a wonderful person. Everybody loved him. He was

friendly and honest and had established a following of customers over the years. The only problem with Dave was that he was as broke as I was.

He explained that it was a simple business, one I could learn in no time, but it was a capital intensive business. I guessed that to mean it was expensive to get into, so I asked him how much. He said it would take a line of credit of one million dollars to start up. A million dollars is not a lot of money to some people, but to a person of my background, it was all the money in the world. I told him I'd let him know when I got back from fishing.

About a week later when I returned, I called two friends of mine who were doing well in the real estate world and asked if they would like to be our financial backers. They had strong ties with the C & S Bank, and on May 19, 1972, Atlanta Waste Control was formed. By God, they had arranged a million dollar line of credit!

We were incorporated under the laws of the State of Georgia. We issued one thousand shares of stock at one dollar a share. Dave and I held sixty percent of the stock, and our money partners were issued the remainder. Dave had to borrow the full three hundred dollars, and my check for the same amount bounced. I had to borrow sixty dollars from Mr. Hunt for the check to clear. One of the financial partners wanted to back out right then, but I talked him out of it. I was finally in business.

Dave was in charge of operations, and I was in charge of sales. With the one million dollar line of credit, we ordered our first truck, a Dempsey Dumpster front-end loader. That meant about as much to me then as it does to you now. All I knew was that son of a bitch cost $40,000.

James Higgins, our first driver, had gone up to Knoxville with us to drive it back. James, a nice man and far and away the best driver in the city, had a fourth-grade education. For some reason, Dave had insisted on having James as part of our business deal. We had gone so far as to give him a small percentage of our stock. I was vigorously opposed to this, but Dave was adamant about having James.

One of those trucks fully loaded weighs sixty thousand pounds. Jesus Christ—it's like a tank. If it got away from you, it could destroy a *small city.*

I rode part of the way back with James, and here was this man with a fourth-grade education driving seventy-five miles an hour in and around traffic like Richard Petty. I couldn't any more have driven that truck than disguise Stone Mountain. Neither could Dave. But old James was handling this ponderous machine like it was a riding mower. We may have been the first company in this country to employ free-flowing vertical management. It finally dawned on me: James Higgins was a flaming genius . . . he *was* our garbage company. Sickness or death to him and we were out of business. He was our million-dollar man.

We set up a small office near downtown and leased a lot down the street with a shed for tools, tires, and storage of our containers, and . . . James started running our garbage company.

I had learned from Don Davis the value of promotion. Our colors were red, white, and blue. Our logo was, "Talk Trash With Us." James wore a clean white uniform. Our white truck was decorated with large red "Pac Man" heads. We actually had "Pac Man" before "Pac Man" did, but we failed to register it.

We hit the streets and alleys of greater Atlanta in search of garbage. Our mission . . . a garbage war. Our opponents . . . Browning Ferris Industries, Waste Management, and the dreaded Fowler Boys. BFI and Waste Management were publicly owned and the two largest garbage companies in the world. Neither was as feared as the Fowler Mob. They had their headquarters over in rural Cobb County. Complete Sanitation was the name of their company, and you spoke of them in hushed tones.

Complete Sanitation was owned and operated by three brothers. Pete, the oldest, was their spokesman. They made their own containers, drove and repaired their own trucks, paid cash for everything, and were politically strong. They operated solely in that county and were totally unchallenged by the larger companies.

Formerly unchallenged, that is, until the new fast gun hit the streets. Vice President in charge of sales, Alex Hawkins, started picking off their accounts. Cobb County was just starting to grow, and I knew the people who were developing it. Getting business was no problem to me. Everybody knew who I was.

How many of you know your garbage man? Dave, having been in the business, both feared and respected the Fowler Boys. He knew that if I kept taking their business, they would soon retaliate.

Finally the call came. The Fowler Boys were looking for a showdown . . . on Fowler territory. We were to meet at their office at eight o'clock that night.

I wasn't sure what to expect that evening. I had heard that the syndicate ran the garbage business in many of the large northern cities. I had also heard talk about the southern Mafia. I was anxious to see what we were up against. And why had they called for a night meeting? When we arrived at their office, it was just getting dark. All the lights were on inside. A few men were still working. As we passed the garage, I counted twelve trucks. We were outnumbered twelve to one.

When we entered the office, no frills were in evidence. Old file cabinets lined the walls, old desks and chairs were scattered about in the open office. Pete, the oldest brother, greeted us with a pleasant smile. He poured three drinks and settled back in his chair. It was his first drink of the day. We made small talk while waiting for the two other brothers. They soon joined us from the garage. They introduced themselves and poured a drink of bourbon, and the summit meeting began.

I took the lead and forcefully announced that we were coming into Cobb County whether they liked it or not. I arrogantly followed this up with "and there is nothing you can do about it." I wanted them to know that I meant business.

Pete did their talking. "We know that. This is a big county now, and it's only starting to grow. The reason nobody else operates out here is because there wasn't enough business. We were like you when we started. Hell, we were going from house to house with hand pick-ups. Just the three of us. But that was ten years ago. Now we've got twelve front-ends and ten roll-ons, but we still drive our own trucks. We started work this morning at five and we're just now finishing up. That's the reason we called the meeting so late.

"Now, we know that you're going to get some business, and more power to you. But everything we've got is paid for. We own the land, the building, and the trucks and containers. We own them free and clear.

"The only thing I'm saying is this. If you start cutting prices below where you can make a profit, then you're stupid. If you're stupid enough to do that, then we're stupid enough to pick it up for nothing."

This made sense even to me. It was getting tougher out here in the real world.

12

Now, fully confident, I looked forward to the 1972 season. I had paid my dues and learned my trade, and I was ready to take on Meredith and Cosell. I honestly believed that at the time, but in reality, I was just like any other athlete who entered the broadcast booth. I thought I knew more than the other jocks, but the truth of it was we all sounded the same, with clichés like, "they came to play," "one heck of an athlete," "he gives 110%," "they're a physical team," "if he breaks the plane of the goal," "they wasted a time out," "control the line of scrimmage," and on and on and on. Only Don Meredith was truly unique.

I was now working with Frank Gleiber, a veteran announcer from Dallas. Frank was solid, dependable, and easy to work with. Frank had but one problem . . . women. Frank couldn't stay married and he wouldn't quit trying. He was fresh off of his third divorce and working on his fourth engagement.

CBS's policy was to keep talent (as announcers are called) together whenever possible; they assigned different producers and directors almost every week. The past year I had repeatedly asked the various producers and directors for ways of improving myself. Without exception, they echoed the same line: "Just be yourself."

It should be obvious by now that I didn't know *who* I was, so this was particularly difficult for me. Every week I'd ask the same question: "How did I do?" Every week I would get the same reply: "Fine, you did fine; just be yourself." It never occurred to me that *they* didn't know *what* they wanted. They were as much in the dark as I was. The truth of the matter was they all wanted the same thing ... the same thing that surrounded Monday Night Football.

The 1972 season was off and running, and so was my mouth. CBS was starting to get mail on me. Most of the mail they received at the network was negative, but mine was mixed. I was amusing to some, downright folksy to others, and offensive to many. Some cities liked me better than others. Either way, I was being talked about. I didn't want to be average, and if these people wouldn't direct me, I would direct myself. I wanted to be like Dandy Don and Howard.

The fifth week we were back in Baltimore for a match-up between the Colts and Cowboys. A rather strange development had taken place in July. A man named Bob Irsay had purchased the Rams from the estate of the late Dan Reeves. Irsay had traded the Rams to Carroll Rosenbloom for the Colts. After having owned the Colts for twenty years, Rosenbloom had suddenly moved to "tinsel town."

The Colts were off to their worst start ever and had lost three of their first four games. As always, John Unitas was quarterbacking the Colts. The Cowboys were in charge of the game when suddenly and without warning, Johnny Unitas was benched. This was impossible, unheard of. For seventeen years this man had been performing last-minute miracles; it was unthinkable to jerk Unitas. To make matters worse, he was not benched by head coach Don McCafferty. He had been benched by Bob Irsay, the owner admittedly, but a man who had been around the game for only five weeks. A man with no previous experience in football or the National Football League.

Furthermore, John Unitas had been replaced by Marty Domres. I didn't even know who Domres was. I can't tell you how incensed I was. How could a man like Irsay with nothing more than money be allowed to do such a thing? Had the National Football League gone completely mad? I out-Coselled Cosell.

After the Cowboys finally defeated the Colts, I *ran* to the Colts' dressing room. By the time I got there, Don McCafferty, who had coached them to a Super Bowl win just two years earlier, had been fired for defiance in regards to benching Unitas. I guess this was when I first realized that the National Football

League was not what it used to be. New owners, with their money, egos, and arrogance, now viewed themselves as bigger and more vital to the game than the coaches and players.

The seventh week of the season, I was back with Gleiber, this time in New Orleans at Tulane Stadium for a game between the Eagles and Saints. I opened the telecast with, "Ladies and Gentlemen, today we have the two worst teams in football playing on *the* worst field in the league. Stay tuned, this should be hilarious."

Throughout the game I made disparaging remarks about the teams, players, coaching staffs, and owners. All of the replays were analyzed negatively: "Let's see on the replay if that was a good run or just bad tackling." As the replay unfolded, I would remark, "Bad tackling here, bad tackling there, and yes, another bad effort there. You see, folks, it really was shoddy."

On a badly overthrown pass, I remarked, "Had it not been for the law of gravity, the ball wouldn't have hit anything." Frank Gleiber was enjoying the whole thing. I felt so cute. The crew in the truck were strangely silent.

After the game, I asked my standard question: "How did I do today?" This time the answer came back: "Well, it was certainly different."

If you know the people of Philadelphia, it will come as no surprise that I got rave reviews. Three different writers praised me as the only honest and knowledgeable announcer in football. CBS got heavy mail both ways. They must have been confused. They didn't know what they wanted, and they didn't know what they were getting. But they knew they were getting *something*.

The final game of the season Gleiber and I were back in Dallas. It was a cold afternoon and the fans at the game were bundled up in their warmest wear. The game was in progress when suddenly the director cut to the stands and on my monitor I saw what looked to be the figure of a flaming man lunging forward in the stands. He was totally ablaze.

I don't know how he got the shot or why he chose to use it, but I had learned to support the director's picture. Without thinking, which is how I usually operated, I announced, "There'll be a hot time in the old town tonight."

I had no way of knowing it wasn't a prankster or a gag. It

turned out the man was wearing a combustible outfit and someone had inadvertently ignited him. He was hospitalized with serious burns. I was judged to be terribly insensitive by the people at CBS, which may or may not have been true.

Frank and I were chosen to broadcast the final game of the season, the Pro Bowl, which that year was played in Dallas.

Back when I was playing in the 1950s and '60s, being chosen for the Pro Bowl was the highest honor bestowed on a player. It meant additional money and an automatic raise of a couple thousand dollars for the coming year. More importantly, it was a status symbol. You were officially recognized as the best. What's more, a major portion of the revenue from that game went towards the players' pension program.

When I arrived in Dallas, I was shocked to discover that no fewer than ten players had refused to participate in the game. The only excuse for not playing in that game was an injury. Yet ten players had claimed injuries. I found this hard to believe. Had the game changed that much in the few short years I'd been out of it?

One player, Jake Scott of the Dolphins, reported with two broken hands. Jake was a throwback to another era in sports when playing with broken bones was expected of you. When informed that he was excused from playing, Jake got right indignant. He claimed that he had played in the Super Bowl game just a week before with the two broken hands, and it is a fact that he had intercepted two passes. He further stated that the only time he was troubled by the hands was when he went to the bathroom. He said that was when he knew who his real friends were.

I carried that story with me into the broadcast booth. There is an old saying in broadcasting, "Be careful of what's on your mind because it may come out of your mouth." Late in the fourth quarter of a customarily dull game, I told the Jake Scott story to our viewing audience.

Gleiber, the spotters, and everybody in the booth were broken up by it. Thousands of people at home were also. The people at CBS were not. The director down in the truck came on with these words, "I don't know what it's like up there, but it's quiet down here." Then I heard a telephone ringing in the background and the director's final words: "It's not quiet now, that's New York." I was fired before I had my headset off.

A week or so later, I received formal notice that my services would no longer be needed by CBS Sports. The people at Black Rock felt I was dangerous and crude.

13

By the spring of 1973, our little garbage company had grown. We now had two trucks and a third one was on order. We hired a full-time secretary and bookkeeper named Sherry Garrett. Sherry had worked for Mr. Davees until he sold the P.T.A. She then went to work for Mr. Hunt until he closed his office. Ms. Garrett was a loyal and capable woman who was highly sought after. To secure her services, we had to make room for Mr. Hunt. Naturally, he paid no rent. Mr. Hunt and I were at opposite ends of the building.

Mr. Hunt was on hand every day to preach, lecture, give advice, dispense wisdom, or otherwise disrupt things, as only he could. He maintained that we were growing too fast and that the local economy was slowing down, as he had still not unloaded his Six Flags property.

Just before he left for Texas, Mr. Davees had offered the same dark forecast. He claimed that there were too many construction cranes in the air in Atlanta. Don had gone down to Houston and formed a partnership with a young, rich Texan named Ferg Ginther. Ginther-Davis Interest (G.D.I.) dealt in real estate, investments, development, construction, finance, insurance, oil, and gas properties.

G.D.I. was putting some cranes of their own in the Texas sky. The Houston economy was bullish, and Don was in the right place at the right time with the right partner. The Ginther family was old, respected, socially accepted, Texas money. The real kind. Mr. Davees had finally found a state that was big enough for him. He was riding high and painting wide.

We only saw each other once a year but we corresponded by phone or mail. Everything was breaking right for Mr. Davees, or so it seemed, as he was not only talking oil and gas, but fast food and gold as well. Don was interested in everything, and I wasn't altogether certain he wasn't serious when I received this letter:

Dear Mr. Hawkins,

I do not know if you will be interested in this, but I thought I would mention it to you because it would be a real "sleeper" in making a lot of money with a small investment—$3,000.00.

A group of us are considering investing in a large cat ranch near Hermosillo, Mexico. It is our purpose to start rather small with about one million cats. Each cat averages about twelve kittens a year; skins can be sold for about twenty cents for the white ones and up to forty cents for the black. This will give us twelve million cat skins per year to sell at an average price of around thirty-two cents, making our gross revenue about $3 million a year. This averages out to about $10,000 per day—exclusive of Sundays and Holidays.

A good Mexican can skin about fifty cats per day at a wage of $3.15 per day. It will take only 633 men to operate the ranch. So the net profit will be over $8,300 per day.

Now the cats would be fed on rats exclusively. Rats multiply four times as fast as cats. We would start a rat ranch right adjacent to our cat farm. If we start with a million rats, we will have four rats per cat each day. The rats will be fed on the carcasses of the cats that we skin. This will give each rat a quarter of the cat. You can see by this, this business is a real clean operation. It is self-supporting and nearly automatic throughout. The cats will eat the rats and the rats will eat the cats and we get the skins.

Let me know if you are interested. As you can

imagine, we are rather particular who we want to get into this; and want the fewest investors possible.

Yours truly,

Mr. Davees

P.S. Eventually it is our hope to cross the cats with snakes, and they will skin themselves twice a year. This would save the major cost of skinning as well as give us two skins for one cat.

I didn't mention this to Mr. Hunt as I was sure that, after the Elephant Walk, he was no longer interested in anything connected with animals, large or small.

14

The 1973 season was fast approaching and for the first time since junior high school, I had nothing to look forward to. I was no longer a part of the game. After fourteen years, ten as a player and four as an announcer, I found myself on the outside of the NFL looking in.

Try telling Richard Petty he is out of racing. Convince Arnold Palmer he is no longer a part of golf. Tell Nolan Ryan he is finished with baseball. While I was nowhere near as big a name as those people, my love for the game was every bit as great. Football was all I ever knew and all I ever really loved. I was scared without it. I simply had to hang on to it any way I could.

Just before training camp opened, I was offered a job by a local TV station to work on the Falcon preseason games. I also agreed to write two articles a week for the *Atlanta Constitution*. Neither of these jobs paid much, but both of them kept me "inside" the game where I felt I justly belonged.

The idea of writing for the *Constitution* was challenging. I had been close friends with sportswriters since college and found them to be totally upfront, honest people who truly loved and cared about sports. There was nothing deceptive or pretentious about these writers; what you saw was what you got. They were, in many ways, fearless.

But why anyone would want to become a sportswriter is well beyond me. The job offers a truly miserable salary, an even worse expense account, the worst working hours imaginable, and a far better than average chance of going absolutely nowhere in life. For these same reasons, it is the easiest way for a writer to get started. Then they get hooked on sports and find that writing is a disease rather than an occupation.

I'm not speaking of the sportswriters of today. I'm talking about the writers of the fifties and sixties. With the exception of a few good columnists, there was little or no variance in sportswriters the world over. They all lived a drunken, disorganized life of near poverty for the simple reason that they just didn't give a damn. They were world-class procrastinators with date line mentalities. They overindulged in everything they did. They got the best of nothing and the worst of everything else. They were belittled and berated by their wives, bosses, editors, coaches, players, and landlords.

They cared nothing about their appearance. On an average, they smoked three packs of cigarettes, drank a case of beer, and ate one meal a day, provided it was paid for. Over the years, the ones I have known have averaged 2.3 marriages. They were undependable, unreliable and unmanageable. Beyond that, these sportswriters had a healthy disrespect for: high-paid athletes who perform below their capabilities, lofty coaches who consider themselves geniuses, and media journalists who look and sound intelligent but have no idea what sports is all about.

Considering their income, appearance, lifestyle and future prospects, sportswriters had absolutely no reason to take themselves seriously. But they truly loved the game, and they went about their lives having fun, taking chances, and making adorable playmates.

There was no reason for excitement in the preseason games. The Falcons had some quality players, but, once again, the Dutchman had no signal caller with which to execute his sometimes brilliant game plan. That year he had traded Bob Berry to Minnesota for their quarterback, Bob Lee. It was a strange trade that made little or no sense, but I tried to take a wait-and-see position.

Once you have been around a winning organization as I had for *nine* of the ten years I had played, there are things you look for in assessing the quality of a team. These are usually small, intangible things but they nevertheless spell out the team's future. The really good teams are loose, confident, and relaxed. Laughter, love, and respect bind players and coaches.

Nothing had changed in Atlanta. The Falcons were a typical Van Brocklin-coached team. The team and the front office were riddled with hate, suspicion, doubt, and fear. The Falcons, as usual, were pulled apart from every direction. I kept these feelings to myself during the preseason telecasts. There didn't seem to be any objectivity in television, and with the exception of Dandy Don and Howard, no one else was big enough or bold enough to get by with "telling it like it is." I was saving my salvo for my weekly newspaper column. The newspapers seemed to be the last bastion of integrity for sports.

Nothing had changed between Rankin, Frank Wall, and myself. They knew my true feelings, but as long as I kept them off the air, we coexisted fairly harmoniously. I was still flying on Rankin's plane to avoid the Dutchman, who had still not spoken to me for almost five years. On our way home from out-of-town games, Rankin would wait until we were both in the cups and then corner me and begin, "Well, genius, what did we do wrong today?"

"Everything, Rankin, just about everything," I would begin, and with the diplomacy of a ripsaw, I would give *my* expert evaluation of *his* team's performance. After downing six or eight vodkas, it was truly amazing how much I knew. Looking back, I'm not really sure who was the biggest ass, Rankin or myself. He seemed to enjoy these verbal castrations, and I, sickly enough, enjoyed administering them.

In my first article on Monday before the opening game, I laughingly depicted the Falcons as a three-part comedy that would soon be closing. I made unkind reference to the fact that the Falcons had not had a winning season in the seven-year history of the franchise. I further pointed out that the Dutchman had experienced but one winning season in his eleven years as coach of the Vikings and Falcons. I labeled Bob Lee a wind-up, rag-armed quarterback, incapable of winning.

They opened the season with a 62-7 win over the Saints, then proceeded to lose their next three games. Each loss was another spike in the Dutchman's heart. Damn, that man hated losing, and when he did, he hated everything and everybody. Norm was going berserk. He ranted and raved, chastised and belittled. His venom spread throughout the team and the entire organization.

It was during this third loss, to the 49ers in Atlanta, that the accumulated hatred spilled over. I was in the press box that day. The Falcons were trailing 13-9, but had driven deep into 49er territory and were threatening to take the lead.

Suddenly, a fight broke out in the *offensive huddle*. The quarterback and the fullback started punching one another, and the tight end joined them. They were flailing away at each other, and the game had to be halted to break up the melee.

Well, sir, I thought that now I'd seen just about everything. The press corps first reacted with shock, goggle-eyed and open-mouthed. Snickers followed and then uncontrollable laughter. Writers were slapping each other on their backs, and tears were streaming down their faces. No one had ever seen a fight in a huddle. The officials weren't sure what to do. The Falcons now hated everyone, even themselves.

The Monday after, I conceived what I thought to be the greatest idea of my life; I decided that the time was right for a hostile takeover. While I had never heard of a takeover, hostile or otherwise, it was pretty much what I had in mind. My only problem was I had not the vaguest notion of how to go about it.

I called Lindsey Hopkins, one of the seven minority stockholders of the Falcons, and invited him to lunch. Lindsey was a sportsman and a gentleman and one of the most respected men in the city. I suggested that we get all the minority partners together and buy Rankin out. I felt we could generate enough bad press, as I was now a member, to embarrass Rankin into selling the franchise to *us*. As General Manager, I felt certain I could turn the Falcons around.

Lindsey listened to me in dumbfounded bewilderment. He was obviously embarrassed for me but he didn't laugh. When I finished, he kindly explained that he didn't feel it was the right time for a takeover, and strongly suggested that I not bring our conversation to the attention of anyone else, now or ever. He further suggested that I should abandon the plan altogether and immediately. I got the feeling it was a bad idea.

It seems I had overlooked the fact that these seven stockholders were relatives, business partners, and associates of

Rankin's. One was his college roommate and, as Governor of the State of Georgia, had been responsible for Rankin being awarded the franchise. All of these men were Rankin's oldest and most trusted friends.

Two articles a week doesn't sound like much, and it isn't if you can spell, punctuate, type, and arrange complete sentences. I could do none of these, so twice a week I was at the newspaper at 6:30 a.m. asking one of the eight staff writers to do it for me. I paid whoever did it fifty of the one hundred dollars I was being paid.

It didn't matter which of the writers translated my story into print, as I was close friends with all of them and all of them could find use for the money. Perhaps the most prototypical writer in the sports department was Frank Hyland.

Frank grew up in Minnesota and played college and service football. He was stand-up and stubborn, with a passion for both sports and journalism. He felt his obligation as a journalist was to educate the fan, and only through honesty could you do that. He had covered the Falcons in 1971 and 1972. He and the Dutchman had traded punches the first week in camp; neither landed any blows, but neither side forgave the other. For two years, they waged a cold war until Frank was assigned to the Braves in 1973. Hyland and I had a mutual combination of respect and disrespect for Norm Van Brocklin, but we both thought he was hilarious.

Over the years, Norm had developed an almost abnormal pre-occupation with the Communist Party. He blamed the "Reds" for almost everything unpleasant that happened in the world. The integration of schools in the 1960s was undoubtedly a Communist plot. The incident at Kent State was, of course, Communist inspired. The prison riots at Attica were the last straw. Dutch could stand it no longer. "Those bastards have taken over the schools, the churches, and now they're taking over the fucking prisons." He strongly resembled Sterling Hayden in *Dr. Strangelove.*

Frank loved to goad Norm, and Dutch took the bait like a large-mouth bass hitting a top-water plug. Frank wore a Russian belt buckle, drove a Volkswagen, and spoke Russian fluently.

Since I was Frank's friend, it didn't take long for Dutch to label *me* a Communist.

Suddenly, the Falcons, with quarterback Bob Lee, caught fire. They reeled off seven victories in a row. But the Dutchman, instead of pacified, became more belligerent and antagonistic than ever. Each succeeding week made him more and more pugnacious.

I stubbornly held fast to the notion that the streak was just a fluke. Each week I would forecast a Falcon defeat. As the winning continued, my credibility and popularity steadily diminished. One does not win friends by downplaying a *winning* home team. But I wasn't doing it deliberately. I honestly didn't think the Falcons were good, and I certainly didn't believe they could win with their quarterback or front office. People who had always accepted my opinion were starting to laugh at me. I couldn't believe it, but then it got worse.

One of the best things about being a jock was you never had to fight. No one ever physically challenged you. People just assumed if you played ten years of professional football you were another Rambo. Oh, occasionally a drunk would get jealous of you and ask you outside. I'd snuff that by telling him to go on out and practice bleeding and falling and I'd be out directly.

Now as a sportswriter, I was being held accountable. It seems that the spoken word is uttered, heard, and then quickly forgotten. But the "written" word is just that. When you put it in writing, you had better mean it and be able to back it up.

No one had ever challenged me, certainly no "civilian." But when the winning streak reached five, I was approached by a little old lady at a fashionable cocktail party who told me that if she were a man she would punch out my lights.

Then a drunken baseball player offered to bite off my ear. The next thing I knew, Frank Wall declared war on me and tried to have me removed from the press box. Then my Buckhead friends, who were better friends with Rankin, stopped inviting me to lunch.

The final blow came on the last day of the season. The Falcons had lost two of their last three games and were eliminated from the playoffs. I was in the dressing room after the game saying goodbye to some of the players. As I saw it, my war was with management, not the players. I was still one of *them*. That hadn't changed. Suddenly, I was confronted by the hulking figure of a naked lineman. He was pilled up and hostile and invited me outside to fight.

He was four inches taller, sixty pounds heavier and twelve years younger, but I had taken all the abuse I was going to. This jerk was not even a starter and had been in the league just two years. The very idea of challenging a veteran of ten years to go outside and fight. I was tired of being treated like a sportswriter, so I marched straight to the door, with him in close pursuit.

In ten years I had learned that there were always one hundred or so relatives, wives, children, and well-wishers waiting outside to see the players. The dumb-ass lineman was almost out of the door before he realized he was naked. The fight never materialized, but I quickly resigned from the paper. That was fifty dollars a week I could well do without.

The following year, the loveless Falcons won only two of their first eight games. After a 42-7 loss to the Dolphins, Norm Van Brocklin was fired.

Paul Hornung, Max McGee, Hawkins, Artie Donovan, and Norm Van Brocklin on "Football Saturday" at Harrison's.

Angela Hornung, Hawkins, and Norm Van Brocklin on "Football Saturday."

Hawkins at work on the Falcon Network.

SPORTS ILLUSTRATED

Front row: *Johnny Unitas, Hawkins.* Second row: *Tom Brookshire, Irv Cross, Brent Mussberger.* Third row: *Tommy McDonald, Phyllis George, Sonny Jergenson.* Fourth row: *Tim Van Gelter, Paul Hornung, Pat Summerall.* Fifth row: *Frank Gleiber, Johnny Morris, Emerson Boozer, Don Criqui.* Sixth row: *Tom Matte, Jim Thackher, Gary Blender.*

CBS SPORTS

Lindsey Nelson and Hawkins.

TRAVIS ELLISON

CBS SPORTS

Hawkins and Frank Gleiber from CBS days.

H. M. cutting cypress knees for Down to Earth, Ltd.

An ad for one of Down to Earth's tables appears in Architectural Digest.

Mr. Davees.

Mr. Hunt, age 20, and . . .

. . . Mr. Hunt, fifty years later, with H. M.

15

A general slump in the nation's economy was starting to play hell with our garbage business. For the first time since my move to Atlanta, the city was at a standstill. Fewer and fewer cranes were ornamenting the city's skyline. Times were bad and getting worse.

Our fourth truck had just been ordered, but new business was hard to come by. In fact, many of our customers were reducing their number of containers or cutting back on service. Some of them were actually going bankrupt. I'd never paid attention to the economy before, so I wasn't all that concerned about it. Ms. Garrett and Mr. Hunt were downright frantic.

"Hawkins, this mess is going to get worse before it gets better. Start paying attention to your overhead. Sell one of those trucks and fire a driver. Start thinking cash flow. I've been through this shit before, and when things turn downward, you find out that bankers can be nasty little bastards. Don't buy another thing," said Mr. Hunt.

I felt we'd already seen the worst of things, and I paid him no mind. I know I shouldn't have felt that way, but it always pissed me off when Mr. Hunt was right.

It was time for Super Bowl VIII and the annual reunion of the old firm. However, since the game was played in Houston, Mr. Davees' town, and since the events that transpired there were largely engineered by Mr. Davees, it seems appropriate to hear his version of the story:

This story begins as the final gun sounded at Super Bowl VII in Los Angeles. I had just returned from Europe when my close friend Mr. Hunt phoned me from Atlanta announcing he had beat the spread and was ready to begin plans for Super Bowl VIII and our annual firm meeting of Hunt, Hawkins and Davees in Houston. Mr. Hunt quickly reiterated he would not be subjected to the embarrassments and inefficiencies that occurred at the firm meeting at Super Bowl VI in New Orleans under the direction of our celebrity firm member, Mr. Hawkins. In other words, Mr. Hunt said, "Davees get your ass in gear, now."

Mr. Hunt is everything that a successful Texan is supposed to be and demonstrates various combinations of these aspects of this presence wherever he is. Mr. Hunt has more sides than a crystal.

This story will just describe a few of those sides, one of which is his demanding and commanding nature. I, of course, was very proud that Super Bowl VIII was going to be in my town, Houston. Here I was in my thirties, a self-made millionaire, healthy, happy, single, and in a great economy with the next Super Bowl on the way. I believed I had what is known as the "home field advantage." As the months progressed, Mr. Hunt reinforced his position with reminders of Super Bowl VI, where Mr. Hawkins had failed to produce rooms, tickets, badges, invitations, and other accoutrements of that Super Bowl. Clearly I was charged with Super Bowl VIII in Houston. This, of course, suited me, as it's my nature not to mind being in charge. I noted, however, that as December rolled around and the teams narrowed down, Mr. Hunt's preoccupation with Super Bowl VIII was taking on an intensity of scary proportions for me. By Christmas, Mr. Hunt was routinely telling anybody who needed tickets, rooms, cars, dates, or anything in Houston not to worry about it. He would just simply call Mr. Davees and get it handled. All of a sudden I realized that my "home field advantage" was quickly turning into the "home field disadvantage."

My relationship with Mr. Hunt has always included a lot of one-upmanship, but pulling something over on Mr. Hunt is not an easy task. I was determined that I had to create some circumstance that would put Mr. Hunt off guard and give me the upper hand as soon as he arrived. Otherwise, I would become his verbally enslaved manservant, in charge of everything, with the dubious honor of "paying the checks." My plan seemed simple to start with: just create a sit-com extravaganza upon his arrival, thereby neutralizing his demands and giving me a position of strength.

Mr. Hunt has few weaknesses; however, one of his weaknesses is his love of and for women. So I knew that whatever I did would have to involve women and sex, if possible. The only time Mr. Hunt is not in charge of himself is when he falls victim to the element of surprise; even then his confusion exists only for those brief moments until he has had time to assess the situation. Then he quickly finds and defines his position and reverts to the demanding and commanding Mr. Hunt. I decided to confront Mr. Hunt with a situation that would not only call forth all of his manly abilities, but would start his Super Bowl off with a "bang" in the literal sense.

The early 1970's was a flourishing time for hippies and hippie chicks, and our Houston/Montrose area was no exception. I decided that I would get such a hippie chick and have her pose as a hitchhiking wanderer. She would be the star of my welcoming committee for Mr. Hunt for Super Bowl '74. My problem, of course, was to find a hippie who would be willing, sight unseen, to fall in love with Mr. Hunt and begin his Houston Super Bowl in memorable fashion. I quickly realized the only alternative was to find a hooker whom I could pass off as an eighteen-year-old hippie and who would play out whatever role that I planned for Mr. Hunt during this welcome. I began interviewing a few hookers, and while I didn't find my hooker/actress right away, I did enjoy several of the interviews.

Finally I decided on a girl named Jeannie, who seemed to fit the bill and wanted to be the actress. Jeannie was twenty-two years old, long-haired, slender-built, and innocent enough looking to be a nineteen-year-old wanderer. She, of course, had no hippie clothes because she was not a hippie. So we went to Montrose and bought her the requisite outfit: a long skirt, a "make love not war" t-shirt, a wine pouch bag, a small knapsack, some dope-type paraphernalia, peace signs, and whatever else was for sale. In addition to cash, Jeannie got to keep the clothes and accessories as payment for her performance. At the dress rehearsal she really did look like a hippie, and a good-looking hippie. She was fun and ready to get into a "just right" performance for Mr. Hunt's welcome to Super Bowl VIII.

Back to the element of surprise: in order to get Mr. Hunt off guard and to bring out his true antic personality, all of this preparation was absolutely necessary. After picking him up from the airport, we drove in my two-door Mark IV through the five o'clock afternoon traffic to Mr. Hunt's Galleria area hotel. I had stationed Jeannie a few hundred feet from the corner of San Felipe and Post Oak Boulevard in front of a shopping center best known for Rudi's Restaurant. By design, we were at an extremely traffic-heavy intersection. As I turned the corner, I said, "Mr. Hunt, look at that hippie over there hitchhiking. Let's stop and pick her up."

Mr. Hunt took one look and bellowed, "Davees, don't stop for that girl. There's no telling what she's got, who she is, or where she's been. She may get us arrested, and God knows I didn't come to Houston to get in any trouble. Davees, don't stop!" He began motioning with his hands and arms to go on to the hotel, whereupon I pulled over and opened the door, and Jeannie's 110-pound body lept in the front seat on top of Mr. Hunt's bear-sized lap. She slammed the door behind her, and the three of us were jammed in the front seat of the Lincoln. Mr. Hunt was beside himself, unsure for once what orders to bark. There was no room for hand waving; the wine bag and backpack were all over him, and her long hair seemed to have him tied in knots. That moment of surprise, that confused reaction was worth all the preparation.

Mr. Hunt was no doubt thinking that to stop would cause a traffic jam, a wreck, or something. Maybe she was carrying dope. His computer mind was playing hell with his decision-making process, but something had to happen in these few seconds to make something else happen. Anything, so we continued through the Galleria area. Jeannie said a polite "thank you for picking me up." I asked where she was going, and she said, "I don't know. I'm leaving home. I just got to get out of Houston." Mr. Hunt is quickly and quietly trying to figure which position he should take. I said, "Jeannie, why don't you stop and have a drink with us at Mr. Hunt's hotel before you go on with your journey." She said, "Who is Mr. Hunt?" I said, "The man you are sitting on." She looked at him and said, "Okay, he's cute."

By this point Mr. Hunt had concluded that Jeannie was not a killer, not a dope peddler, and not crazed. Jeannie was, in fact, a very attractive, long-haired, no make-up, good-looking young girl with all her belongings in tow. Obviously, he would have to come to the rescue of the hitchhiker, so he immediately reverted to his dictatorial self: "Mr. Davees, let's get in this lane. Davees, why aren't we in the other lane? Davees, why is there so much traffic? Let's move right along. Mr. Davees, does my hotel room have a view and room service for proper food and drink for Jeannie?"

"Mr. Hunt, would you just wait a minute. I'm doing my very best."

"Well, Davees, I don't know that that's good enough." Mr. Hunt continues badgering me while smiling, winking his baby-blues, and otherwise displaying his affectionate side to the hitch-hiker. Unbeknownst to Mr. Hunt, I had directed Jeannie to just tell her story of woe and neither reject nor encourage Mr. Hunt's advances. Jeannie's story was even better than we had rehearsed—no money, no shelter, a misunderstood life, no fun, no travel, etc. And there is nothing Mr. Hunt would rather do than solve other people's problems.

We got to the hotel, and, of course, Mr. Hunt signaled me: "Mr. Davees, get the bags. Is my room in order? This is your town. I'm a guest, and Jeannie's my guest." So Jeannie has been elevated from wandering hitchhiker to Mr. Hunt's guest in less than a mile. And naturally I am relegated to being Mr. Hunt's "Hey Boy." We go up to the room, and Mr. Hunt orders me to order room service to bring food and drinks.

Mr. Hunt now fully realizes that happenstance has put him with a very good-looking young lady, early in the trip, with a good story and a great personality, so he launches into his routine of all the Super Bowl plans for the long weekend ahead; all of his past experiences and accomplishments, including building Six Flags; and all the fun things he had done and does now. Jeannie, of course, was very happy, impressed, and thor-oughly enjoying her drink and hors d'oeuvre. Things couldn't have gone better. I got my phone call and left to go to the lobby, assuring Mr. Hunt that I would be about an hour or so and that he should get dressed to go out for dinner that night.

Flemin Gaskin had chauffeured our Texas Taxi, a yellow GMC super mobile home, to the hotel in readiness to transport Mr. Hunt and Mr. Hawkins around Houston for the weekend. The Texas Taxi was one of those giant RVs with card tables, TV, stocked bar, and all the comforts of home. While I was seeing to my other Super Bowl-host chores, I assumed that Jeannie and Mr. Hunt were having their hitchhiker affair.

When I returned to the hotel some two hours later, Mr. Hunt was in rare form. "Davees, you little shit, I ain't been in Houston but two hours and I've already been laid. This is going to be one hell of a Super Bowl."

On the way to the airport to pick up Mr. Hawkins, Mr. Hunt opened a deck of cards and insisted we play gin rummy. I didn't want to play gin rummy for two reasons: I hate to play cards, and Mr. Hunt is an excellent gin player.

At this point, I had already paid Jeannie $300 and bought her clothes, and now I was having to play gin and listen to Mr. Hunt tell of his sexual exploits with a nineteen-year-old hippie.

Hunt told me what a lovely girl she was and how she really liked him and they really had just gotten so close so fast, even mentioning his sexual prowess during that hour or so in the bedroom. Mr. Hunt normally doesn't relate these kinds of stories, but this had been so action-packed and so sudden that I thought, "Well, he's got to tell me all this" and I listened. All the while he is beating me at every gin hand. Not only are the tables turning very quickly on me, but the reverse sting is on. "Jeannie thinks she loves me," he says, continuing to beat me $25 a hand. I'm down a couple hundred in the gin game, I'm paying for the Texas Taxi ride, I'm listening to Mr. Hunt, I'm providing the whiskey, I'm providing everything and getting beat every which way.

When we picked up Mr. Hawkins, Mr. Hunt was still blowing hard: "Hawkins, you asshole, what's been keeping you? I haven't been here three hours, and I've already screwed a nineteen-year-old hippie. Get in front with Flemin; Davees and I are playing gin.

"Davees," he continues without a pause, "I was lucky to find this girl, but you should learn that you always have to make your breaks happen." So now I'm getting a lecture from Mr. Hunt. Then he announces that he's invited Jeannie to go with us to dinner. I'm floored, speechless, as Mr. Hunt asks, "Davees, where are we going to dinner, Tony's or Rudi's?"

"Mr. Hunt, where is Jeannie?" I ask.

"I have sent her out to buy clothes and get dressed. I told her we would be going to some nice restaurant."

I now realized that Jeannie had gone beyond her role; things were out of control. I had set up a situation impossible to carry on for three more days. Mr. Hunt didn't know Jeannie was a hooker, and I don't dare tell him at this point. I couldn't believe this was really happening to me. What did "Sweet Jeannie" have in mind? We doubled back to the hotel where Jeannie appeared with a complete outfit and makeover. She was now Jeannie whatever-her-last-name-was, and she was Mr. Hunt's dinner partner and date for the evening. Had Mr. Hunt really done an outstanding job, or was Jeannie playing me for additional cash, knowing I would pay more now rather than ruin my setup?

I quickly made my way to Jeannie to make sure that she had not misunderstood me and let her know she was not still on my payroll. Jeannie had the same intent and immediately let me know that she had completed her work and this was now a personal matter between her and Mr. Hunt. What in the hell was going on here! The thought of my paying for Mr. Hunt's pleasure beyond my sit-com had about made me sick. Meanwhile Mr. Hunt was strutting around in a fashion that would make a peacock look drab. The bottom line was that Jeannie was going out with Mr. Hunt, not as a hooker, not as a hippie, not as a hitchhiker, but just as a fine lady and one hell of a woman. She told Mr. Hunt that she had to leave early the next morning and was not likely to ever see him again. They had a wonderful night together, and it had become so real to Mr. Hunt that I couldn't tell him the true story.

So, once again, Mr. Hunt had reversed the joke and the sting was on me. I had done all the paying, all the setting up, all of the doing, none of the screwing, and he had ended up with the best-looking girl at the whole dinner party, except, of course, my date. I told Mr. Hawkins and the few people who knew about the hitchhiker that I didn't want the story to be told for at least ten years. And when Mr. Hunt reads these pages, it will be his first knowledge of the truth.

Mr. Hunt told this hitchhiker story all weekend and is still telling it today—the story of his prowess and how the girl just fell in love with him. I am sure that even now he still believes that she was not a hooker, and I don't know—maybe she wasn't.

16

In March of 1974, it was announced that Don Meredith had left ABC and signed on with NBC for what was reportedly $200,000 a year, plus. It was a sudden and shocking move, but it was manna to me. I was the perfect replacement for Dandy Don. ABC told it like it was, and the thought of working with Howard Cosell had me climbing the walls. I couldn't help but become a star!

I picked up the phone and called ABC Sports and asked for Roone Arledge. He wasn't in so I left my number. When he didn't call back, I phoned him again. I called him the next day. And the day after. As a matter of fact, I called him once a week for over a year and he hasn't returned my call yet. But I'm getting ahead of myself.

I hopped on a plane for New York. Monday Night Football was what I was after, but another matter also interested me. A newly formed World Football League was to start playing in July. Television Sports (TVS) was going to televise the games. A new league starting up with plans to go global — that was my cup of tea.

The plane trip to New York was like any other. As you get closer to the city, things get testy. People get antsy, nervous, and slightly rude. The passengers beside you, the stewardesses, everybody starts feeling trapped. A feeling of anxiety creeps over you until you finally land, and then it's sheer panic: the mad scramble for books, papers, and carry-on luggage and the stampede to the door. Then the pace quickens, and it's a foot race for the luggage bin and the fight for a cab.

Over the bridge or through the tunnel? By now, you don't

care. They know you're a tourist. You've already been had. You give him the address, and he doesn't understand you. You repeat it again, only louder.

"Between 52nd and 53rd?"

"I don't know."

"You don't know? How in Christ's name am I supposed to know?"

You rarely get one that speaks English, and if you do, he can't understand Southern, so where are you then?

You get there, you always do. Whatever you tip them is never enough. Or if it is, you can't tell. New York, New York.

Unannounced, I marched into the sports department at ABC and asked to see Roone Arledge. Roone was not in, so I left my name and number where I could be reached. I went on over to CBS, said hello to some friends and asked to see the powers that be. I was kindly told that I was wasting my time. Once you're fired from a network, you're never rehired by that same network. They play hardball in the city.

I called Roone again — still not in. I found this place called T.V.S. It wasn't a building, but it was in a building. I hadn't expected much. The man I needed to see was Eddie Einhorn. Eddie wasn't in, but I was ushered into the office of his partner, Allen Lubell. We talked for awhile and he was excited. They had settled on Merle Harmon as the play-by-play man, but no decision had been made on the color man. Allen told me that he had seen my work and liked it, but couldn't promise anything. He would have to discuss it with Eddie and Gary Davidson, the commissioner of the World Football League. Just as I was leaving, he got serious.

"Alex, I like your style. But there is one thing that you must understand. The game has got to be *sold*. We have got to do the best work imaginable. We're brand new and we're all in this together. There is no room for criticism or *honesty*; you've got to be a shill. We've got to *sell* the league. Do you understand what I'm saying? The League is counting on us to *sell* it."

I faced a moral decision here. I'd come up here, highly principled, looking for work with ABC so I could "tell it like it is." And that is the way it should be. Now I was looking at a job description that read, "house man." I did what every nonworking announcer in the country would do. I told him I'd take the job.

Leaving no stone unturned, I made another unannounced visit, this time to NBC. The head of sports there was Carl Lindemann, and for some strange reason, he agreed to receive me.

I had never met Carl, but I introduced myself and sat down. He never got up or offered his hand. "Carl," I began, "I'm looking for work." That's about as far as I got when he broke in.

"I don't like or appreciate having people drop in on me without an appointment. I want to make that point very clear. I know who you are and I've seen your work. What happened to you at CBS?"

"You probably know more about that than I do. Anyway, I'm looking for work. Can you help me?"

"We don't have any openings this year, but if something comes up in the future, I'll keep you in mind. I hate being ugly, but I meant what I said about coming in here unannounced."

"Carl," I said as I stood up, "If you're worried about being rude, don't. You're the nicest person I've talked to all day."

Some really weird things were happening in Atlanta that spring. People were going broke. Not any of my Buckhead friends; their pockets were too deep. But, a lot of my real estate friends were. The bloom was off the rose in the land business. The banks were calling notes and bankers were getting fired and the loan officers were getting real nasty.

Atlanta Waste Control was holding on. Customers were calling *us* shopping prices. It's funny, but people somehow resent having to pay for trash removal. Our prices were generally lower than the competition, so our customer base was at least stable. Our fourth truck was ready for delivery, but Dave, who handled that, was out of town. I had to talk to the loan officer about the financing of the new truck. What I knew about finance was less than nothing.

All I knew was we had not used up our million-dollar line of credit and we were operating in the black. I'd been bullshitting my way through life, so why not try it at the bank?

My bookkeeper explained that we were paying two percent

above prime. I didn't have any idea what prime was, but I went on down to the bank.

C & S was our lender, and they were getting killed by land loans. Personnel were shifting like leaves in the wind, and people were losing their jobs. Across from me sat their third loan officer in as many months, a nice young man trying to talk sternly but obviously unsure of himself and his job.

"Good afternoon, Mr. Hawkins, have a seat. What can I do for you?" he said coldly.

"We've got this truck that needs financing and I don't know a lot about it, but I guess we could do it like we did the last one, couldn't we?" I asked.

He started in on how the rates had gone up and loans were being called and it was indeed starting to get bad in Atlanta, when all of a sudden, his secretary called on the speaker phone and exclaimed that the governor's office was on the phone. The governor wanted *me* in his office as soon as possible. Burt Reynolds was having a press conference in Jimmy Carter's office to announce that he was going to be filming *The Longest Yard* somewhere in Georgia. He wanted me in on it.

Well, I puffed up like a pumpkin and looked at that banker for the moment it took him to volunteer that I was on my way there. He assured me, as he walked me to the door, that the papers would be delivered to my office the next day, at the same rate as before.

I was a shrewd negotiator. It was great being a celebrity.

17

Deliverance had been a smash hit and opened up the world for Burt Reynolds. He was the most talked about property in the motion picture industry.

When I arrived at the governor's office, it was overflowing with media. The State Capitol was buzzing with excitement; it was clear that something bigger than day-to-day legislation was taking place. Local politicians were ignored; Governor Jimmy Carter was a secondary figure. Burt Reynolds was in town, and that meant fun and excitement; he had an aura about him.

Deliverance had grossed well over $100,000,000, and the Waycross-born Georgian was superstitious and loyal to his native state. He announced that his next movie, *The Longest Yard,* was going to be filmed somewhere in Georgia that fall. It would prove to be the second of eight movies he would film in the state.

Deliverance had showcased Burt, but it wasn't the movie that had vaulted him to the top. Nor was it his appearance on talk shows, though that had helped. It was when he posed nude for *Cosmopolitan* magazine that America went wild. *Playboy* had featured nude women for several years, but, to my knowledge, Burt was the first nude male. And it wasn't his body that stirred the nation; it was that little-boyish, "I don't give a shit" smile. America fell in love with this laughable, unassuming, mischievous, self-deprecating little boy. He was naughty but nice, the man the ladies wanted to dance with and their husbands like to drink with.

Pandemonium broke out when the press conference ended.

Secretaries abandoned their work and chased after Burt. Young women and little old ladies, women who would never dream of cheating on their husbands, were frantic to get near him. An autograph, a word, a look or a touch. They all wanted to be near the blaze. It was scary. He could have had any woman he wanted.

Being the center of attention was not new to me. I have been there for most of my life. But even the superstar jocks like Unitas had not affected people anything like this. These women didn't want his attention, they wanted *him*. And Burt handled it so well. He honestly didn't know why people reacted to him as they did. But he didn't spend a lot of time worrying about it. He didn't know what he had, but he knew he had *something*. His confidence level was well off the charts.

Even men were attracted to Burt. For some reason, they didn't feel threatened by him. They envied him, yes, but they were not jealous. Burt didn't take himself seriously, so he wasn't judged. He had the greatest laugh in the universe, and he exercised it freely. Being with him, I just stood back and stared. He had IT—whatever that mysterious quality is that sets you apart. He was a Star. Better still, he was a Movie Star. Everyone wanted a piece of him, but there was only so much to go around and he was so unselfish.

The Longest Yard was about a pro football player who had a run-in with the law and was sent to prison. While there, he was coerced into forming a football team with the inmates to play against the prison guards. Not only was it a perfect role for Burt, but there were any number of parts for me.

The next day, we went on location. We toured three prisons. In each prison we visited the reaction was the same as at the capitol. These inmates were falling all over themselves trying to get a look at him. They kidded and joked with him through the bars, and he with them. Somehow they felt he was one of them. It was strange that they cheered him. Burt had everything going for him, and they had only an eight-by-ten cell.

Then we found Reidsville Prison. Reidsville is a maximum security prison in the southeastern part of the state, famous only for its solitude and remoteness. We would be staying in Reidsville for eight weeks. Being in prison for two months was not my idea of a good time. I decided to forego my movie career for the time being.

It was late June when I received the news that I had the job with T.V.S. They had tried to land Alex Karras as their color man, but had not succeeded. I was warned, once again, that the league had to be sold. Everything was to be positive. Negative would not be tolerated. I accepted the job on those terms.

The World Football League was the creation of League Commissioner Gary Davidson. Gary was a West Coast attorney who had previously founded the American Basketball Association and the World Hockey Association. He had been successful with both, so he was viewed with respect and fear by the owners of the NFL.

Players' salaries had risen sharply in basketball and hockey as a result of his ventures, so the NFL owners were anxious and suspicious. The NFL had just awarded franchises to Seattle and Tampa for $16,000,000. The asking price for a franchise in the WFL was only $400,000. This was threatening to Pete Rozelle and his staff. The price of an NFL franchise had doubled in eight years, or so "they" said.

The All-American Conference formed in 1946 went under in 1950, yet three teams, the Colts, Browns, and 49ers had been absorbed by the National Football League. The American Football League, formed in 1960, had successfully merged into the NFL in its entirety. Now the WFL, with a television contract, was posing some serious problems. What was a WFL team worth?

In 1973, the WFL announced that twelve teams would commence play in July of 1974. In January, the WFL held its first college draft. By the end of the month, they had signed some of the top collegiate players in the country. In March, it was announced that Larry Csonka, Jim Kiick, and Paul Warfield had signed with the WFL. Their contracts were reported to be a $3,000,000 package deal with ironclad guarantees.

In April, Ken Stabler signed with Birmingham. Soon after, Calvin Hill, Bill Bergey, Daryle Lamonica, and John Gilliam joined on. By June, a total of fifty-nine players had defected and signed with the WFL. Football is a labor-intensive business. It was now starting to become a capital-intensive business as well.

The price of everything was going up.

The WFL appeared to have the NFL reeling. Every announcement was positive. But just beneath the surface all was not well. Some of these WFL owners were rich and respected. Others were not. An assortment of personalities were involved in ownership, and franchises were swapped about weekly.

The Memphis Southmen had started out as the Toronto Northmen. Owner John Bassett was a recognized and respected Canadian businessman with interests in television, newspapers, and film. Entertainers Charlie Rich and Isaac Hayes were also involved. Similarly, The Honolulu Hawaiians were owned by Chris Hemmeter, a successful developer and businessman. On the other hand, the Philadelphia Bell was represented in league meetings by a lifeguard from a local swimming pool. He and his partner had each borrowed $25,000 as a down payment for the $400,000 franchise fee. His partner backed down at the last moment, and the franchise was picked up by John B. Kelly, Jr., from one of Philadelphia's foremost families.

A player agent became owner of the Houston Texans. He rented the Astrodome. The Jacksonville Sharks were owned by a man named Fran and his wife named Douglas. They hired the high school coach from New Smyrna Beach to head up the coaching staff.

The Florida Blazers started out in Washington, moved to Norfolk, and then shifted to Orlando. The owner was a former college and pro footballer who just happened to be the first black assistant coach in the old AFL. His resume stated he was "self employed."

The Birmingham Americans were owned by a former underwater demolition expert. A secretary of his became part owner and president of the club. She was tall and blond and had the body of a beauty queen.

The Detroit Wheels were owned by a twenty-eight-year-old black lawyer. The team's identity as a Detroit franchise was foiled when they had to play their home games in Ypsilanti, thirty-seven miles from Detroit. Franchises in Tokyo and Mexico were being discussed.

It was apparent from the start that the league had its pros and cons, its pluses and minuses, but it was all so exciting. It was *new.*

I personally had been growing more and more disenchanted with the NFL. There seemed to be a sameness creeping into the league. All the teams were starting to look alike. Businessmen had replaced sportsmen as owners, and the players were getting what I termed "greedy." Money was replacing loyalty. Both owners and players were growing increasingly arrogant. In short, the game was changing and I hated the change. Pro football was now Big Business.

The WFL was to open its season on Wednesday, July 10. Our opening telecast would be the following evening. Because of the fifty-nine NFL players signing contracts with WFL teams, interest was building in this new league.

Just before the NFL training camps opened, the startling news came down that the NFL Players' Association had called for a players' strike. Rookies reported to camp but the veterans stayed out. The College All-Star and the Hall of Fame games were cancelled. Just that quickly the World Football League was the only game in town. At that point, I was the only working color man in America.

Sports fans did not care to read or hear about labor relations, so all attention was focused on *our* opening night.

18

On Wednesday evening, July 10, 1974, the World Football League commenced play. I was in Jacksonville preparing for the first of twenty-two nationally televised games. Thursday night's game featured the New York Stars and the Jacksonville Sharks.

The Thursday morning papers had proclaimed that opening day had been a total success. Two hundred thousand people in five cities had turned out on day one. Attendance exceeded expectations. The front page headlines boldly announced the league was off and running. There was no mention of the NFL. That *other* league had seemingly vanished.

Eddie Einhorn and his T.V.S. crew of thirty had been in Jacksonville since Monday. Preparation for this game was almost impossible, since everything and everybody was new. It was far and away the biggest challenge of my career.

T.V.S. was basically a four-man operation with President Eddie Einhorn in central control. Eddie had started T.V.S. with a briefcase and an idea. In the sixties he started buying the TV rights to various sporting events. He contracted with stations, both independent and network-affiliated and sold commercial time to advertisers. By the early seventies he owned the rights to every college basketball conference except the A.C.C. Eddie was a gambler, but a good one. T.V.S. had paid $1.5 million for the rights to televise the WFL. If this league proved successful, he would be a very wealthy man.

One hundred ten stations had signed on to carry the game, giving the league exposure in eighty-five percent of the country. The future of the WFL rested in our hands.

The success of Monday Night Football had influenced everyone. Basically, we had the same opportunity as ABC. T.V.S. was the second network to televise prime-time football, and we would be judged more critically for that reason. While ABC used nine cameras, one hand-held and four replay machines, we were limited to about half of that hardware. It was indeed a challenge.

Merle Harmon had been hired to do the play-by-play. Merle, a veteran of fourteen years, was currently the voice of the Milwaukee Brewers. The only hitch was, Merle's contract with the Brewers was so demanding he would not be able to arrive at the site of our game until the day of the contest.

The success of ABC's three man broadcast had tempted the other networks to try it. No one else had successfully pulled it off. I had been involved in one attempt while at CBS, and it proved awkward. T.V.S. was not only going to try it; they were putting a new wrinkle in it. Each week, a different celebrity would be added to our team. The celebrity was not necessarily an expert on football. What and how he or she would contribute to the telecast was solely up to me.

Our first guest commentator was sports novelist George Plimpton, of *Paper Lion* fame. I had breakfast with George that morning, and we'd discussed various approaches as to how he could be brought into the game. He'd confessed to knowing little about football, less about the rule changes, and nothing about the players. I concurred with him on two of the three, so we agreed to "throw a bunch of stuff against the wall and see how much of it stuck."

George was bright and humorous, and I knew he'd do fine. My work required a little more imagination. The league had been hurriedly put together, and competent media relations people were hard to find. The team-by-team media guides, so important to broadcasters, were sketchy, vague, and downright inaccurate. The name NFL players who had signed with the league would not be joining the WFL until 1975 and '76. Meanwhile, the rosters were made up of unknown players from obscure schools from all over the country. Who were these guys? I was supposed to know.

For three weeks I stayed buried in media guides searching for players whom someone might know or remember. Oh, there were a few with name recognition like George Sauer, John Elliott, and Gerry Philbin, but not nearly enough. What was I going to do with names like Reggie Oliver, Keith Kripple and Wimpy Winther? My reputation for candor and honesty was going to be seriously stretched.

In an effort to generate some interest, I ferreted for information. To my astonishment, I found that every player in the league had been all-*something*, somewhere or another. Over a hundred had been All-Americans, and roughly a half-dozen had been runner-up to the Heisman Trophy winner. Since nobody ever remembers the runner-up, it was a safe out.

We arrived at the Gator Bowl well before six. The traffic there was horrendous, and they were expecting a near sellout. Merle and I were wearing our T.V.S. blazers, which were hard to describe. The fabric was polyester, but the color was neither red nor orange. I think it is safe to say that there is not another color that looks good with it.

After checking to see if everything was working in the booth, I went down on the field to talk with the players and coaches. Allen Lubell had earlier made the statement that we were "all in this together." I have never before experienced so much cooperation. Both coaches spoke candidly and openly about their respective philosophies and approaches to the game. They told me which players could play and who were the pretenders. Both coaches gave me their opening series so we could isolate on key players. Everyone knew how important TV was to the survival of the league.

This was such a departure from the tight-lipped coaches in the NFL. Everything there was top secret, Pentagon stuff.

At nine o'clock we opened the telecast with a shot of the traffic crossing the bridge to the Gator Bowl. It was backed up for miles and looked impressive on camera. Fifty-nine thousand people had shown up on a hot Florida night to view what they could have seen on television at home. The World Football League was now being watched by most of the country.

We had plenty to talk about that night. Merle had to explain the ten new rule changes and why and how they had come about. He announced that over two hundred thousand people had attended the five opening night games. Forty-two thousand in Memphis, fifty-three thousand in Birmingham, fifty-five thousand in Philadelphia and now fifty-nine thousand in Jacksonville.

We talked about the bright future of the league and how much greater it would be when Csonka, Kiick, Warfield, and Stabler joined us. We praised the new owners, players, and cities that had joined in on professional football.

At halftime, we introduced Eddie Einhorn and Gary Davidson. They talked of future plans to expand the league into Mexico and then Europe and the Orient. I was already thinking up names for those teams. The Chinese Walls, Spanish Flies, and Brussels Sprouts all sounded good to me. Everything was smooth and positive . . . until the seven-minute power failure after halftime. I doubt that we lost a viewer.

George entertained with trivia, observations, and a rough explanation of how the "dickerrod" worked. The dickerrod was a new method of measuring first-down yardage. We had been warned by league officials that it was nearly impossible to explain how it worked, but they were certain it did. They were partially right. It *was* impossible to explain, and it *didn't* work, but we didn't know it at the time. Nevertheless, it proved a theme for comedy throughout the entire season. Whoever heard of anything called a dickerrod?

Aside from the seven-minute power failure, everyone was relatively pleased with the telecast. George was both pleasant and humorous, and Merle and I worked well together. Everything was upbeat and positive. The ratings were higher than anticipated. Interest and curiosity had peaked, as we were the *only* game in town. Nearly everyone was pulling for the league to succeed. No one was more pleased than the NFL Players Association. There was now an option as to where you could play and the salaries were escalating rapidly.

Our second game was in Memphis, featuring the Portland Storm and the Memphis Southmen. My routine was to leave for the home city on Tuesday. I'd watch the home team practice and then visit with the coaches, players, and front office people.

John Bassett, the Memphis owner, was confident, capable and cordial. His coach was John McVay, a small college coach for the past ten years with no previous experience in the pro game. But these people knew what they were doing. The franchise was being run as smoothly as any NFL club. The stadium seated fifty thousand and it was sold out for our game.

I spent Wednesday with the Portland Storm. Their coach was Dick Coury. He had coached two years with the Denver Broncos. Neither team could have been nicer or more helpful. Again, it was understood that we were all in this together, and all knew the importance of TV exposure.

We had announced that our celebrity guest would be Elvis Presley, but it turned out to be Alex Karras, whom I knew from his playing days in Detroit. An outspoken and very funny man, Alex was now pursuing a motion picture career. League attendance was once again high in the second week of play. Things were going well and our confidence was growing.

Alex was easy to work with. He knew football but, more importantly, he understood "interior line play." Memphis had an outstanding offensive line, and that is where our cameras spent most of the night. Once again, neither team had players with name recognition, so we focused our two replay machines on the interior line. The networks weren't doing much of that back then, and it proved to be an interesting and innovative experiment.

Our third game was in Philadelphia. The Bell was hosting the New York Stars. Bell owner John B. Kelly, brother of Princess Grace, was a member of one of Philadelphia's finest families. They played their home games at J.F.K. stadium, which seats 102,000. While it wasn't a sellout, a large crowd was expected.

Our guest celebrity was Jane Chastain. She was formerly "Coach Friday" from her TV days in Atlanta. She had worked at a local station there as a so-called "sports personality" and then had moved on. As for her knowledge of football, well, she didn't know if you blew it up or stuffed it.

I spent my customary Tuesday with the home team. Their head coach and general manager was Ron Waller. Ron had been an all-pro performer with the Rams and had spent the previous year as interim head coach of the San Diego Chargers. A renegade player and coach, his flamboyant and Cavalier attitude was well known in the football world. Other than his quarterback, his team was comprised of unknowns.

James "King" Corcoran was the quarterback. King, as he preferred to be called, was our league's answer to Joe Namath. The WFL needed a star and King was anointed. He had played a year or so with the Jets and the Patriots, but had never distinguished himself. His only success had come with the Pottstown Firebirds in the semi-pro Atlantic Coast League.

King was outspoken and witty and more or less handsome. He had played well in his first two games, and the word came down from the league office that this was the star. I knew he couldn't play, but what's a person to do?

With two bad teams and a "Coach Friday" to work with, I had no idea how to handle the game. I went to Jane and suggested she ask me obvious questions about the game that women don't normally understand. She vetoed that flatly. She said we had the entire afternoon to study film and I could teach her the game so that she could explain it like the other jocks. We watched film for three hours before she settled on confining her efforts to the explanation of the "seam" in such a way that an audience could understand it.

Two hours later, Jane had it down. As she understood it, the seven defensive backs divide the field up into seven sections and the seam was merely the eighth section. I figured that was as confusing as I'd ever heard it, so I let it go at that. A record crowd of 80,000 expectant, excited fans had turned out for our game.

It was hard to believe the Bell organization could muster up so much support. They were a confused and scattered front office, nothing at all like the Memphis Southmen. But, still, here were these 80,000 people whooping it up like Monday Night Football.

It was a slow, poorly played game, but we masked it as well as we could. The 80,000 in the stands didn't seem to mind. They were a vocal and jubilant crowd, and if they didn't know the difference between professional and semi-professional, far be it from me to tell them. We spent most of the evening on crowd shots.

Late in the fourth quarter, I was asked to go down on the field and do commentary from the sidelines and interview the winning coach. I didn't have any trouble getting down from the box as there didn't seem to be any security. With less than a minute to play, Philadelphia was punting to New York. All of a sudden, the field was flooded with people from the stands. They were coming in waves. The punted ball was being fielded by a New York player when two fans shot in front of him and caused a three-way fight for the ball. One of the fans won out, but was immediately tackled by the other. Before he hit the ground, he astutely lateraled to yet another member of the mob. The contest between the Stars and the Bell was forgotten.

Whistles were blowing and people were stampeding and the public address system was pleading for everyone to clear the field. The fans kept coming until finally thousands of people were running all over the place, grabbing chin straps, trying to get a souvenir of any kind. When they tried to get my hand-held microphone, it dawned on me . . . I was in the middle of a riot!

T.V.S. sent a mounted policeman down to rescue me, but the officer fighting his way through the crowd ran into my back and sent me sprawling. Then the horse stepped on my foot. With the officials unable to clear the field, the remainder of the game was called off. I didn't stay around for interviews.

19

The next week, the story broke. Philadelphia admitted to giving away tickets. Lots of them. In fact, only thirteen thousand had been sold for their first game, six thousand for their second game, and only two thousand for the third. The Bell had given away *78,000* tickets for our game!

Then all hell broke loose. Jacksonville owned up to committing a similar sin. John B. Kelly resigned as President of the Bell. The owner of the New York team was rumored to be in financial trouble.The check to pay for the Orlando franchise bounced. It had been issued by a convicted felon who had served a year behind bars.

With the league's credibility plumetting, the newspapers turned against us. They had been lied to, and they struck back with vengeance. The formerly quiet NFL broke their silence with a barrage. This was the opportunity they had waited for, and they pounced on it. They discredited the WFL from every angle. Who was this Gary Davidson and who were these other owners? Ypsilanti, for God's sakes, and high school coaches? Randall's Island and dickerrods? The NFL went for a quick kill. After all, they had a vested interest here. Their players were still on strike. They needed to eliminate all forms of competition. They labeled us the "Whiffle" League. The NFL didn't even have troops, but they were winning the war. The death knell had been sounded.

The newspapers also went to work. They had to settle this issue once and for all. Was this new league for real, or what? All eyes turned to Gary Davidson. He was the man of the hour and he stood tall. The commissioner of the league spoke calmly and positively about the reported scandals. He admitted to the ticket scam and announced that the Philadelphia Bell was being taken over by the league. They were looking for a buyer and the asking price was now $4.2 million. Gary confidently turned the situation around. The press was quieted, but it would be watching carefully.

The first eight telecasts had already been set. T.V.S. had three major sponsors and our ratings were still strong, so there was no problem with us.

The fourth week passed smoothly with guest Don Perkins. The fifth week was in Jacksonville with Paul Hornung. I knew Paul from my stint with Green Bay. Our paths had crossed several times since. He liked the excitement of an event—a Super Bowl, a heavyweight title fight, a Kentucky Derby, a Master's Golf Tournament, or a side-street bar. Paul turns up in the strangest places. He is a delightful little boy. When you're with Paul, something always happens.

That was the night Richard Nixon resigned his presidency, but Paul couldn't have known that, or could he? He ran around with the damnedest people. We fed the network and scooped the big boys; we had beaten the eleven o'clock news. I didn't understand the significance of that but everybody else seemed pleased.

The sixth week we were in Houston with McClain Stevenson, and while there I got to visit with Mr. Davees. He and his partner were still going strong. He was wearing a $2,000 beaver cowboy hat, and his secretaries looked like the Ford Modeling Agency.

It was now late in August and the NFL players were still on strike. We remained the only game in town, and although our ratings had fallen, we were still bettering our share. The last preseason game in the NFL was right around the corner, and the labor dispute was still not settled. The networks were worried; so were the owners and players. This was getting expensive. The owners had underestimated the strength and resolve of the players' union. They were having to explain to the networks why they didn't have a product.

The NFL had backed off of our case. They had problems of their own. Their PR people were devoting all their time and resources to making their own striking players appear gluttonous and greedy. Our seventh game was in Detroit . . . pardon me, Ypsilanti, thirty-seven miles west. The Detroit Wheels were hosting the Chicago Fire. The Wheels were 1-6, and word had it that payrolls were not being made. I never knew what I'd find from one week to the next.

When we landed on Tuesday, I was met by the assistant PR man who drove me to Ypsilanti in his *un*-air-conditioned car.

"What's wrong with your team?" I inquired.

"You'll have to ask the trainer," he reported.

I thought it strange that he referred me to the trainer rather than the coach. But then he continued: "We're broke and about to go under. Morale is bad, and the players haven't been paid for a couple of weeks. Then there's the problem with the soap, towels, and tape."

"What's the problem there?" I asked.

"We ain't got any. The players have to bring their own. The coaches do too."

"You've got to be kidding?"

"No, sir, I'm telling you the truth. We're behind on our laundry bill, and they've cut us off too. A Johnson & Johnson salesman in Philadelphia gave us some tape, but that was four weeks ago. It's all gone now. The players haven't been taped for two weeks."

When we reached the practice field, all was confirmed. The trainer took me aside and whispered in my ear. "I've lied to the team. I've kept back enough tape for the Thursday night game. We're not going to be embarrassed on national TV."

Gale Sayers was beside me when the Wheels lost their seventh game. But let the record show that the entire team was taped.

On Wednesday, August 28, the striking NFL players went back to work. We were no longer the only game in town. Then, in September, the WFL came apart. After losing ten of eleven games, the Detroit Wheels folded. The newspapers, now with the NFL to cover, only wrote about the negatives within the WFL. They had more than enough to talk about. The IRS lodged a tax lien of $168,000 against the Portland Storm. Their players were not being paid, but the team played on. Charitable citizens were feeding and housing the players.

Upton Bell took over the New York Stars and uprooted them

to Charlotte. In Jacksonville, the owner borrowed $27,000 from the head coach and then fired him. The California Sun owner pleaded guilty to submitting a false financial statement when negotiating a bank loan to buy the team. The IRS claimed the Birmingham owner owed back taxes. As in all the other cases, these "gluttonous and greedy" players were playing for nothing.

But the worst situation was taking place in Orlando. Managing General Partner Rommie Loudd hadn't met a single payment to his team or coaches in weeks. Gary Davidson ordered Loudd to raise two million dollars. Loudd sued the league and a partner. Loudd was indicted by a Federal Grand Jury for tax fraud. He later went to prison. The Jacksonville franchise was taken over by the league. The team continued to play for one-fifth of their back salaries.

We didn't know if there was going to be a game from one week to the next. Eddie Einhorn and a few of the owners were holding the league together. Gary Davidson had run out of moves. Having lost all credibility, he was soon asked to resign.

I, very frankly, was having the time of my life. The whole thing was so bizarre you couldn't help but love it. Each week was a brand-new experience. I was working with Rosie Greer, Paul Hornung, Don Perkins, Dick Butkus, Burt Reynolds, and Jack Kemp. Each week was a new challenge. We never knew *where* or *if* we would play. I was told to stay in my office until twelve noon on Tuesdays. I'd make reservations on flights to Memphis or Portland. Then the phone would ring and it would be Eddie Einhorn. "Alex, we're on again this week. Go to California."

This was tough enough for me, but it was a nightmare for Merle Harmon. He was still doing the Brewers games, and he seldom made the game site until late afternoon on the day of the game. Getting in and out of Orlando, Birmingham, Jacksonville, and Shreveport is not that easy. Merle often worked with only a couple of hours sleep. He was a professional.

Howard Zuckerman, our director, owned the mobile unit that we telecast from. He, too, was a gambler. Three of our cameramen all but lived in the unit. They got the same news I got every Tuesday. They had two days to get the truck to the game site. It could be Portland, Orlando, or anywhere in between—no one ever knew. They usually drove to Kansas City on Fridays, the center of the country.

Working with the same crew from week to week was a new experience. Sharing the same chaotic conditions and experiences can bring people pretty close. The Thursday Night Game didn't end until after midnight, and where do you go in Shreveport at that hour to relax and come down? We set up a bar in a room wherever we stayed.

We'd stay up most of the night and rehash every play or situation. We developed a team spirit. I know that sounds silly, but we really did. We worked so closely that we could anticipate each other's thoughts and movements. I've never worked harder or had more fun. Our November 28th game was nominated for an Emmy.

This was easily the most fascinating league ever spawned. Teams were folding, owners were dropping, players were changing, and schedules were altered. Still, they played on.

We were in Birmingham for their game with Houston when it was announced that Houston was moved to Shreveport. When they heard this news, just prior to boarding the plane, over half the Houston team defected. The head coach was fired and the remaining players didn't get to Birmingham until a few hours before the game.

Paul Hornung was our guest commentator, and he too was late arriving. I was down on the field before game time checking out lineup changes when I was approached by one of Houston's coaches.

"Any changes in your lineup?" I asked. "Yes," said the assistant. "We've got a new head coach and several other changes. Over half the team quit, and we've got four new starters on the defensive line. Our offensive team has six new faces, but we're not sure who'll start. Some of them haven't gotten here yet. We've been on the phone getting local talent. Oh, by the way, both of our quarterbacks left so we got this new kid from the University of Houston. We'll be using the veer offense tonight. He doesn't know any other."

About that time, Paul came up to me and asked about changes. When I told Paul what was going on, he just froze for a moment. You could see the wheels turning.

"What are we doing here then?" he asked.

"Where should we be?"

"On the phone to our bookmaker," he announced as he quickly left the field.

Birmingham covered the line.

That the league didn't fold is a major miracle. Only two or three teams were making their payrolls. Still these "gluttonous, greedy" gridironers played on. I have always maintained that most players, the real competitors, will play the game for nothing. Well, here was living proof of it. I fell in love with the league. I no longer felt I was "shilling." I truly admired these people. They loved the game and they proved it. Since they were only getting a portion of their pay, they referred to themselves as semi-pros.

Two of our telecast games were cancelled, but somehow they patched things up again and played the following week.

It was late November, and once again Paul Hornung was our guest for the Philadelphia-Florida game in Orlando. This was the final week of regular-season play. Late in the game Paul was down on the field doing interviews with coaches and players while the game was in progress. Philadelephia was trailing but was now on the move with its hurry-up offense. Bell coach Ron Waller was sending in a play, and Paul had stepped in with his microphone. Our cameras shot tightly on the coach and his messenger. Merle and I silenced our microphones so we could hear his instructions. "Now, listen carefully," Ron told the player. "Tell King to call 41 straight and you be sure to pick up the linebacker. He's blitzing like a c---s-----!"

Merle looked at me and I looked at him and we glanced at our monitor. Paul was trying to muffle his laughter, but his microphone was shaking violently. I could hold my silence no longer. "Well, Merle, I believe in telling it like it is, but this is carrying it too far!"

Memphis, with a 17-3 record, was the best team and organization in the league. Birmingham, 15-5, was next, followed by Orlando with a 14-6 record. No other team was a contender, so the playoffs got changed. Birmingham drew a bye and Orlando upset Memphis in the first round.

Orlando was the miracle team. Everything about it was

incredible. Head Coach Jack Pardee had held his team together for the fifteen weeks despite the fact that no one had received a single paycheck. The coaches and trainers were in the same fix. For nearly four months these people had stayed together for nothing but the love of the game. In the course of that time, they had but one defector. Everybody washed his own uniform, furnished his own soap, towels and tape. The coaches furnished the toilet paper. Still they hung together. These athletes wanted only to play.

On December 5, 1974, Orlando faced Birmingham in the World Bowl. This would be the last telecast game in the World Football League. We at T.V.S. knew it, but like Orlando we were proud to have gone the distance. It was the most outrageous year of my life, but the most rewarding.

George Mira led the Americans to a narrow 22-21 victory over the Blazers. At the end of the game, one of the Florida players scooped up the game ball, but was chased down underneath the stands. The ball was reclaimed by the Americans. After the game, a sheriff repossessed the Birmingham uniforms. The Orlando Blazers disappeared as they had arrived ... into oblivion.

20

With Super Bowl IX drawing closer and closer, things got a little tense around the garbage shop. Mr. Davees and I were on the phone daily. He had forgiven me for my poor performance at Super Bowl VI in regards to tickets, badges, and accommodations.

Mr. Hunt had not. He was in my office three or four times a day. "Hawkins, have you taken care of your duties? Are you sure we've got twenty tickets, and where are they? I'm not going to sit down low or near the end zone. And what about the badges? I'm not going to let you embarrass yourself like you did the last time we were down there."

By Monday, I'd had it, so I called Mr. Davees and told him I was on my way to Houston to spend a couple of days before escorting him on to New Orleans in proper fashion. After spending a couple of spirited evenings together, we left Houston on Wednesday afternoon, as Mr. Davees refuses to rise before noon.

When we arrived at the Fairmont Hotel, Mr. Hunt had everything under control . . . his control. Before we got to the registration desk, we heard his bellowing voice, "Boy, here's twenty dollars, get me six of the best cigars in the house. I'm Mr. Hunt from Dallas, so let's move right along."

When we asked to register, we were informed that Mr. Hunt had already taken care of that. He had gone on and *assigned* us rooms.

"Davees, you go on up and unpack while Hawkins and I go over to Stonebreaker's office and pick up the tickets. I ain't going to relax until they're in my hands. His friends probably ain't no more reliable than he is."

Steve Stonebreaker had gone to New Orleans in 1967 in the player allocation draft. He had won the hearts of the locals and was a celebrated player and personality. He had a couple of radio shows and published a weekly sports magazine. Stoney had secured us tickets and badges for both the game and Rozelle's party.

When we reached Stoney's office, Mr. Hunt once again took over. "Boy, let me see those tickets." When Stoney handed them to him, he quickly counted them, twice, and ordered me to pay for them as he had left his checkbook in his room. Stoney gave me a puzzled look, and I just winked back.

Back at the Fairmont, I found Mr. Hunt's and Mr. Davees' rooms were directly across the hall from one another, while my room was around the corner and far down the hall. Mr. Hunt had assigned me a suite and had taken the trouble to stock the bar fully. He had even been thoughtful enough to buy a coffee maker, knowing full well that Mr. Davees and I did not drink coffee. Mr. Hunt had considerately arranged for three keys to my room in the event we got separated.

We freshened up and went to dinner at Moran's. Now, with his tickets in his coat pocket, Mr. Hunt went to work. He would order a drink and count out his tickets. Everybody at the Super Bowl was looking for tickets, and Mr. Hunt had plenty of them. He planned to be increasingly popular as the week wore on.

During dinner he must have recounted the tickets a half-dozen times. This got the attention of the neighboring tables. The spotlight was squarely on him.

"Hawkins," he spoke less loudly, "I don't think these are good seats. Are you sure Stonebreaker has clout? I ain't all that happy with my room either. I don't care for the color of the drapes, the ice machine is way down the hall, my bed is not wide enough, the air conditioner makes too much noise, and the towels ain't big enough to dry my balls.

"I've never liked this city and I ain't seen a decent looking woman since I got here. If things don't pick up by tomorrow, I'm going home.

"Davees, get the check. I left my billfold in the room. Hawkins, where are all the celebrities you're supposed to know?

I ain't seen a damn one of them. Let's go to the Absinthe House. And, Davees, you tip too damn much. You keep spending money like that and you're going to be broke again."

Mr. Hunt is not a sound sleeper. A moth on a marshmallow will wake him, and when he is up, so is everyone else. He was pounding around in the suite fixing coffee. He is neither a quiet nor a considerate person. "Wake up, wake up; the sun is up and the bird is on the wing. Hawkins, get your lazy ass moving. We've got things to do and people to meet. If I don't find a date today, I'm going home." With his hundred dollar bills and his pocket full of tickets, Mr. Hunt was ready to take on the city.

We toured the French Quarter looking for "hippies," and while there were any number of those, none took a fancy to Hunt as the one had in Houston.

Thursday was a reenactment of the previous evening—dinner at Moran's, a stroll through the Quarter, and drinks at the Old Absinthe House. Mr. Hunt did manage to steal away with Mr. Davees long enough to explain his new plan for the disposal of his Six Flags property. I was never allowed in those "top secret" meetings, but I could tell when they adjourned that his new plan would not work.

Friday morning, Mr. Hunt announced he was bringing in a date from somewhere in Louisiana. I knew she would be driving as he would not foot the bill for airfare. Late that afternoon, this beauty descended upon us. Mr. Hunt's dates share one thing in common; they all arrive late and leave early. This was to be no exception.

That afternoon, Mr. Hunt was strolling his "arm piece" on Bourbon Street and flashing his tickets, which by this time were pretty well worn. Mr. Davees and I were off in another direction, and it was after seven o'clock when we got back to the Fairmont.

Stonebreaker had left our tickets to the Rozelle party at the desk, but when I asked for them, I was told that Mr. Hunt had already claimed them. When we went to his room, he was not there.

It seems Mr. Hunt had neglected to turn back his watch to Central Time and he was running on Eastern Standard Time. He assumed we had gone on without him, so rather than be embarrassed in front of "Miss Louisiana," he did what comes so naturally to him; he picked up all the tickets and looked after himself.

So I called a friend of mine, Jerry Lisker, who was the sports editor of the *New York Post* and had him run us over some extras. By the time Lisker reached us, Mr. Davees had concocted a "sting." Jerry, a former Golden Gloves boxer and pro football player, had never met Mr. Hunt, but when told of the theft, he offered to take part in our plan.

The weather had turned cold in New Orleans; the wind was kicking up and it was getting downright uncomfortable. When we got to the armory where Rozelle's party was being held, there must have been five thousand people inside. Certain areas were roped off for "badge" people, with non-roped areas for ticket people. Mr. Hunt was both ticketed and badged and was milling around with the "badge" people. He was easy to spot on the dance floor as his style was, well, unique.

We located Stonebreaker, explained our "sting," and spread out around the arena. First, Mr. Davees walked up to Mr. Hunt with his best hound-dog look. Mr. Hunt sensed the seriousness of his expression and stopped dancing.

"Davees, you little shit, why did y'all leave without me?"

"Mr. Hunt," Don began in his most somber tone, "we've got a *problem*."

"What's that, Davees?"

"Those tickets you picked up at the desk were not ours."

"What tickets? I didn't take no tickets. I don't know what you're talking about."

"Stonebreaker left some tickets at the hotel in Mr. Hawkins' box. They were for Adolph Hammerschmidt. He's the CEO at Burger King and Burger King is Stoney's biggest account. They sponsor the back page of his magazine and that's worth $250,000 a year. Somebody took those tickets and Stoney is about to go crazy. He can't find another ticket anywhere and Hammerschmidt and his wife are outside in the freezing cold. If you've got any tickets, let me have them now. If Stoney loses that account, the magazine goes under. It's just that simple."

"I told you, I don't know anything about any fuckin' tickets. Now leave me alone." Mr. Hunt, not yet aware of the gravity of the situation, went right on dancing. Mr. Davees disappeared.

After fifteen minutes had elapsed, Mr. Hunt was approached by Lisker. Jerry, like most boxers, had that crazed stare in his eyes and a snarl on his face. Mr. Hunt had never met Jerry, but his expression was enough to make Mr. Hunt stop dancing.

"What can I do for you, boy?"

"You can stop dancing long enough for me to whip your ass, you big, fat piece of shit." His fists were clinched and his eyes narrowed.

"You took those tickets, and it's going to cost Stoney his magazine. I ought to whip your ass, but you're too old. I'll tell you one thing, you better hope you don't run into Stoney. He's going to kill you." Mr. Hunt was visibly shaken.

Lisker withdrew, and Mr. Hunt, now apprehensive, was less enthusiastic about dancing.

Fifteen minutes later, up strolled Stonebreaker.

"Hunt, you fat tub of horse piss, I ought to tear your lungs out, but I hate you too much for that. You've cost me my business, that's what you have done. I know you took the tickets. The desk clerk told me. I don't want to ever see your cheap ass again." Stoney hurried away. Mr. Hunt, no longer eager to dance, went straight for the bar.

Guilt is a strange thing, but it was relatively new to Mr. Hunt. I let him down three or four Scotches before I approached him. "Mr. Hunt," I spoke calmly, "I should hate you, but I don't. I know you took the tickets, and I can't believe even you could stoop so low. Stonebreaker got us hotel rooms, Super Bowl tickets, and passes to this party, and you, you selfish bastard, have ruined his life. Now, if you've got those tickets, let me have them now. Hammerschmidt and his wife are outside shivering in the cold." Then I reached for the white envelope inside his coat pocket.

You would have thought I was reaching for his tongue. "Goddamn you, Hawkins. Has everyone lost their minds? I didn't take no fuckin' tickets, and I don't know what you're talking about. Get away from me!"

Tears were welling up in his eyes, and his arms and hands were going in every direction. "Miss Louisiana" didn't know what to think, but she sensed she was not in the company of

Mr. Wonderful.

I disappeared, but kept surveillance on Mr. Hunt, who three drinks later marched to the main entrance and went outside. I followed and when I got to the door, Mr. Hunt was waving the tickets wildly in the air and screaming at the top of his lungs. *"Hoganschultz, Hammerfelt, Finklestein,* goddamit, is there anybody here from Burger King?"

But the evening was far from over for Mr. Hunt. Back at the Fairmont, Mr. Davees was up to more of his mischief. We had gotten in about four o'clock. I had retired to my suite, but Mr. Davees was on the phone with a wake-up call.

"This is Mr. Hunt in room 1106. I've got the most important meeting of my life in the morning. Now listen closely, I want a wake-up call at 7:00 a.m. I'm a very sound sleeper, so I want another call at 7:15. I'm grouchy as hell in the mornings, so don't pay any attention to anything I say. I may tell you I'm awake, but I may not be, so you ask me if *both of my feet are on the floor.* I want another call at 7:30, and I want room service at my door. I want *cold* oatmeal, two pieces of dry toast, and a glass of lukewarm spicket water in a plastic cup. Do you have all of that? O.K., there's a hundred-dollar tip if you do exactly as I've asked." Mr. Davees retired for the evening.

Mr. Hunt and "Miss Louisiana" got in about 5:30 a.m. At 7:00 the phone rang in room 1106. Mr. Hunt picked up the phone. "Mr. Hunt, this is your wake-up call. It's seven o'clock."

"I didn't ask for no wake-up call, you asshole. Don't call me again."

At 7:15 the phone rang again. "Mr. Hunt, it's 7:15. It's time to get up; you've got a big meeting."

"What in the hell are you talking about? I ain't got no god-damn meeting."

"Are both of your feet on the floor?" came the cheery reply.

"Is everybody in this city crazy? Both of my feet will be up your ass if you call me again." He slammed down the phone.

At 7:30 the phone rang again. "Mr. Hunt, it's time to get up; it's 7:30." In the middle of a tirade of profanities too foul to record, there came the knock on the door.

Mr. Hunt, exasperated, bolted out of his bed and threw open the door. In came the bell captain with his cold oatmeal, dry toast, and the lukewarm spicket water. "Good morning, Mr. Hunt, it's exactly as you ordered."

"Get that goddamn mush out of here, you stupid bastard." The cart was rolled unceremoniously out of the room with considerable force. He may have imagined it, but Mr. Davees, still awake, could have sworn a body struck his door five seconds after 7:30. Mr. Hunt could not get back to sleep, so he and "Miss Louisiana" had the entire day to sightsee and count his tickets and badges.

21

On Saturday night in New Orleans, I had been introduced to a man named Bob Wussler. Bob was thirty-nine, a year younger than I, and had just been appointed head of CBS Sports. At five-feet-ten, one hundred sixty pounds, he was not a physically imposing figure, but he had a charming, impish smile and a whip-quick laugh that never lasted long. He was sharp. You knew that immediately. Still, there was something about him that made me uneasy. He was so smug. He seemed to know more about me than I knew about myself. He studied me more than he talked to me. I felt like an insect under a microscope. I got the distinct impression I amused him.

Bob praised my work on the World Football League. He said that under the circumstances, it was the best work ever done. I had to admire him for his splendid taste. We talked for awhile, and just before parting he told me I'd be hearing from him. I somehow knew I would.

When I related this conversation to Mr. Hunt, he told me I was out of my mind. "CBS ain't going to hire you back after they've fired you. Those people don't work that way. I saw you talking to that pig-eyed little bastard. You can't trust those people. They're all out to protect their own asses. Besides, you were never worth a shit to begin with, so forget it."

Back in Atlanta, business conditions continued to deteriorate. Finally we did, in fact, sell one of our trucks and let go a driver. We were eight hundred thousand dollars in debt, and the C & S Bank was starting to panic. They were foreclosing and calling in notes on some of the real giants in the business community. All I could think of was how I could pay back eight hundred thousand dollars!

Mr. Hunt was always there with his sage advice. "Hawkins, if you can't make your payments, you can always throw the keys at the C & S and let them run the damn business. Take my word for it, they don't want to own a garbage company."

I started bearing down on delinquent accounts. Twice a week I stayed in the office and phoned people on past due bills. If you want to get your customers' attention, just tell them that if their payment isn't received in three days, you're going to bring their garbage back. Cash flow improved.

For the past two years, I had been home on weekends in Atlanta. It had become my habit to have drinks with a group of sports and trivia buffs who gathered every Friday. This group of a dozen or so regulars was far removed from my Buckhead Boys. It was comprised of Jews and Italians and a Canadian. They had come from New York, New Jersey, Chicago, Baltimore and Miami.

There was a lawyer, a promoter, a rag man, a furniture salesman, and two or three ad men. One was the head of the Anti-Defamation League. Most were peddlers who had settled in Atlanta about the same time I had. Despite the soft economy that persisted, they were doing far better now than they had been back home.

They were street smart and savvy and found Atlanta an easy mark compared to their harsh native grounds. They stuck together, helped one another, and mutually prospered. They had come to Atlanta without the benefit of friends or introductions. They were, by and large, social misfits who could forget about country clubs, much less the Piedmont Driving Club. Ours was an ethnic assemblage that resembled the United Nations.

We drank, joked, teased, played liar's poker and talked sports just like I had in my days in Baltimore. It was a culture I both understood and missed. None of them had come up easy, and nothing had been handed to them. What they had acquired had been hard earned and deserved. They paid the price, but it was rarely retail.

It was through this association that I was gradually received into the Jewish community. I was laughingly referred to as their token "goy." I got a lot of their business and then referrals from their friends. They were quick to help me, and I accepted even quicker. Soon, I had what I referred to as my "Yiddish route."

The closer we became in business, the more socially involved I became. I was brought up a Methodist, but had no strong thoughts in matters of religion. I didn't go to the synagogue, but I did attend several other related functions such as bar mitzvahs and a bris. I was curious and intrigued by these cere-monial events. I went, watched, and learned as much as I felt a celebrity garbage man needed to know.

Libby, a devout Presbyterian, was rock solid in her beliefs and feared only that she might offend someone. She went along with everything without so much as a question. What she didn't understand, she felt she could well do without. This just wasn't always the case.

One afternoon we were at a friend's house to attend the bris of his son. One of my more imaginative friends had called Libby the week before and cautioned her about the importance of the occasion. He explained that she was the token gentile and, as such, would have the honor of aiding the Rabbi in the removal of the foreskin by holding it gently between her teeth while the Rabbi circumcised the child.

This had been a matter of great concern to her for over a week, but she didn't say a word to me until we were at their front door.

"Alex," she said, "I know how important this is to you, and I'm not going to embarrass you by not going through with it. I'll do it, but I'm not going to like it. I want you to know that this is my last bris." When she wasn't called on, she was greatly relieved.

It was nearly spring when the call came through from my new friend, Bob Wussler. I was invited to New York to have lunch and talk contract. I was being invited back to work with CBS.

We had lunch in the posh executive dining room with a chef and the whole works. Bob was a charmer, but I honestly felt he liked me. He laughed at everything I said, but somehow I kept getting the feeling he was laughing *at me*. He had me labeled as "blue collar" and I must have confirmed it when I ordered a cheeseburger, French fries, and milk. We came to terms on a contract when I accepted his offer. He was the boss, and I was made aware of it. We were the only two in the dining room. Without knowing it, I had become one of his "projects."

During my tenure as a sportswriter, some journalism had rubbed off on me. My experience with the World Football League had schooled me, and I felt more comfortable about the TV business. But the most beneficial lesson, for me, was realizing that it *was* a business. Television football was by now Big Business. I finally accepted this fact. I had a new-found respect for broadcasting, but a profound grief for the game. Pro football was losing itself to television. Commercials were more important than kickoffs, and *don't you forget it*.

Nevertheless, I was back working with Don Criqui and Frank Gleiber, and it was as much fun as before. I was being paid fifteen hundred dollars a game for flying into a city, sitting in the broadcast booth for three hours, and talking about the game with talents like Criqui and Gleiber.

The first week in November, I was suddenly assigned to work with Lindsey Nelson. Our first game together, we were at Shea Stadium in New York. Ordinarily this would not be a big thing, but Lindsey Nelson is no ordinary man. He was a legend in the broadcasting business and more particularly in New York. He had been the voice of the Mets for over fifteen years.

I had grown up listening to Lindsey on radio. Now I would be right there beside him doing a game on television. Not only that, but I would be working the game between the Jets and Giants. In ten years of pro ball, I had never played in New York City. Added to that was the fact that I had never broadcast a game from there. What I'm saying is, for me this was a big deal.

I had just met Lindsey for the first time that morning at breakfast. We had never met before because of his heavy workload. He now did the San Francisco Giants baseball games on Tuesdays, Wednesdays, Thursdays, and Fridays. He then flew out to do the play-by-play on Notre Dame football games on Saturdays. He worked Sunday on NFL games and flew to a different city on Monday to announce Monday Night Football on radio.

How he could remember the names and numbers of all those players bewildered me.

Lindsey didn't talk much at breakfast. He is naturally a quiet, retiring man, but what impressed me was the respect shown to him by our producer and director. They were almost reverent in their adulation, and I was impressed by their homage. On the cab ride to the stadium, the producer made nervous conversation, and Lindsey, in deep concentration, would placate them by an occasional um-hum or yes.

But when we entered the ballpark, his presence was felt. People were running up to him shaking his hand, patting him on the back, and making one-sentence conversations. It was like a king or an emperor had arrived at the stadium ... in a plaid jacket! Lindsey never stopped or changed pace. He was polite, attentive, and cordial as he marched on towards the press box. It seemed that everyone in Shea Stadium knew him personally. I had fallen back two steps behind him for obvious reasons. I was certain of only two things: nobody knew *or* cared who Alex Hawkins was.

But the intimidation didn't stop there. As we took our positions in the booth, I looked out at the skyline of New York City. Damn, it was big and powerful. Damn, it was important. I've laughed at people who felt that way about this city on more than one occasion, but that day, I felt its power. Whatever it may be, it's still the capital of the world. This was the Big Apple!

If that wasn't bad enough, in walks Jack Whitaker. Well, there are broadcasters and there are broadcasters, but Jack Whitaker is the classiest, most talented talent in the business. For poise, skill, and imagination, the industry knows not his equal. I'd worked with him before and had drinks with him many times, but I have always been in awe of his combination of confidence, sincerity, and humility. He is the gentleman's gentleman.

Jack was there to do what he does better than anyone who ever lived: a two-minute vignette. No prompters, no writers, no rehearsals—he just sits there scribbling on a piece of paper, reads it back to himself, tears it up and goes on. The next two minutes are filled with the most beautiful rhetoric ever uttered by a human being. He completely captures the moment, the event, or the summation of the day. He is the highlight of many of the most prestigious sporting events, and no one has ever done it better . . . or even come close. The director decided to tape Jack's piece and get it out of the way. He went on camera for *exactly* two minutes of perfect eloquence, then thanked the crew, smiled, and sat down to watch the game.

By this time, I am shaking in my shoes. Being in the company of men like these was just too much for Ma Hawkins' little boy, Alex. It was time for the rehearsal of the opening, and I was completely unglued. The microphone was shaking in my hand like an earthquake had hit. My eyes were darting all about, and my mind, what was left of it, was running all over the globe.

Lindsey's introduction was, of course, perfect, and then it was my time to strut my stuff. My mouth felt like sand, and my tongue was six inches thick. I was out of my league and knew it. There was nothing to do but laugh. The producer and director were in stitches. Lindsey looked at Jack and they broke up too. It was all too obvious that I was not ready for the major leagues. I had learned, but not nearly enough.

"Gentlemen," I announced. "I'm going to take a leak. If I don't make it back, go on without me." I left and returned in time to salvage some of my dignity. I made it through the opening.

I worked the remainder of the year with Lindsey. What a story-teller the man was. He'd been everywhere and seen and done more than most. Yet next to his wife, sports remained his main love. He saw the changes in broadcasting but refused to change with them. "Just remember one thing," he told me; "the game is the thing. Nobody is bigger than the game. Don't make it less or larger than it is." Paint the game. And that is about all anyone ever taught me about broadcasting.

The season ended and I looked forward to Super Bowl X in Miami. It was Pittsburgh against Dallas, and CBS would be televising it. More important to me was the fact that I would be doing some work on the pregame show before 60,000,000 viewers.

Most "big-league" announcers have a breakthrough broadcast. Howard Cosell's was Monday Night Football. Jim McKay's was the Olympics in Munich. Would mine be Super Bowl X?

22

I headed for Miami. It was once again time for the annual meeting of the old firm of Hunt, Hawkins and Davees.

My flight was in the late afternoon, so Mr. Hunt arranged an early departure. He and Mr. Davees were staying at the Jockey Club in Dade County. CBS had us headquartered on Miami Beach. Since one hundred and eleven blocks separated us and I would be working, the old firm would not be together nearly as often. Mr. Davees had already taken this fact into consideration.

He had with him a lady from Houston by the name of Charlie. Knowing that nobody could get along with Mr. Hunt for four days alone, he had brought Charlie as a buffer. The new firm of Rich, Pretty and Hunt was thus formed.

Charlie was adorable. She was Texas to the core, tall and lean with a curley blond mane. She was a bundle of energy. Her eyes were brighter than Edison's first bulb, and her smile was so big it nearly ran off her face. Charlie could make friends with a biting dog. She had a keen sense of humor and a quick, wholesome laugh. She was there to have fun.

She loved Mr. Hunt and was a great straight man. Mr. Hunt needed no more. Give him an audience of one and he would perform all night. Charlie was also a fine "gofer," and, as always, Mr. Hunt abused the privilege.

Since Mr. Hunt hated Miami, our Wednesday-night dinner was held at the Jockey Club. Mr. Davees and I got to visit a lot as Mr. Hunt was dancing with Charlie most of the evening. A dance partner was not something Mr. Hunt came by easily; his style was something out of the forties and had not yet been recycled.

When the check came, Mr. Hunt took me aside and explained that he would not be seeing a lot of me that week. With the exception of the CBS and Rozelle parties, and the game, he would not be coming to Miami. He did expect tickets and badges for these events, and he made it clear that he expected the firm to be shown on national TV somewhere during the telecast.

"Hawkins," he barked, "It don't mean nothing to me and you know that, but it would mean a hell of a lot to Mr. Davees. Just handle it."

Now that Mr. Davees had settled up the check, we returned to the table. Mr. Hunt made it known to all that the new firm would be featured on national TV during the Super Bowl.

I don't remember the exact year that the Super Bowl coverage expanded from three hours to ten, but it had to have been along about this time. I do know this: Bob Wussler was not going to be outdone. He was a spender with both style and substance. He brought everybody who worked at CBS down from New York, and he dispersed the talent to every conceivable location between Ft. Lauderdale and the Keys. CBS crews were on boats, barges, bridges, helicopters, hotel lobbies, shoeshine stands, and of course, bars. Jack Whitaker and I were assigned to the Bowl Bar along with a newcomer named Al Michaels. Jack was stationed outside the bar, and Al and I were set up inside.

The Bowl Bar is just that, directly across the street from the Orange Bowl. It was the only place for blocks to get a drink or watch the game if you didn't have a ticket. It was an old run-down place that under normal conditions probably seated a couple dozen people. I would guess that the fire marshall would set the capacity at sixty or seventy.

Wussler had me cast perfectly in the bar, but the same could not be said of Al Michaels. Al was a West Coast boy of some refinement. This was not his element. Tom O'Neill was our unit producer and Dave Fox our director. If either of these two actually gave a shit about anything, it was a closely guarded secret. O'Neill, a good-looking, fun-loving bachelor, would try just about anything, and Fox would try the rest.

The bar itself was horseshoe-shaped and took up all but six

feet of the entire room. Al and I were set up at the center of the horseshoe with the crowd all around us. Our initial assignment was to conduct interviews with the customers.

On Saturday we were to report at the bar at 1:00 p.m. for rehearsal. You can easily see how this might be necessary for the cameramen and technicians, but it's hard to rehearse an interview with someone who wouldn't be there until the next day. But since this game was more important than the Invasion of Europe, we all went along with it.

We put on the IFBs and checked out the microphones, cameras, and whatever else they do in the truck. Then we checked them again and still again. We sat there at the bar until five o'clock. We sat there with a couple of winos and drank beer for over four hours. You didn't dare abandon your post. This was the Super Bowl, by God, a Global Telecast. It was Wussler's project. He had to outdo the previous Super Bowl.

By the time I got back to the hotel, I was feeling no pain, so I sat down at the bar with a Texan with golf shoes on. Well, it turns out that even though he's snockered, he's still a mighty funny guy. He tells me the story of how he was playing golf in Fort Worth on Wednesday and lost $500 on the match. He then lost another $500 at gin, so he and his partner get on a plane for Miami to get their money back on the Super Bowl. Why they had to go to Miami to do it, only a drunk knows. Their plan was that they didn't have a plan. So, anyhow, he has been down here four days in the same clothes he played golf in. His buddy had gone back that morning. He then calls home and finds that his Daddy has fired him, and his wife, Mary Alice, is suing him for divorce. He had already spent another $2,000 since he got here. He tells me that he can't bring himself to either sober up or go home, so what should he do?

I tell him it's a very sad story but funny also if you look at it that way. I wished him good luck.

We got up the next morning and went to the stadium. It was hours before game time and the Orange Bowl was already half-full. Hundreds of Pittsburgh fans were trying to find tickets. It seems a travel agency in Pittsburgh had booked a trip for about 1,400 people, but had yet to locate tickets. They had the accommodations, but not a single ticket. Having known these people from Pittsburgh, I was certain they didn't have the scalper's fee of $200 per ticket, and I could see we were going to have most of them in the Bowl Bar.

I wasn't wrong. When we got there, it was wall-to-wall blue-collar Pittsburgh Steeler fans. They had found their seats for the game. It's a shot and a beer here and a shot and a beer there, and keep in mind, it's still hours before game time. Al's and my position was roped off, so that wasn't a problem. The camera was behind the bar, so that wasn't a problem. So what was my problem? How to get the old firm on camera, that was the problem.

Well, about that time I spotted Mr. Hunt and Mr. Davees and Charlie in the doorway. Mr. Hunt was wearing his finest hat and a bright yellow blazer with a large cigar jammed in the side of his mouth. Mr. Davees was wearing his 30X beaver hat and a leather jacket. Charlie looked more like *Lady* Charles. She was resplendent in about $2,000 worth of North Beach leather, a dynamite pair of boots, a hat, and about six pounds of lipstick on that big, beautiful, wide-open smiling mouth. She must have had fifty teeth and they were all showing. There was no way I was going to keep her off TV. I turned to these three men behind me and asked if they could make room for my father and his friends. Mr. Hunt had already started towards me.

We got set up and the lights went on and with Mr. Hunt, Mr. Davees, and Charlie as a backdrop. Al Michaels did his thing and I did mine, which was interviewing the new firm as to the probable outcome of the game. All three picked the Cowboys and we went back to Brent, Phyllis, and Irv.

The new firm of Rich, Pretty and Hunt went across the street to the Orange Bowl, and Al and I headed back for the control truck. Inside the truck, folks were busy, but they smiled and lied about how "well you did." And then I saw Wussler with that mischievous little smirk on his face. It was impossible to know what he was thinking, so we just shook hands. Al looked pleased with himself. He had done well and he knew it. We were through until the postgame, so we stayed there and watched the game from the truck.

Pittsburgh was on top 21-10 with 3:02 remaining. I was thinking about how happy the Steeler fans would be back at the

Bowl Bar. The point spread was six and they were winning by eleven. Then Staubach went eighty yards in five plays to bring the Cowboys to within four. Now that they were beating the point spread, Cowboy fans were happy and excited. Steeler fans were low sick.

A minute and forty-eight seconds still remained when Wussler ordered Al and me back to the bar. I assured Bob that that would be a huge mistake, as there would be nothing but Steeler fans there and they would be drunk and surly. Bob strongly suggested that he make that decision, so we got in a golf cart and rode the three-quarters of a mile back to the bar.

When we got to the door, we couldn't get in. There must have been four hundred people in there watching Dallas threaten to take the lead. I did not miscalculate the mood of the Steeler fans. Pittsburgh was still winning, but they were not going to cover the spread. To make matters worse, the Cowboys had the ball back and Staubach was on the move.

There was no way we could get into the bar. The place would not hold another body. I looked at Al and he looked at me, and I could see how he felt. His first year with CBS and he knew he had talent, but he couldn't afford a "no show." There are too many talented people who would kill to get where he was—network announcer. All you've got to do is mess up once and you're history. He was sick with worry. I'd already been fired by CBS once, and *nobody* gets a third chance. I knew *my* fate.

I surveyed the situation and took a thought from Patton. "When you're surrounded from all sides . . . attack." It was a noisy bar, but if you screamed at the top of your lungs, you could make yourself heard.

"Get the hell out of the way," I screamed. When all eyes turned to me, I finished with, "Because I'm going to put every one of you bastards on national television."

The seas parted. They started cheering us as conquering heroes, and a path to our bar position just opened up. By the time we got to the bar, Staubach was intercepted in the Steeler end zone and the game was over. The Steelers had won, *but* they had not covered the spread. There would be a lot of vulgarity in the moments to come.

Suddenly I saw over my shoulder a familiar face. It was the

Texan in his golf shoes. "They're coming to us next," said David Fox. "I'll count you down from ten." I looked at Al. Sweat was pouring off of his forehead. All this had been pretty chaotic, but more than that, Al was a West Coast boy and these were rowdy, drunken steelworkers. There wasn't a cocktail drinker in the place. Al had no idea what they might do or say. Neither did I.

"Ten seconds," said Foxy. And a cheer went up from the patrons. Foxy stepped away from the camera and approached us. "They're not coming to us," he whispered. "Wussler changed his mind!"

"What do you mean 'they're not coming to us?'" I asked.

"They're just not going to use us," he said.

"How are we going to get out of here?" I hissed. Foxy smiled and said, "Do you want to fake it?"

"You bet I do!" I exclaimed.

So O'Neill turned off the bar TV sets and with a countdown from five and a hand pointed towards us, we were *ON*.

Al identified himself and gave our location, set the score and turned it over to me. With Steeler fans hanging from the ceiling and on each other's shoulders, the "dead air" interviews began. They just knew we were live. I took the microphone, smiled at a Steeler fan and said, "They are the best fucking team in the world." He responded with, "Nobody can beat those c---s------." And for the next six interviews, those were the cleanest words spoken. Everyone wanted to one-up the other.

Finally, I turned to the Texan: "Being the only Cowboy fan in here, you might want to say a word." He grabbed the microphone and started in. "Listen, Dad, I know you're mad and you should be, but we can work everything out when I get back. And, Mary Alice, don't leave or change the locks or do anything foolish. We've always worked it out before and we will again. By the way, I did win a couple thousand on the game, so everything is going to be all right. I miss y'all and I'll be back tomorrow. Mary Alice, I love you and tell the kids 'hi.'"

At that, Al sent it back to CBS control and the Stadium Bar exploded with cheers. The path to the door opened, and we were escorted out with cries of, "You two are the only announcers in the world who tell it like it really is."

When we got outside, Al looked at me and said, "Hitler used to do that!"

I learned a big lesson at Super Bowl X. It had taken me all those years to find out the only thing I had ever done in big-league fashion was get along well with drunks.

23

Christmas of 1975 had not been a happy time at Atlanta Waste Control. There were no Christmas bonuses, not even a party. It was all we could do to make payroll. Interest rates were still rising, and we were on the verge of going under. Finally Mr. Hunt made the declaration that we were just going to have to sell out. As much as he hated losing his rent-free space, we had no other choice.

"Hawkins," Mr. Hunt said, "get on the phone and start trying to sell this dump. You're the perfect person to negotiate the price. The minute they realize how dumb you are, they'll be interested in buying you out. Trust me, start with the smaller companies and work your way up. The larger the company, the larger the greed. They'll figure if you two dumb asses can stay afloat for four years, they can turn it into a profitable operation."

So I got all these figures from Ms. Garrett and went to visit the Fowler boys. They looked at our numbers and offered me $50,000. They wanted our company, but allowed that that was all the business was worth.

I arranged a meeting with Waste Management and the offer doubled. I then talked to Browning Ferris and the price doubled again. In less than a week the price was up to $200,000. By the end of January, Dave and I were taking turns getting paid. We were desperate to sell, but Mr. Hunt argued that it still wasn't time. If Mr. Hunt understood anything, it was greed.

When I told Waste Management about the new offer from BFI, they kicked their bid up to $300,000. BFI then countered with $350,000, and Waste Management brought their corporate lawyer in and jumped the price to $400,000. The lawyer looked me straight in the eye and affirmed that it was their final bid. There was a stern look in that lawyer's eye, and when I mentioned that look to Mr. Hunt, he said it was time to sell.

On February 16, 1976, Atlanta Waste Control was "dissolved" into Waste Management.

Our money partners had long since signed their stock over to us to get off the note. Waste Management offered us stock or cash or a combination of both. We settled on cash, so with $200,000 in our pockets, Dave went to work with Waste Management, and I put my share in my *checking* account and went fishing. It was great to be rich!

Two hundred thousand dollars was more money than I had ever dreamed of, certainly more money than I had made in ten years of professional football. Everything in my background was middle-class, and this sudden wealth threw me. I bought the children cars and Libby a new house and built her a tennis court in the back yard. I treated myself to about fifteen new leisure suits and thirty flowered polyester shirts. With my zip-up half-boots, I was the best-dressed redneck in the city. Nationally, Billy Carter may have outdone me, but I didn't mind taking second to the president's brother.

One afternoon I got a surprise call from Paul Hornung. I had known Paul for fifteen years. I had played with and against him, gambled with and against him, and downed more drinks with him than I care to remember.

I've met a lot of people in my life, but Paul doesn't remind me of any of them. He is simply Paul Hornung, the Golden Boy. Life has been good to him, and he has been good for life. He enjoys himself to an embarrassing degree. He is the most uninhibited person I know. In fact, Paul is not really a person; he's an attitude. Or better still, an experience . . . an out-of-body experience. People just like him and they love to do things for him. He has grown to expect it.

One night we were out drinking, and at about four in the morning he turned to me in a stupor and uttered, "Damn, it's scary knowing when you're fifteen years old that your entire life is going to be one continuous scholarship."

"What does that mean?" I mumbled.

"People just like to do things for me," he answered. "They always have, so I let them."

And come to think of it, who else do you know who won the Heisman Trophy quarterbacking a team that won but two games? Who else owned up to betting on football games, got suspended, but ended up making more money than he would have had he played? And Paul, an alien to discipline, nevertheless was the favorite of both Vince and Marie Lombardi. Paul was a charmer and he lived a charmed life. He just accepted the fact.

Actually we're not all that close, but haven't you had friends like that? A person you seldom see, but still love to be with? Well, that's how I feel about Paul. Back on the phone I asked him, "What's on your mind?"

"Do you want to work the New Orleans Saints preseason games with me?"

"How much does it pay?" I asked.

"That doesn't matter. It ain't but four hundred, but it'll be fun. I used to live down there."

That was all I had to hear. Paul more or less invented fun and ran around with funny people.

"Deal me in," I answered, "but who's going to do play-by-play?"

"You can, I will, what difference does it make? We'll have a good time."

The New Orleans Saints were without question the worst team in football. In their nine years of existence, they had never posted a winning season. Only three times had they won as many as five games. Hank Stram, the new head coach, was hired to change all that. The Saints had drafted well that year, getting number-one choice Chuck Muncie and number-two pick Tony Galbreath, two big running backs with great ability.

On the other hand, quarterback Archie Manning was lost for the season, so Stram had to settle on Bobby Douglas, a quarterback known better for his running than his passing. Not much was expected of them, so our job was simple. Paul and I were to play the part of a "homer," a positive supporter of the home team. We were to praise this fine, young team and call attention to how bright their future looked.

Everything went smoothly for the first couple of games. Paul did the play-by-play, if that was what you called it, and I did my thing. That's what I called it. But most of all, we *were* having fun.

Paul's New Orleans friends were outrageous. From Jim Moran's to Al Hirt's and on over to Pete Fountain's, these were free-living, hard-drinking, heavy-eating, high-rolling, fun-loving people. They had a good time, all the time.

No one enjoys eating or drinking more than Paul. Dinner was an occasion with him, and he spent freely. I, now rich, didn't mind, but the simple fact remained that we were making four hundred dollars a week and spending a couple of grand!

Finally I brought this to his attention. "Paul, we're making four hundred bucks a game and we're spending four times that amount."

"So?" he questioned.

"Well, how are we going to come out like that?"

Paul thought for a minute and then announced, "We'll just have to start betting the games."

The next night the Saints were playing the defending World Champion Pittsburgh Steelers, with the Steelers favored by nine. Paul came into the booth and told me we were down for $5,000 on the Steelers and were giving nine points. I admired his choice of teams, but balked as to the amount of the wager. While I was still rich, I was not a high roller. That's the most I had ever bet on a game, by far. Paul's mother and girlfriend were seated behind us with headsets on so they could hear the telecast.

Pittsburgh scored three unanswered touchdowns and kicked a field goal to lead at halftime 24-0. We had a fifteen-point cushion. What a fine first half of football. We were praising the Steelers for the World Champions they were. Paul compared them to the once-proud Green Bay Packers.

I made excuses for the Saints and glorified their effort. They were, after all, a young team with no quarterback, but oh, what a future! With the score at 24-0, it was hard for us to find fault with either team.

We concurred that what it really took to win in this league

was *patience*. Hadn't it taken the Pittsburgh Steelers forty-two years to win a championship? Then along came Chuck Noll, Terry Bradshaw, Rocky Bleier, and Mean Joe Green, and all of a sudden they were winners.

Hadn't Hank Stram guided the Kansas City Chiefs to a World Championship in 1970? Now with players like Muncie, Galbreath, and Archie Manning back . . . well, anything was possible. We were having a good time.

In the third quarter, the Saints scored and cut the lead to 24-7. We applauded their offense. We still had an eight-point cushion.

Midway through the fourth quarter, the Saints scored again. This made it 24-14 and our cushion was cut to one. Even a field goal would beat us. Somehow the game was no longer so enjoyable.

The Steelers took the kickoff and drove seventy yards to the Saints' ten-yard line and fumbled. New Orleans recovered. With a little less than four minutes remaining, they started their drive.

"Douglas back to pass, can't find anyone open. He scrambles forward for a gain of nine.

"It's Galbreath up the middle for the first down. The Saints are on the move.

"Douglas scrambles again, this time for fourteen yards. What's wrong with the Steeler defense?" cried Paul.

"It's Muncie sweeping the left side for twelve yards and into Pittsburgh territory. The Saints are playing like champions. I don't know what's wrong with the Steelers!"

Paul's voice was now changing. His pitch was now higher and his voice more excitable, maybe even frantic.

I looked back behind me to see if Paul's mother and girlfriend could detect the difference. The smiles on their faces suggested they could.

"It's Douglas out of bounds at the Steeler thirty. Muncie for five. Galbreath off the right side for the first down inside the twenty.

"What in the hell is wrong with the Steelers? They'll never repeat as World Champions playing like this. This is ridiculous."

Paul's voice, now critically shrill, was louder by the second.

"Muncie off the right side to the Steeler nine and another first down. Do the Steelers have no pride? This is disgraceful. New Orleans shouldn't even be in the game. I can't believe what I'm seeing. They should be ashamed.

"First down at the nine, trailing by ten and a field goal won't help them. Douglas back to pass. Looking, looking, throws into the end zone and IT'S INTERCEPTED BY PITTSBURGH. THE GAME'S OVER. PITTSBURGH WINS IT BY ONE!"

"Paul" — I spoke up for the first time in four minutes — "The score is 24-14."

"Whatever!" said Paul as we went off the air.

I don't think that Paul ever realized I had been totally silent throughout the entire drive.

24

It was still very much grass-roots time in America. Willie Nelson was topping the music charts, and Kris Kristofferson's popularity as a singer, songwriter, and actor was soaring. Jimmy Carter from Plains, Georgia, announced he was running for President of the United States. The Sunbelt swing was well on its way as America continued getting back to the "basics of life."

By 1975 Burt Reynolds had become the nation's number-one box office attraction. This may have changed some people, but not Burt. He was a good ole boy and good ole boys were in.

That fall I received a call from Burt's "people" that he was shooting yet another movie in his native state. He insisted I play the part of a sheriff and would not take no for an answer. The movie was being filmed in Savannah, and Burt was trying his hand at directing. The movie *Gator* would showcase his new girlfriend, Lauren Hutton, and country singer Jerry Reed. They assured me that my part would be shot in four days and wouldn't interfere with my broadcasting. And since Burt was no stranger to Savannah, I signed on.

I've always loved the movies and was excited to see what went on during the filming of one. Four days and nights with Burt in Savannah couldn't help but be fun, and Lauren Hutton was the highest paid model in the world. Lauren and Jerry were both making their movie debut.

I had never been with Burt when he wasn't fun, but I had never been with him when he was working. I didn't even get to see him the first night because he was watching the "dailies." It turns out that there is nothing fun about making a movie. It's early to bed and early to rise. Time is money, and these people were serious about their careers. Burt was both starring and directing, so he was working night and day.

I only had four scenes in the movie so I spent most of my days standing around waiting. Waiting has never appealed to me, but finally I got to see myself on camera. After watching each scene several times, Burt and I concurred that my movie career would best be served on the other side of the camera, if at all.

Back with CBS, I anxiously awaited the scheduling of assignments for the 1976 season. Pat Summerall and Tom Brookshire were clearly the number-one broadcasting team, but no one had come to the front as the number-two team. By this time, the AFC was dominating the National Football League, and NBC was telecasting nearly all of their games. Only five or six NFC teams finished the season with more wins than losses, and since Pat and Tom were going to get the better games and the Super Bowl, it didn't leave much for the rest of us. The number-two broadcasting team might get a Minnesota-Dallas, or a St. Louis-Washington game, but little remained after that.

Bob Wussler decided to alternate the announcers. He hired more talent than he had games and rotated the announcers from week to week. I'm sure before the year was over, every color man had worked with every play-by-play man at least once. All this scheduling was being decided by one Robert Wussler, my patron. I got letters from him, memos, telegrams. His communications always offered encouragement and friendly advice, though he repeatedly included the phrase, "in good taste."

While I seemed to amuse him, he still viewed me with some suspicion. Now it's true I was fired for my bathroom story on Jake Scott. And it's also true that I ordered a cheeseburger and fries with Wussler in the executive dining room at CBS. But now that I was rich and dressed out so adorably in my polyester leisure suits, I could not understand his concern in regard to my taste.

Bob Wussler—or Robert, as I referred to him—was an odd man. He was the youngest of three children born into a lower-middle-class family in New Jersey. A Catholic gentile in a predominantly Jewish neighborhood, he vowed to succeed. After graduating from Seaton Hall, he went to work in the mail room at CBS in 1957. Driven by this passion to succeed, he rose rapidly through the ranks and learned every facet of the CBS operation. A brilliant negotiator, he knew how to play the game. More importantly, he knew how to please his bosses.

Although he was never athletically gifted, sports remained his love, and by 1974 he headed up the sports department at CBS. By 1976, at the age of 39, he was president of the entire network. There was nothing ordinary about this man. His wife gave birth to four children in eleven months.

Robert had an inventive mind and thought years in advance. He moved Irv Cross out of the booth and into the studio and developed the very popular "NFL Today Show." He had already moved Pat Summerall from color man to play-by-play and was the first to illustrate popular songs through slow-motion action football footage. He "popularized other people's work" as he put it.

A lightning decision maker, he nevertheless hadn't decided on who the number-two broadcast team would consist of. He continued to shuffle the talent throughout the 1976 season.

For the first time in over half a decade, the Super Bowl would have to be played without the old firm of Hunt, Hawkins and Davees. Super Bowl XI was taking place in Pasadena, and Mr. Hunt wanted nothing to do with those weirdos in California. Besides, he was afraid that he would run into his first wife, although the odds against that occurring were twenty million to one. Mr. Davees and his partner were out of the country touring Europe. Ginther-Davis Interest now had a net worth of over ten million dollars.

Mr. Hunt and I had plans to watch the game together at his apartment where he had control of the channel changer. After each play, he would be able to go to another station to watch thirty seconds of "The Jim Dance Fishing Show," "Bowling for Dollars," or a rerun of "I Love Lucy."

One Thursday I had taken the family over to South Carolina to visit my in-laws. Just before leaving I had given Mr. Hunt the keys to our house. He had a hot date lined up for the weekend, and there was nothing he liked more than a warm fire on a cold night. His apartment had no fireplace, and I had just stacked a cord of wood in the carport.

We were later than expected getting back on Sunday, so I had Libby drop me by Mr. Hunt's apartment. The game was just starting when I entered his place. Mr. Hunt had wagered on Oakland and was already cursing an official who had levied a penalty against the Raiders.

"Look at that flat-faced son of a bitch," he said, pointing to the referee. "He knows how I'm betting. I don't know how much money that bastard has cost me over the years, but he's after me again. I wouldn't have bet the game if I had known he was officiating. The son of a bitch hates me."

But Oakland quickly started dominating the Vikings, and we were getting along reasonably well. Mr. Hunt is far more agreeable when his team is winning. Just before halftime, I got a call from Libby.

"Alex, who's been in the house?"

"Why?" I asked.

"When I walked inside, I saw two half-burned crutches sticking out of the fireplace and all the bed slats are gone."

Sure enough, Mr. Hunt had parked his car six inches from the cord of firewood, but had not seen it. Rather than be inconvenienced, he had promptly built a fire with my crutches and every bed slat in the house.

Two things were proven that afternoon: One was that John Hunt has absolutely no sense of shame. Number two was that referee Gene Barth could not make enough bad calls against Mr. Hunt to prevent Oakland from coasting to a 32-14 win over the Vikings.

1977 was another prosperous year for the Hawkins family. We sold our old house which we had been renting and netted thirty thousand dollars. An aunt, whom I had never met, passed away and left me ninety thousand more. Soon after, another relative died, and I inherited an additional forty-two thousand. Money was coming to me from every direction. I was honestly bored with it. I started taking it for granted.

I bought a custom black Checker Marathon cab, an interest in a coal mine, and made some real estate investments. I just wanted to get rid of this money . . . *it was starting to make me think!* I also expanded my playground. I started hunting and fishing in the Keys, Cozumel, the Exumas, the Yucatan, and the Baja. I was playing where the big boys played. I was too busy and rich to work.

I was just turning forty, and life was still a game—one I was very lucky at. My big earning years were still in front of me. Football had taken no toll on my body. I had escaped the pain suffered by so many other players and was still young and full of energy. I played tennis three or four times a week. I was popular in the bars and spent lavishly. I didn't know what a hangover was and was always ready for the next day or night, which sometimes ran together. However, I was dissipating both my time and money, and it started to concern Mr. Hunt.

"Hawkins, you're acting like a goddamn fool. You're pissing away more money than Don Davis. Things are going well for you now, but that won't always be the case. You've been lucky so far, but luck ain't nobody's favorite. You ain't earned a dime of the money you're throwing away, and you sure as hell ain't smart enough to make it again. Get your head out of your ass and come to your senses, but get me another drink before you do."

Most of what he said was true, but try convincing a blue-collar jock who had never had money, never grown up, never taken life seriously, never assumed responsibility, and never cared about anything but the present. I lived my life one day at a time and enjoyed doing it. Fun was the one thing I knew about, and I was good at it.

The future was way down the road, so why should I worry about it *now*? Life had been good to me, so why not enjoy it? I was special. I was reminded of it daily. I still had a jock mentality. I thought I could do anything. I was indestructable, invincible, and immortal. Good Lord, did I have it going.

25

It didn't destroy me when CBS renewed my contract for only eight of the fourteen games that fall. My friend Bob Wussler would look after me. I didn't need the money, and pro football was starting to bore me. Players were starting to act like wrestlers. Coaches were talking like geniuses, and owners were more talked about and powerful than governors. Although attendance and TV ratings continued to climb, I was disenchanted. Pro football was losing the honesty, sincerity, and purity of the game I once played. Television was turning the *game* into a *show*, a corporate sales tool.

Once again CBS had hired ten color men to cover seven games, meaning that each week three analysts would not be working. This did not set well with anyone, but it was senseless to argue. It was all in Wussler's hands, and no one had ever won a dispute with him.

With ten analysts and seven play-by-play men, it was back to the juggling act. Each week you were working with a different announcer, producer, and director. Only Brookshire and Summerall stayed together. Still no one had won the battle for the number-two spot.

Dallas and Minnesota were the only quality teams in the NFC, as the AFC continued its dominance. If parity was what the league was looking for, they had succeeded beyond their wildest dreams. You can't be competitive in football without a top-flight quarterback, and the AFC had five of the top six.

You would have thought the viewing audience could detect the disparity between the two conferences, but the fact was that the American public couldn't tell the difference as long as the announcers were upbeat and enthusiastic. The unspoken credo of the networks was to keep the audience any way you could. We were in the "Entertainment Business." Stay *up*, baby. This is show business.

As the 1977 season dragged by, it was hard to make the dull games sound interesting. All of us felt the same way, but all of us wanted to keep working so we stayed upbeat and positive. My feelings were a little hurt when I didn't get an assignment each week, but I was still convinced that my patron and friend Bob Wussler was taking care of me. I worked eleven of the fourteen games, and since no one had emerged as the number-two team, I had no reason to be any more discouraged than anyone else.

At season's end, I was awarded the final playoff game between Minnesota and Dallas to determine which team would represent the conference in Super Bowl XII. Since Summerall and Brookshire would be doing the Super Bowl, it was an honor to have been chosen to work the second biggest game of the year with Vin Scully. In fact, I was so appreciative of the assignment that I had stopped by Neiman Marcus and bought an eleven-foot pole as a gift for Wussler. The eleven-foot pole was for people you wouldn't touch with a ten-foot pole. He accepted it in the manner it was intended.

At the opening of the *show* (that's how T.V. people referred to the game), Vin asked me which team would likely prevail and represent the NFC in the upcoming Super Bowl. Without thinking, which was still my usual way, I said I hoped it would be Dallas as Minnesota had already lost four out of four Super Bowls.

This naturally sparked a wave of protest from Minnesota fans before the game even started. The switchboard lights at Black Rock lit up like a pinball machine. They estimated that over five hundred calls came in denouncing my lack of diplomacy and downright partiality.

Then late in the fourth quarter with Dallas leading 23-6 and the game all but wrapped up, Minnesota called a time out. I was watching the monitor as Roger Staubach trotted to the Dallas sideline to confer with Tom Landry. I suddenly noticed something strange about his trotting gait. Staubach was a great athlete and a respected runner. He walked like Gary Cooper. But it struck me that he trotted in a feminine fashion. Again without thinking, I observed "Roger kind of trots like a sissy." Vin, well schooled in the do's and don't's of broadcasting, looked at me and asked, "Did you wear a helmet when you played?"

Well, that did it. The switchboards at CBS in New York were jammed. The same thing was occurring in Dallas at the local affiliate station. The switchboard at Texas Stadium was flooded with angry and indignant callers. It was two hours of pure bedlam.

I, in my innocence, naiveté, and stupidity was oblivious to any wrongdoing. I knew that Roger was a great athlete. He had boxed at the Naval Academy. Still, for that brief second, he looked a little feminine. I thought it was funny. Where I grew up, we openly referred to men or boys with feminine qualities as sissies. I had hardly ever heard about gays. I certainly didn't intend the inference.

It so happened that a former player in the NFL had just come "out of the closet," admitted his own homosexuality, and claimed he knew at least three quarterbacks in the NFL who were gay. I had ignored his suggestion and scoffed at the accusation, but a lot of people hadn't.

After the game, the CBS crew gathered together in the Cowboy Club. The coolness when I arrived was apparent, despite the customary congratulations from everyone. Wussler was aloof and disgusted, and that "you've done it again" look was on his face.

The next day I got a call from the Cowboys' front office. They told me that Staubach was upset with me because of my remark. His teenage daughter had come home from school crying after having been teased by some classmates about her daddy's being gay.

I called Roger at home and apologized to him and his daughter for the misunderstanding. They were more forgiving than CBS. I was not invited back for the '78 season. I had been fired again.

26

Super Bowl XII was being played in New Orleans. The Big Easy was not one of Mr. Hunt's favorite cities, but since his Dallas Cowboys were playing Denver, he consented to attend.

We were staying at a charming little hotel in the French Quarter. As usual, Mr. Hunt had flown down earlier and by the time Mr. Davees and I arrived, he had already assigned us rooms. This time Mr. Davees had the suite.

The first couple of days are always the most difficult with Mr. Hunt. He has to make sure that tickets and badges are assured, and he is most demanding about party invitations. "I'll not be dicked about, Hawkins, and get us some drinks, Davees. Let's move right along. Where the hell are the women in this town? If I don't have a date by Friday, I'm going home."

It is true that the Super Bowls we have attended together have not been Mr. Hunt's finest hours. Why he continued to go was anybody's guess.

And Super Bowl XII was no exception. Mr. Hunt was pickpocketed sometime Friday night, and without money, credit cards, or identification, he was more or less at the mercy of Mr. Davees and myself. We showed our compassion by putting him on a twenty-dollar-a-day allowance, which, I might point out, was more money than he normally spent since Mr. Davees picked up all the checks anyway. However, because Mr. Hunt is a voracious eater and Mr. Davees and I are late sleepers, it was an inconvenience for Mr. Hunt's breakfasts and late-night snacks.

Since Mr. Davees has had the opportunity to describe Mr.

Hunt and I have chronicled his every action, it is only reasonable to allow Mr. Hunt to give his account of the old firm:

To begin with, I don't normally run around with dull or shallow people, and I'd like to point out that Hawkins is the lone exception to that rule. The son of a bitch is the most hard-headed, undependable asshole I have ever met in my life. The best thing about him is his wife and those two shitty children. He ain't got good sense, he won't take advice, and you can't believe a goddamn thing he says. He wasn't worth a shit as a player, was even worse as an announcer, and is the dumbest businessman I've ever known. He's pissed away more money than he'll ever make again, but he doesn't have enough sense to worry about it.

He has absolutely no fear of rejection and can sell just about anything, but the bastard won't go to work. He still thinks he's a celebrity. I paid for him to go to real estate school and even drove him to his first class to show him where it was. The shitass never went back again.

He ruined Super Bowl VI when he didn't take care of his obligations. We didn't have rooms, tickets, badges, party invita-tions, nothing. He was too proud to admit he'd screwed up, and he stayed drunk for four days. He slept on the couch in my room the first night. The second night he ended up sleeping in a bed with a Green Bay linebacker and two drunken women who were bigger and uglier than the linebacker. The third night he came staggering in my room about the time I was getting up. I undressed him, put him in my bed, tied a yellow ribbon around has little dick and brought people in to show them what a big-time network announcer looked like. He had a little bit of char-acter when I first met him, but I'll be damned if he didn't lose that.

And Davees? Shit, he ain't one goddamn bit better. Once a person becomes my friend, I accept him for what he is and I don't judge him. But if Davees wasn't already my friend, he wouldn't be taken into consideration as a candidate. Oh, he's a smart little shit, but he's as hardheaded and stubborn as Hawkins. He didn't have an ounce of character when I met him, and he's only now developed the little bit he's got. If he had come back to Atlanta when I told him, he'd be worth fifty million dollars, instead of sitting on his ass down in Houston and suing a billion-dollar bank.

But back to Super Bowl XII, it wasn't just that I got pickpocketed and the little bastards gave me twenty dollars a day to live on.

The tickets to the game weren't worth a damn anyway, and after the game I took my last ten dollars and stopped by this little pizza place down in the Quarter for a last-minute bite. I ordered and paid for my pizza, and while I was waiting, three goddamn thugs came in and held the joint up. They started shooting up the place, emptied the cash register, and made everybody empty their pockets and lie down on the floor. I thought they were going to kill me because I didn't have any money. But, by God, once the thieves left, I wasn't going anywhere until the sons of bitches cooked me my pizza.

One more bad experience and I ain't going back to no more Super Bowls. The game ain't never worth a shit anyway.

27

As long as I could remember, people had warned me about turning forty. Their descriptions were morbid. Lack of energy, failing memory, receding hairlines, paunchy waists, arthritic pains, fears of the future, you name it. But forty had come and gone and nothing had changed. I was still playing tennis, hunting, and fishing. I was a regular in the bars and played poker all night a couple of times a week. My weight remained under two hundred pounds, and while my belt was a little tighter, I still wore a size thirty-six. My hair was full and blond, and I had more energy than most young people.

My financial picture was not as bright as it once was, but I was still solvent. Mr. Hunt constantly nagged me about getting a job, and now that my broadcasting career was over, I was starting to wonder when I would find my niche in life.

Then one afternoon I was visiting a friend of mine when I noticed her new coffee table. She was a woman of great, but expensive, taste and I liked to kid her about her extravagance. She liked to tease me about my leisure suits and overall lack of refinement.

"How much did the coffee table set you back?" I asked.

"Number one, it's a cocktail table, and number two, if you have to ask the price, then you can't afford it," she responded.

"No, I'm serious," I said. "I like it."

"Twenty-eight hundred," she returned offhandedly.

I was flabbergasted. It was an attractive table, but it was nothing but a bone-colored stump, leveled on the top and bottom.

"What kind of wood is that?" I inquired.

"White cedar from the northwest," she answered.

It was an attractive piece and oddly shaped, but it looked like the base of a cypress tree. The swamps in the Southeast are full of cypress trees, and I had friends in South Carolina in the lumber business and friends who owned swamp land. I told her I could get her all the cypress stumps she wanted for nothing.

She suddenly became interested. She was a mother and housewife, but being interested and enterprising, she was always dabbling in things. She was socially connected and she dealt in gold, jewelry and antiques. She knew the price of everything, as well as its value.

"Let's go take a look at them," she said.

"Have you ever been in a swamp?" I asked.

"No, Hawkins," she said, "but I've been to Africa three times, and I'm going to the Amazon. Does that qualify me?"

So I called my friend in the lumber business, and we drove over for a look. We hired a man with a chain saw, cut twelve cypress butts from the lumber yard and two dozen cypress knees from the swamp, rented a truck, and headed back to Atlanta. Why she wanted the cypress knees was a mystery to me.

The larger the base of these stumps, the greater the configuration of the table. Some of these stumps weighed a couple of hundred pounds. Two-thirds of the weight was water, so we had to rent a kiln to dry them out to make them light enough to handle. Then we scoured the city for a woodworker to finish our tables. Woodworkers are a breed unto themselves. Irrespective of their talent, they all view themselves as artists, which means that for the most part, they are undependable, undisciplined, emotional, temperamental, and childishly sensitive.

We interviewed a dozen or so and looked around the city at their work. One man's work stood out. Fred Lindahl was the Van Gogh of the woodworkers. Fred was born in 1952 and was a product of his time. An average student, he stayed in college two-and-a-half years studying sex, drugs, and rock 'n' roll. Half way through his junior year at Maryland, he decided to attend Mardi Gras and wound up in New Mexico for the next six months.

Then it was on to California for a year with his friends, "Lightning Lewis" and "The Earl." In Berkeley, he took to commune life and gravitated into woodwork. The boy fell in love with redwood burl. After a year in Berkeley he got restless and wandered to another commune in a small town in Pennsylvania. Less than a year later, the seven-man cooperative broke up, and Fred took his act to Atlanta. He established himself as Atlanta's best at redwood burl, and that's why we picked him. H. M. liked the best!

H. M. Hull was her name, and she wasn't afraid of the devil with a handgun. She was a black-sheep blue blood. She liked movies and books, antiques and horses, eating and drinking, hunting and fishing, sailing and diving. She is a *very* interesting woman . . . *amen.*

The three of us were a comical alignment of personalities with little or nothing in common. We were a contemporary version of Tarzan, Jane, and Boy. But here we were: two forty-year-olds and a twenty-seven-year-old going into business together. A Berkeley flower child with the sensitivity of an infant; a beautiful Buckhead lady of exquisite taste and refinement; and a beat-up jock with a child's view of life, no taste, no organizational ability, no input, and no idea what was going on. And I was their *leader.*

We formed a partnership and incorporated under the name of "Down To Earth Limited." Fred's job was to finish the stumps. H. M. was in charge of selling to the showrooms and helping with design. I was in charge of procuring the stumps, which are hundreds of years old and antiques themselves. In fact, H. M. refused to use the term *stumps.* She referred to them as sculptured pieces . . . sculptured by God.

While waiting for the stumps to cure, Fred got interested in the cypress knees. Fred would stare at them with what seemed like dementia, and under his artist's eye they would take form and shape. He took five or six of the knees, doweled them together, leveled them, and drew a design for a glass, free-form table top. We found a glass cutter who could cut this design and sold both tables, in one day, for eighteen hundred dollars apiece.

"To hell with the stumps," said Fred. "They're too heavy to work with and take too much time to dry out. With the proper knees, I can sculpture a masterpiece." So, it was back to the swamps in search of more knees. We only wanted the unusual pieces that were gnarled and twisted. None of those straight up pieces that you see in Stuckey's.

Now, a swamp is not a pleasant place to hang out, especially in the summer. But that's when the water level drops, and you've only got a few months until the water rises again. So I got busy and lined up friends who had swampland. We were very selective about the pieces we used and only cut about one in a thousand.

We confined our activities to an area just outside of Columbia, South Carolina, where I had a friend who owned a motel and restaurant and knew everyone who owned land. He had trucks and boats and knew the neighboring swamps. That familiarity was important because if there's one place you don't want to get lost, it's a swamp. It's a dangerous and disagreeable place.

It was late June when we started cutting in Eastover. The three of us located a lumber yard where labor could be hired. We paid from five to nine dollars an hour, well above the standard fee. We needed a chain saw man and two men to carry out what he cut. Sometimes the walk to and from the truck would be as much as a half-mile, which is a long way in ankle deep muck that sucks tenaciously at your boots and the temperature well into the 90's.

Everything about the swamp is dangerous and foreboding; you cannot relax for a moment. What's more, a chain saw is an unforgiving machine, and the sound of it running all day is maddening. Then there are the mosquitoes, ticks, leeches and yellow flies, snakes, alligators and spiders. Nothing in the swamp likes you, and something is biting you every minute. But worst of all is the stifling humidity. There is never the least flutter of a breeze, and you stay wet with perspiration from the time you enter it. We stayed there from daylight to dark, but never for more than three days at a time. It was too intense.

All that summer we went back and forth from Atlanta to Eastover until we had stockpiled enough pieces to fill the largest of Ryder's rental trucks, and then we drove them back over to Fred's workshop.

He pieced together a dozen tables of varying designs, shapes, and sizes. We customed the glass tops and H. M. accessorized them. We had brass plates made with Fred's signature, along

with brass business cards. We had the tables professionally pho-
tographed to go in our suede catalog and then sent H. M. out on
the road. She was selling the sizzle, and she was *damn* good at
it. She placed them in decorative arts galleries around the country. At last, I was in business . . . the interior design business.

I had kept myself so busy that summer I had completely
forgotten about football. The regular season had cranked up,
and for the second time, I had no involvement with the game.

I watched every game, of course, but I was more interested in
the announcers than the football. Naturally, I was more critical
now that I was not working. The first two weeks were all I could
stand. Being at home on the fall weekends and out of the spotlight was killing me. On Tuesday, after my second weekend at
home, I hopped a plane for New York. A strange development
had occurred at CBS that spring. Bob Wussler had resigned.
After twenty years with the network, he had left them to form
his own production company.

I stepped off the airplane in New York and took a cab straight
to the Black Rock headquarters. I had not called ahead or made
an appointment. I didn't even know who I was there to see. I'd
already been fired by CBS twice, but I made my way to the
thirtieth floor and asked to see the president, who turned out to
be Barry Frank. To everyone's mutual surprise, I was invited
into his office.

If I had met Barry before, I didn't remember it. "What brings
you to the city?" he asked.

I waded right in: "I came up here for work. Outside of
Brookshire, I'm the best color man you've got. I've waited for
two weeks for you to call me, and when you didn't, I thought I'd
bring it to your attention."

He stopped me right there. He picked up the phone and
summoned Clarence Cross, a vice president, and we began
again. Five or ten minutes later, after I had exhausted myself, I
was interrupted by Barry.

"Can you work with Vin Scully?"

"Certainly I can work with Scully," I replied. "I've worked
with him before."

"We know," he replied with a smile. "We all remember that.

Vin is one-half of our number-two broadcast team, and if you can stay out of trouble and work with Vin, you've got a job."

"Starting when?" I asked.

"This weekend," he answered.

So, just like that, I was hired for a third time by CBS. I had gone from unemployed to the number-two job without an appointment.

28

Now that I was into interior design and working alongside the poised and polished Vin Scully, I had to do away with my leisure suits. Brooks Brothers and Neiman Marcus were getting my business. I was trying to create a new image.

The AFC continued its dominance over the NFC, with Dallas and Los Angeles the only competitive NFL clubs. But because of Vin's strong contract with CBS, we were getting most of the better games.

Keeping up with football was never a problem for me, but now that I had been out of it for ten years, it was a different matter. Nearly all the players I had played with and against were retired. There were ten new coaches in the league that year alone. The regular-season schedule expanded from fourteen to sixteen games to accommodate television, which was paying the owners five million dollars a year per team. I was now starting to think before I talked, and I surprised myself at how dull and boring I was becoming, but I made it through the 1979 season without incident.

Down to Earth Limited was doing quite well, thank you. H. M. had targeted seven showrooms across the country that she wanted to handle our line. She got all seven. We were in decorative art centers who catered only to the trade in Atlanta, Miami, Palm Beach, Houston, Dallas, and New York. Phyllis Morris handled us in Los Angeles ... on Rodeo Drive. Our tables were in *Interior Design* and *Southern Accents*, and *Architectural Digest* featured us four times that year. H. M. could talk that talk, and we were wholesaling our "one of a kind" tables for eighteen hundred dollars a pop. A custom retail sale would go for five to seven thousand. Our tables were in some of the finest homes in the country. Cher had one, as did J. B. Fuqua, the Duke of Bedford, and His Royal Highness, Prince Faisal. We were appealing to the people who don't ask about price.

H. M. was comfortable with these people. She dressed the part, acted the part, and looked the part. She could sell anything she believed in, and she believed in our tables. It was funny to me. I just stood back, far out of the way.

Our biggest problem was product supply. Sales were exceeding production. Fred was the only person who could sculpture these tables to H. M.'s discriminating taste and satisfaction. She had an eye for perfection and perfection takes time. Fred had his own business to look after, so sometimes we were put on a back burner. This galled H. M. Her clientel wasn't accustomed to waiting.

H. M. wanted perfection, but she wanted it *now*, and this is where I came in. I had to act as arbitrator and peacemaker between the two. H. M. couldn't design the tables, but she knew what she wanted. And while the two of them usually got along ... well, there were those other moments. Both parties were high-strung and temperamental. Both were erratic and sensitive. Both were short-fused and emotional. Emotions run high with artists, and both were artists in their own way.

It would normally start with a minor disagreement.

"It needs another piece right here," she would suggest.

"I tried that and it didn't work," he would explain.

"Well then, move this piece over here and connect it with a runner," she would offer.

"I don't have a piece that fits," he would counter.

"Damn it to hell," she would say a little louder. "Find one in that pile," pointing to the mountain of stacked pieces.

"Find it yourself, you spoiled brat," he would answer, just short of screaming. "I've got to have a cabinet done by noon tomorrow."

"You promised me the table would be ready a week ago. I can't sell promises," she would scream back.

"Then do it yourself, you bitch," he would roar as he turned around and flung whatever he had in his hand against the far side of his workshop. Then he would disappear into his office and slam the door.

"Let's go, Hawkins," H. M. would say, "It's *his* signature on the tables, not mine. All I'm trying to do is make him famous."

She would storm out, and he would return to me teary-eyed and apologetic. The next day the table would be perfect.

All in all, it was a fascinating study in culture shock: H. M., a socialite, reliable, known for saying and doing the right thing; Fred, a flower child from the sixties, confused and defiant, resentful of authority and power; and me, an ex-jock, not sure of anything, suspended between two worlds and living in a third.

29

Christmas and New Year's came and went, and once again it was time for the Super Bowl and the annual firm meeting. For the fifth time Miami was the host city. Super Bowl XIII would feature Pittsburgh against Dallas.

Optimism was high as Mr. Hunt had a foolproof plan for his Six Flags property. Ginther-Davis Interest now had a net worth of over fifteen million dollars. I was back with CBS, and "Down to Earth Limited" was showing a nice profit and a promising future.

Mr. Hunt, still at odds with Miami, rather forcefully suggested we stay outside the city. I borrowed a friend's two-bedroom condo at the Jockey Club and arranged for two rental rooms for the remainder of the firm. Twenty tickets and badges were secured and handed over to Mr. Hunt. Mr. Davees brought with him Lady Charles and a satchel full of money.

But let's get back to *serotonin* for a moment. If you drive serotonin down in the monkeys, you make them nasty, hostile, bitchy, and even crazy. (The advantage of studying animals is that you can switch them from dominant to subordinate and back again and look at the same animal in both conditions.)

I had gone down on an early flight to inspect our accommodations. All was in order for the firm's afternoon arrival. Mr. Davees checked into his modest, but comfortable, room. Mr. Hunt was not so pleased. Immediately he was pounding on my door, and when I let him in, he lit right in on me.

"Hawkins, you asshole, I'm not staying in that room. It's hot, it's pink, I can't see the ocean, and I can't sleep or screw on twin beds. I'll stay there tonight, but not one night more. Now you get busy and find me a decent room. I'll not be dicked about." With that, he was off to the bar in search of a dance partner. I phoned the front desk, and they were already aware of Mr. Hunt's dilemma. They were trying to relocate him but could not promise anything. It seems that Corporate American was buying up blocks of tickets and rooms to entertain its clients.

The Jockey Club was the hottest club going at the time. At dinner that night, I informed *my* group that they had me to thank for everything. I also boasted that in addition to the rooms, we had a fishing boat and captain at our disposal (compliments of my friend who loaned me the condo). Mr. Davees and Charlie were thrilled by the prospect. Mr. Hunt was not.

"I don't care about no goddamn boat. I'm interested in a bigger room with a larger bed. Hawkins, you're up there with an extra bed overlooking the ocean while I'm in a rat hole that looks out onto nothing. If you don't get me a better room, I'm moving in with you."

The idea of spending five days and nights in the same room with Mr. Hunt was unthinkable. No one in Atlanta will share a golf cart with him, and that is the sad but brutal truth. I excused myself and went to the bar. I located a friend of mine from Atlanta and offered the spare bed to him. He graciously accepted, and a near catastrophe was averted.

Later that night after Mr. Davees had paid the check and shot holes in Mr. Hunt's proposed plan for his Six Flags property, we retired to the bar when an unheard-of development occurred. Mr. Davees and I had *words*. In the thirteen years we had known one another, we had never had a misunderstanding. I had seen him turn on other people. Not always is he a perfect gentleman. Sometimes he can be downright mean. I, too, have had rare moments where I have been less than a gentleman. Not often, mind you, but there have been nights when the wine and my neck got redder and redder until . . . well, a small flaw in my character surfaced.

On this occasion, I demanded an apology. Don, stubborn and proud, demanded the same. I, hardheaded and insolent, went to my room. Thursday morning I received a call from Mr. Hunt. The hotel had found him another room, but he was only going to stay there for one night. He pleaded with me to apologize to Mr. Davees.

"You know how stubborn that little shit is. He ain't going to apologize, so you're going to have to. You're like two children and you're ruining my trip."

Being the mediator was something Mr. Hunt loved, but he wasn't really good at it. Whatever he was telling Mr. Davees was not working, either. Mr. Davees did not call.

I spent Thursday morning with my friends from CBS, some ex-players, and my new roommate. I invited them fishing Friday morning. I contacted the boat captain who had already been notified by my friend, his boss, that he was to be at my disposal. But Friday morning found the captain hung over and tired. He made up an excuse that something was wrong with the boat and we couldn't go that day. We made a date for Saturday morning at 6:00 a.m. I called his boss and told him of the incident. He assured me it would not happen again.

Back in my room, the phone was ringing. It was Mr. Hunt.

"Hawkins, quit acting like a child and call Don and apologize. You know how hardheaded the little fucker can be. He ain't going to call you, and I ain't having any fun. Don't ruin everyone's trip. It's bad enough having to change rooms every day. They've got me a new room and I think I'm going to like it. If I can compromise, why can't you?" In just three days, Mr. Hunt had been in more rooms than the maid service.

Mr. Davees did not call.

That afternoon Mr. Hunt called me again.

"Hawkins," he said sternly, "meet me at the bar in ten minutes. And, goddamn you, act like you've got some sense."

When I entered the bar there stood Charlie, Mr. Davees, and Mr. Hunt. I walked towards the threesome, but my eyes were firmly fixed on Mr. Davees. I guess my eyes softened as I drew closer because I know his did. We didn't say a word but our eyes did all the talking. He was as ashamed as I was. We shook hands, and no apologies were exchanged. A few drinks later, we were making plans for the next morning's fishing trip. All three of us had managed to remain the *head* monkey.

It was 5:45 when the captain called and informed me that a storm had come up and he was taking the boat down to Isla

Morada. We were to meet him at the Holiday Isles Marina as soon as we could muster. His trip down would take him about four hours.

I phoned Mr. Hunt and suggested breakfast. I dialed Mr. Davees but there was no answer. Mr. Davees is a notorious late sleeper. He wants no part of the early bird or the worm.

Mr. Hunt and I had breakfast and phoned his room again. Still no answer. An hour and five phone calls later we went to his room. We banged on his door, and finally a voice told us he would be down in thirty minutes. Three hours and ten phone calls later, he and Charlie appeared in the coffee shop. They were fresh but famished and insisted on having lunch before departing for the Keys.

By now Mr. Hunt, always known for "moving right along," was beside himself. He cursed Mr. Davees for the two hours it took us to reach the marina.

"Davees, you inconsiderate little shit, no wonder Hawkins stayed pissed with you for two days. You only think about yourself. We've been up for nine hours, and you've kept us waiting while you laid around in bed. I came down here to fish, not wait. If you make us miss our fishing trip, I'm through with your worthless ass."

When we finally arrived at the marina, it was well past two in the afternoon. "El Capitan" had been waiting for us for four and a half hours.

During the drive down, Mr. Hunt had announced to all that he was to take the first fish. He made this clear to the captain also as he assumed his position in the fighting chair. We were less than a mile from the docks when the first fish struck. Mr. Hunt was handed the rod. We were fishing for sailfish, but whatever Mr. Hunt had on the line was not acting like one of those. The captain slowed the boat down, but Mr. Hunt could not advance the fish. After more than five minutes nothing had broken water, so that ruled out a sail.

Mr. Hunt was pumping the rod and cranking the reel feverishly, but was making little headway on this fish. Whatever it was, it had to be "big."

"Hang in there, Mr. Hunt. Stay on him," we cheered. "It could be a marlin or a giant tuna."

Ten minutes went by and still nothing surfaced.

Mr. Hunt was tugging away and sweating and swearing profusely. At two hundred fifty pounds, he filled all of the fighting chair. He was pulling and pumping and turning and squirming. That fish was playing hell with him, but he was playing hell with that chair!

Twenty minutes had passed and Mr. Hunt was making some progress, but not much. My patience and attention span is almost as short as Mr. Hunt's, so I started chiding him: "Get the damn thing in; we want to fish too." He was as excited as a little boy over this world record whatever it was and he exploded with anger, "Goddamn you, Hawkins," he raged, "just shut the fuck up."

"Just get the fish in. Quit babying it," I barked back.

"This is a big son of a bitch," he screamed at the top of his lungs. I have never seen him more furious. "Keep your fucking mouth shut." He went back to pumping the rod, but this time more violently and frantically than before. He was wild with both anger and excitement. There was always a chance this world-record fish would get off.

He was gaining on the fish, and the captain was poised with the gaff. Down in the water went the gaff and up it came . . . with a twelve pound bonito, *foulhooked*.

During the course of this struggle, Mr. Hunt had torn two screws out of the fighting chair and split the cushioned seat from front to back.

We were back fishing now and hadn't gone over a hundred yards when suddenly all three spinning rods went down. Charlie took one, Don got the other, and I manned the third. Up in the air leapt three beautiful sailfish. Twenty minutes later we landed all three.

"Turn the boat around; let's go back to the docks," I commanded. "This fishing trip is over." Mr. Davees seconded the motion, and Charlie agreed. The fishing trip that had taken nine hours to begin was now over in less than an hour. For the first and last time in his life, Mr. Hunt was speechless.

Mr. Davees and I agreed that this day called for a party. We were going to invite a dozen or so friends to my suite. We stopped and picked up a reasonable amount of liquor, beer, wine, and snacks for a small gathering. When we arrived at the Jockey Club the bar was filled. Late arrivals had come in that we had not seen or talked to. A lot of ex-players were there, and women were plentiful. The excitement of the game was gaining force. Super Bowl XIII was just hours away.

We had to be selective in choosing our guests since my suite could only accommodate about fifty people comfortably. Over half of our invitees were ex-jocks. We figured we might as well invite them because jocks feel they're always welcome and would come anyway.

Mr. Hunt, still seething over the events of the day, had run into an old girlfriend and angrily declared that they would not attend our bash under any circumstance.

Our party was going along nicely, and all was under control until about ten o'clock that evening when Mr. Davees went up to the penthouse to inspect it for future consideration. He had been in an excellent mood all evening . . . and then came that horrible moment. Mr. Davees was refused entry to the penthouse party! He had politely explained to these Pittsburgh corporate people that he would only be staying for a moment, that he just wanted to look around. A spokesman for the group vetoed the request.

When Mr. Davees returned to our party, which now consisted of about two dozen friends and growing, he took me aside. I could tell by the narrowing of his dark, beady eyes that Mt. St. Helens was about to erupt.

"Mr. Hawkins," he said, "I think we should expand our party. I was not invited into the penthouse, so it's time to put them out of the party business."

I could tell by the insistent and determined look in his eyes that he would do just that.

"What do you want me to do?" I asked.

"Just look after Charlie and get ready for a crowd," he said as he left the suite.

I had seen him "create" too many parties to doubt him, and when the room started filling, I knew why. In less than an hour the food and beverage table had quadrupled. Soon the suite was filled and spilling out into the hall. Glasses and ice magically appeared, and women outnumbered men three to one. I expected a band but there wasn't room for one. I'd never seen half of these people before. I knew the Artful Little Dodger was at work.

Shortly after midnight, a new bar was set up in the hall. Each arriving elevator brought more and more "friends." Then Don reappeared. A slight smile of satisfaction was on his mouth, but his eyes remained hostile. I started being introduced to a lot of Pittsburgh people. Then I was summoned to the door. It was the spokesman from the penthouse party.

"I wonder if you'd mind if I joined your party?"

"Not at all," I replied, "Come right on in."

He was a little man, about Don's size.

"A little earlier one of your people was refused admittance to our party upstairs. I was a little short with him. I'd like to apologize. There he is on the balcony," he said, pointing to Mr. Davees.

We walked out on the balcony together. The two shook hands and began talking. The look in Don's eyes had not relaxed. The subject of betting came up, and the sparks started flying.

"I'll bet you thirty thousand and give you five points," said the spokesman.

"I don't bet on football," Don answered calmly.

"Make it ten thousand then," spoke the spokesman.

"I don't think you heard me," growled Don. "I don't bet on football."

The two men squared off.

"Then make it five thousand, if that'll be easier on you," teased the spokesman.

The loaded shell in Don's brain exploded.

"I'll bet you five thousand you're a loser," Don hissed as he reached in his pocket for a fist full of bills that would easily cover the bet.

"What are we betting on?" said the spokesman.

"We're betting on you being a loser," said Don as he reached in his pocket and came out with a quarter and slammed it on the table.

"You flip it and call it," said Don, "because I know you're a loser."

The spokesman picked up the quarter, looked at it, and said,

"Let's make it five hundred."

"Cash," said Don throwing down five fresh cat-eyes.

"Done," said the spokesman, producing a wad of money easily as large as Don's.

Up went the quarter. "Tails," called the spokesman, but it came down heads.

"You're a loser," spat Don.

"Let's do it again for five thousand," countered the spokesman.

"This is not a gambling casino," I interrupted, "and I'm going to have to ask you to leave."

"This is just a nice party for some of our friends," I explained as I walked the spokesman to the elevator (just as a Green Bay linebacker heaved a television set over the railing).

"We're just having a little fun," I told him (as a Redskin safety ripped the shower curtain from the bath).

"Come by after the game tomorrow," I invited (as a Dolphin lineman drove his car through the closed front gate).

"It was really nice having you," I assured him (as a Ram defensive end made off with a hotel golf cart).

Mr. Hunt never showed that night, but we had breakfast together the next morning.

"Hawkins," he said, "this is the last time I'll attend a Super Bowl with you or Davees. While we were out on that cheap-ass boat yesterday somebody stole my tickets to the game. Then that bitch I was with vanished last night, and I saw her having coffee with that shit-kicking roommate of yours. I've put up with your dumb ass and that sorry little shit Davees for the last time. It's my last Super Bowl."

And it was!

Hawkins and McClain Stevenson "selling" the World Football League.

At the Heavyweight Championship of Pro Football in Pompano Beach, Hawkins takes on Jerry Quarry . . . and takes a nine-count.

Mssrs. Hunt and Davees, transacting business.

Flemin Gaskins meets Hawkins and Country Lee Cummings at the airport for the Houston Livestock Show and Rodeo.

Hawkins, Mr. Davees, and Country Lee have "gone Texan."

Ted Turner and Hawkins at the "strike game" in December, 1982.

The historic Kennesaw House.

Hawkins welcomes patrons to his new restaurant.

CHARLES R. PUGH, JR.

Hawkins, Robert Wussler, Jeff Van Note and entourage in front of the restaurant.

Libby Hawkins.

Kennesaw House staffers include (left to right) Sissy Gibson, Maxine McLarnan, and Hawkins' daughter Elizabeth.

The Hawkins boys: Steele (son) and Alex (dad).

30

It amuses me when I hear someone say, "I don't know what I'd do if I didn't work." It had been four years since I'd actually had a job, and I hadn't been bored one minute. Every day is somebody's day off, and I knew whose it was. I was never without a companion. I was hunting and fishing in the Carolinas, the Keys and Mexico. I didn't have time to work. It is true that I was spending more money than I was making, but isn't that the great American way?

CBS renewed my contract, but for only eight of the sixteen games. Now that I was their number-two color man, I felt I deserved better. If they wanted me, they would have to commit for the entire season. They needed me, I didn't need them. And I told them just that. They responded with "take it or leave it." I told them I'd leave it.

Mr. Hunt went bonkers. "Hawkins, for the first time in your life *will* you listen to me? You call those people up and take the eight games. You need them, they don't need you. You've been out of the game for ten years now, and without television you're just another washed-up jock. A year from now nobody will know you. You've gotten a lot of mileage out of a very average career, but you've got to remain visible. Every year there are a dozen bigger names than you retiring. They all want to be color men and some of them will. Be thankful for the eight games. You need the exposure that goes with the job, so use your head and take what they offer. When you're out of that business, you're out of business. Now, please, do like I tell you; I know what I'm talking about."

"Mr. Hunt, I've got too much pride to back down now. They need me. I ain't just another jock, and sooner or later they'll realize that and come around. You watch what I tell you."

They never did.

While waiting to be needed, I got a call from my friend Bob Wussler. Bob had resigned from CBS and formed Pyramid Enterprises, a production company doing sporting events for syndications. "Alex," he said, "what are you doing from June 17 through June 25?"

"I can make myself available," I told him. "What's going on?"

"Boxing," he reported. "I'd like for you to co-host the Heavyweight Championship of Professional Football. You'll be working with Jerry Quarry and Larry Csonka. We've invited one lineman from each of the twenty-eight NFL teams to Florida. They will box to determine who will be the Heavyweight Champion of Pro Football."

"That's a hell of an idea," I said.

"I know," he answered.

"But why Csonka and me?" I asked. "What do we know about boxing?"

"I have my reasons," he returned.

"What does it pay?"

"Twelve thousand dollars and expenses."

"Fifteen," I countered.

"Twelve," he said smugly, "and no leisure suits."

June 17 found me at the Palm Aire Resort in Pompano Beach. I've always been fascinated by boxing. I boxed a little in college, but I knew very little about the sport. I couldn't imagine why Wussler paired Csonka and me with a man like Jerry Quarry, who had fought for the world heavyweight title on three different occasions. But, then again, that was Bob Wussler.

And like Bob Wussler, he did it up right: no expenses were spared. He brought in some of the best referees and trainers in the business and a top-flight ring announcer. The ring and all the equipment was the best that money could buy. Our rooms and meals were first class. We just signed for anything we wanted. Wussler had style; I'll give him that.

I had met Csonka before and he was a nice guy, but he had his wife with him, so I paired off with Jerry Quarry. What a fascinating man. His life had been no open box of candy. He was born in California but moved all over the West. His father was a roofer who liked to stay one step in front of the rent. I asked Jerry how he got started in boxing. He said he had been fighting all his life. He attended twenty-three different schools in one year. Each new school represented a fight because the new kid on the block had to establish himself. His serotonin level was high.

Jerry's career was a checkered one. He was always the challenger and never the champion. He had been unsuccessful in dethroning Joe Frazier for the crown in 1969. He was beaten by Muhammad Ali in 1970 and again in 1972. Always a bridesmaid, but never a bride, he was denied that which he coveted most—the right to be called *champ*.

The big payday had always eluded Jerry. The most he had ever made on a single fight was two hundred thousand dollars. That seems like a lot of money, but out of that comes salaries for the manager, trainer, sparring partners, cut man, bucket man, and, of course, the IRS takes its bite. When it's all over, there is little left for the fighter.

And when the fighting is over, what then? Only the champions are offered analyst jobs. Only champions do commercials. None of them become corporate spokesmen. It's not like baseball, football, or basketball because people deep down are afraid of boxers. Maybe it's that look in their eyes or the aura about them that repels the average man. Boxers make the civilians of this world real nervous.

To prove this point, Quarry would come to my room every morning, and we would ride the small air-conditioned elevator the six floors to ground level. He would fake jabs and hooks to my body, never touching me, but every morning by the time we reached ground level, my underarms would be wet. And the things he could do with his hands. He could make a small bag dance forever. The heavy bag would almost explode from his thunderous punches. He could generate more power from a short left hook to a heavy bag than Csonka and I could with a full kick of our leg. I respected his talents to the point where I would stand and let him snap jabs at my face and he would brush the tip of my nose as lightly as an angel's breath. The force behind the blow, if miscalculated, would have crushed my face.

It irked Jerry that pro football players were held in such high esteem for their macho. After viewing the twenty-eight NFL linemen, he declared he could knock them all out in the first round in the same day. He was right and I knew it, but when he claimed I could not last one round with him and he wouldn't even hit me, it was too much. I bet him a dinner that I could.

The days flew by as we watched these two-hundred-sixty to two-hundred-ninety pound linemen eliminate each other en route to the championship. They were using sixteen-ounce gloves and boxing headgear to prevent injury. Each fight went three rounds. By the fifth day, we were down to two fighters, Ross Browner from the Cincinnati Bengals and Jackie Slater of the Los Angeles Rams. After Browner defeated Slater for the title, Jerry and I held our bout.

The rules were simple; I could hit him but he couldn't hit me. All I had to do was stay on my feet for one three-minute round. How could I lose that bet? Could I not just stand there for one hundred eighty seconds? I told the people in my corner to notify me when the first minute was over, again after the second minute, and then to count me down for the final thirty seconds.

We went to the middle of the ring. Jerry, using the famous stare-down, looked into my eyes and said, "Hawk, you know I love you." I nodded the affirmative. "But are you really sure I won't hit you?" I blinked and wondered. He gave me a strange look and went to his corner.

Suddenly I was confused and shaken. I don't know what came over me, but I realized I was in his arena. The ring was the only place he was truly comfortable. This was his home and his workshop. It was alien to me. And it seemed about the size of a phone booth.

The instant the bell rang, he charged across the ring like a bull. I started moving away from him, but I couldn't *get* away. He was all over me, not hitting me, of course, but *moving* me. I *couldn't* stand still. Soon I started throwing punches, but always he kept me moving. He was inviting me to hit him and I took the bait. I landed my best right hand to his forehead, but his nineteen-inch neck cushioned the blow. He didn't even blink.

Then he started me around the ring again. I felt like I was on roller skates. My legs were getting rubbery. The three minutes *must* be up by now . . . I just hadn't heard the count.

He baited me to hit him again, but I couldn't. The bastard was making me miss. My arms were now heavy and my legs were like lead. Finally I heard it. "One minute is up." *One minute!* I was finished already and could hardly move, but this man was mysteriously *making* me move. I thought my heart would explode.

"Hit me, Jerry, hit me."

"Those aren't the rules."

"I'm going to die of a heart attack if you don't. I need a nine count. I can't just fall in front of all these people."

He tapped me with a soft left, and I gratefully fell.

I can tell you one thing: nine seconds lying down goes by faster than one minute of boxing. I took the full nine count, but he was back at me again. He was the cutting horse, and I was the calf. I was trying not to move, but I just couldn't stay still.

Finally, when I was too exhausted to go on, I heard, "Two minutes are gone." With fifteen seconds remaining, I threw in the towel and collapsed on the ropes. I hadn't trained for such a long fight.

So take my advice: if a really good boxer offers you this same bet, *don't take it*, or you may end up paying for a four-hundred-dollar dinner like I did that evening.

31

Now that my boxing career was over, I turned once again to my interior design business. Down to Earth Limited was badly in need of raw material. H. M. had sold nearly fifty tables that Fred had sculptured, but more knees were needed. Having exhausted the area in and around Eastover, I turned to south Georgia and the swamps that encircled the Okefenokee.

With the help of foresters and some newly acquired friends with Georgia Pacific, we lined up trips to such places as Homerville, Fargo, and Folkston. These little towns along the east Georgia-Florida line were a trip back into the forties and fifties. Life here was slow, simple, and uncomplicated. Children and teenagers still walked barefooted to the old swimming hole carrying cane fishing poles. Everything was "yes, sir" and "yes, ma'am" and when they tell you they'll do something, they will. It is "Andy of Mayberry" all over again. H. M. and Fred were going through their second childhood, and I was still in my first.

All three of us fell in love with the Suwannee River. It starts just above Fargo where it trickles black and beautiful out of the Okefenokee Swamp. You can almost jump across it in the summer months, but then it winds and twists and turns its way out of Fargo and into Florida, getting wider by the mile until just above Live Oak, where it meets the Withlacoochee. It then becomes the loveliest body of water I've ever seen. Stephen F. Foster had never seen the Suwannee when he wrote "Way Down Upon The Suwannee River," and it makes you wonder how much more beautiful the song would have been had he seen it.

We cut about a hundred knees and stockpiled them in our chain saw man's yard. Then we went west into the Tallahassee area and located a forester who knew every swamp for miles around.

Everything about the Panhandle area is intriguing. Many of the people who settled there were fugitives from justice. They made their way there from all over the Southeast and settled in the swamps to avoid capture. They were desperate and dangerous, and not many lawmen were dedicated enough to give chase. Those fugitives who survived were tough and determined, and so were their offspring.

Then it was southeast to Perry, Florida, where the Panhandle proper starts. This is tough country, make no mistake about it. It is a sparsely settled area, and the few people who inhabit it are one way or another engaged in the timber business. Many carry guns and nearly everyone carries a machete. We were real tourists, naive and innocent. We didn't even have a pocket knife. We were oblivious to danger or fear of any kind. We were interior designers.

Then we went due west to the swamp of Sumatra, about twenty-five miles north of Appalachicola. This is really rugged territory with only about two persons to the square mile. I feel confident we were the only tourists the town had ever seen. But, then it really wasn't a town. There were a few houses and a lumber company and a general store. The store served as the post office and gas station as well.

When we couldn't locate the lumber yard, I parked the Honda hatchback between the gas pumps and went in the store to ask for directions. About the time I did, a man pulled up on his motorcycle and raced to the telephone on the outside of the store. Inside I was told the lumber yard was two miles down the paved road and the first dirt road to the left after I crossed the bridge. Armed with this information I started back to the car. Just as I reached the door, I was greeted by the damnedest volley of profanity I'd heard since John Hunt. The motorcycle man was on the phone and he was not happy. He sounded like Hitler with a hangover, and I was delighted he wasn't talking to me.

When I got behind the wheel, I noticed a bushel basket had fallen in front of the car. Rather than run over it or get out of the car to pick it up, I chose to back up. It was a horrible decision. In the excitement of knowing where I was going (which is rare), I had not noticed the motorcycle parked behind the car. It was not the sound of the car hitting the bike that got my attention. It was the screaming "STOP!!!" that preceeded the falling bike as the biker nearly tore the phone from the wall.

I quickly shut down the motor and exited the car. It was a tender scene — the biker fondling his bike like a mother holding her wounded child. He was patting and stroking and examining it for wounds or abrasions like a kind veterinarian looking over an injured animal. The man obviously loved his machine. At a moment like this, an introduction or a handshake seemed out of place.

He was a barrel-chested man about five feet ten, and I judged by his neck and buffalo-sized head that he weighed over two hundred and fifty pounds. He was dressed only in boots and bib overalls, no shirt. His arms were like tree trunks, and his rhino-like torso was designed for strength. But most terrifying of all were these festering sores that covered his shoulders and chest. He looked like the survivor of the atomic blast at Hiroshima. I wouldn't have touched him with borrowed hands.

As he stood his bike upright, I began to speak: "I'm sorry, so terribly sorry. It was all my fault, and I'll be glad to pay for any damages. It was so stupid of me not to see it. I don't know how I could be so blind. I will pay for any damages I've caused or I'll buy you a new bike if you like. Just please forgive me."

I started looking all over his bike for anything new or old I could repair. I would have paid him a couple of hundred bucks for a scratch on his kickstand. I wanted *out* of there!

"You stupid bastard," he growled and kicked his bike. "You dumb, blind son of a bitch. I ought to stomp a mudhole in your ass. I ought to pinch your fucking head off," he roared as I retreated back to the car.

"I'm certainly glad there was no damage. I'll be more careful from now on. I've got a bike of my own," I lied as I got behind the wheel, closed and locked the door, and started the engine.

"Get me anything I can use as a weapon," I whispered to H. M.

"I've already looked," she whispered back. "There's nothing in the car but a road map."

"Oh, shit," I replied as I put it in gear and flattened the bushel basket.

The man from Sumatra was still cursing me and stroking his bike as I sped down the paved road toward the lumber yard. I looked through the rear view mirror and didn't see him, but as I got within view of the bridge, the man from Sumatra was in hot pursuit. It was decision time, and he was coming on fast. What could I do? I'd rather be killed and eaten than to touch his mangy body, and my only weapon was a road map.

Then off to my left I saw the dirt road to the lumber yard. Did I dare make the turn? Would he kill me in front of witnesses? *Make up your mind. You've got to turn now; he's gaining on you.* There wasn't enough time for my normal decision-making process, which is to flip a coin, so I signaled and turned on the dirt road to my left.

I was no James Bond, so I looked for anything that could be used as a club. Then in the mist of confusion came clarity. There was a wide place in the road, with enough room to make a U-turn. If he turned left at the dirt road, I told myself, I'd turn the car around and run over him, I'd kill him. My eyes were fixed in the rear view mirror as the man from Sumatra flew on past me and on down the paved road.

"H. M.," I sighed, "let's don't even go into the lumber yard. I think we've got enough knees already. We've been down here three days and it's time to go home."

Somehow the luster was gone from Down to Earth Limited. We sold another twenty-five tables that fall. Then Fred got busy with his own business, and H. M. started dating a friend of mine. The two of them were soon traveling all over the world. She did, in fact, make it to the Amazon as well as the Galapagos Islands, Peru, and most of Europe.

This left me in charge of sales, and while I can get along with most people ... well, dealing with decorators, designers, and people in the trade was not exactly my long suit. They were a little too ... let's say, sensitive for my liking. So, Down to Earth Limited kind of faded into the sunset, and I was once again unemployed.

32

In the spring of 1980, a rather startling development was unfolding. *Ted Turner was in trouble!* The one-time billboard mogul had branched out into radio and then television. Everything he touched seemed to work. He was a man of uncanny vision, unbridled ego, and balls of steel.

In 1970, he bought a tiny little UHF station that nobody else wanted and set out to conquer the television industry. He and his two dozen employees went to work with the slogan, "Watch us grow," and grow they did, despite the fact that they had no news, sports, or network programming. They showed old movies, reruns, and sitcoms.

In 1976, he beamed into satellite, and Channel 17 became the Superstation. His erstwhile viewing audience of a hundred thousand now numbered over three million. Ted was positive, brilliant, and arrogant, and he charged on unflinchingly. Cable television was the wave of the future, but he was convincing to only a few.

In 1976, Ted also bought the Atlanta Braves. The following year he acquired the Hawks. One year later, he purchased the Chiefs, a soccer team whose attendance was so sparse they did away with turnstiles and started using guest books. In between, he found time to bring the Americas Cup back to the United States. He was tactless and crude, but he somehow got his way. He was making big noises. His competition scoffed at his recklessness, but "Captain Outrageous" kept right on coming.

In 1980, he launched CNN. There was no turning back now. He was committed. Ted was fearless, relentless, and ambitious.

Some thought he was crazed. Others weren't sure. One thing was certain: here was a man who wouldn't back down. He was making a run at The Top.

Ted was now shooting at the big boys. He wanted to compete with the networks. He wanted to go big time, but he had one problem. He didn't know how.

Sure he had been a nuisance to the networks with his outspoken and boastful comments. Yes, he was quoted regularly on his distaste for their programming. But while Ted had flair and a certain style, he still lacked experience and, more importantly, class. He had never been to The Mountain. He, himself, didn't know the ins and outs of big-time television. He had never competed head-on with the big dogs. He needed a man who had been there.

And Bob Wussler was just that sort of man. Pyramid Productions was in trouble. Spartacade, a forerunner to the Good Will Games, had been a disaster and the Heavyweight Championship of Professional Football was never aired. He had lost a lot of money on these projects and was looking for an opportunity.

Bingo. Bob was introduced to Ted, and time and chance came solidly together. Here was Ted's missing piece. Poised, confident, and savvy, Bob was the man needed to lend credibility and class to Turner Broadcasting. He had the experience of having been there before, and he knew television from top to bottom. He was the perfect choice to be president of Turner's network.

Bob was an expert in news and sports, and he was never without an idea. And ideas were something that Ted needed as he was running short of his own. He had one very large idea that he needed time to pursue. He had the idea of becoming the next president of the United States. Or so I was told when I picked Bob up at the airport on his arrival in Atlanta in April. I drove him to the SuperStation, and we talked about life in Atlanta. It was a big comedown from his past position of President of CBS, and he made no bones about it. Here there would be no unlimited expense accounts, penthouse apartments, chauffeur-driven limousines, or executive dining rooms. Here he would be flying tourist because Turner flew tourist and those were the rules. Here he would rent an apartment, eat in a restaurant, and drive a medium-sized car. Here things were different, but he would make do. He always had.

I only hoped he would look after me. I was his "project," and I needed the work. But projects for Bob came in two sizes. He felt he knew talent and could spot it in the rough. He would polish and hone it and then let it shine. But his other projects were poor, pathetic creatures who could not get along without the help of Bob Wussler, people who couldn't take care of themselves. I was never sure which of these "projects" was me.

It wasn't long after Wussler joined Turner that the sales department came to him with half an idea. They had sponsors who were interested in a football show on TBS for Saturday night. Since TBS had no football or football shows, they had thrown together a rough format of what might work for local consumption. They had approached the right man and wrong man at the same time.

Wussler had total contempt for local programming. That was not why he was here in Atlanta. He had been hired to bring class and network style to Turner Broadcasting, and that's what he intended to do . . . at any cost. After all, this was the man who conceived "The NFL Today" and discovered Phyllis George, Brent Musburger, and Jimmy "The Greek."

So he took this four-thousand-dollar-a-week budget idea of theirs and "Wusslerized" it. He wanted not only scores and highlights of college games, but through the satellite, he added some night games in progress. Understanding the importance of gambling, he added forecasts of the Sunday pro games and predictions by the point spread. Then he threw humor and variety into the mix. He insisted on a live audience of three hundred people, and he wined and dined them as well. In short, he wanted one hour of solid entertainment for sports fans and non-sports fans. The four-thousand-a-week budget idea had mushroomed to six times that amount, not including salaries for the talent, which consisted of Bob Neal, Norm Van Brocklin, Paul Hornung, Kathy Wilson, and myself.

"Football Saturday," it was called, and we shot it live from the Fulton County Stadium Club. It was new, bold, and exciting, and anything went.

Bob Neal was the host and ringmaster. He was the only professional, and his job was to hold the show together and produce and direct from the floor. Norm Van Brocklin specialized in the pro game and caustic comments. Paul Hornung was the college expert and pro betting guru. I was the humorist and antagonist. Kathy Wilson was a school teacher. The reason for her being there was never determined.

Terry Hanson, the general manager of the now defunct Chiefs, was hired to assemble an audience of three hundred and seat them. The liquor tab alone exceeded the original budget of the show. It was a strange group of talent and personalities conjured up by the inimitable Robert Wussler. All of us had one thing in common: we needed the work.

Bob Neal was an enthusiastic announcer trying to get established in sports. His first broadcasting job was covering a pumpkin festival in Illinois. I had worked his first football game with him in 1972. He was likable and friendly, and he truly enjoyed sports. He was one of the few announcers who actually cared for athletes. He was one of the very few announcers whom players liked.

Norm Van Brocklin had been fired by the Falcons after the 1974 season. He had retired to his pecan farm in Social Circle, Georgia, but his obsession for the game had never diminished. His reputation for what some termed lunacy had prevented him from rejoining it. Too proud to accept an assistant coaching job, he farmed his pecans and fretted. His volatile disposition and contempt for the media excluded him from broadcasting. In 1979, Norm had had a stroke that required brain surgery.

No one is sure whether it was the brain surgery or turning fifty, but something had mellowed the Dutchman, and he accepted a job as *assistant* coach at Georgia Tech in 1979. Then to the total disbelief of anyone who had known him, he took the TV job on "Football Saturday."

"Football Saturday" premiered in the fall of 1980. We had a loose, rough format for every show, but it was never concrete. It changed from minute to minute and week to week. So did the time slot. One week we would air it from 9:00 to 10:00 p.m. The next week it would start at 8:00. This changing time slot would have killed most shows, but not "Football Saturday." It only added to the irreverence of the show. Nothing was rehearsed or written. It was completely off the wall and off the top of our heads.

The first three or four weeks we had trouble getting an audience. After that, we were the toughest ticket in town. Waiting lists were five and six weeks. It is truly amazing how you can gather a crowd with free food and drinks. What's more we were having fun. Although we never took a drink until after the show, the audience always thought we were loaded.

Kathy Wilson, Wussler's attempt at another Phyllis George, was axed after six shows. Squeezed for air time by four larger egos, she never had a chance. But otherwise the chemistry worked. Bob Neal was strangely at ease being nervous, and we were always putting him under pressure. If we were running late on a segment, we continued right on. It was Turner's network, so we could do anything we wanted. Sometimes the show lasted an hour. Other times it would be an hour and a half.

At first the Dutchman was hesitant and suspicious, still distrustful of the media. But little by little he loosened up and relaxed to such an extent that many people felt he should have had brain surgery earlier in life. He became a nice person. He was even laughing and joking with me, a man he had labeled a communist and hadn't spoken to in more than eleven years.

We were building a cult following. People were planning their weekend around our show. We finished the season as Turner's second best rated program. Only "Atlanta Live Wrestling" drew a larger viewing audience.

33

By the spring of 1981, I was once again in a financial bind. I could have gotten a job, I suppose, but I was still having too much fun. Instead, I decided to do some creative financing. I took a thirty-five thousand dollar second mortgage on our home and went right on enjoying myself.

"Football Saturday" was back, and it was bigger and better than ever. With the growth of the cable industry, our ratings were constantly higher, but the show was still losing money.

Bob, Norm, and I were all making seventeen hundred a week, and Paul was being paid four thousand plus expenses. This disparity brought me into negotiations with Wussler.

"Seventeen hundred was what I was making last year," I argued.

"Yes, and that's what you'll be paid again," he said.

"Aw, come on, Bob, make it twenty-five hundred. I need the money."

"Seventeen hundred is the figure," he said as he waved me out of his office with the hand that held his unlit cigar.

After one year of doing this show, the Dutchman was fully relaxed and enjoying himself. It had taken him fifty-five years to rid himself of his obsession for this sport, but he was finally freed. Super Bowl XVI may have been a contributing factor in the changes in the Dutchman. He had gone to Pontiac, Michigan, to interview 49er coach Bill Walsh and Cincinnati coach Forrest Gregg. Gregg was receptive to the request, but Walsh denied him. The Dutchman may have interpreted this rebuff as the game of football turning its back on a Hall of Fame player.

Either way, Norm's attitude changed radically. He now enjoyed laughing at the game he had once revered.

The once legendary media-hater had joined it. Not only that, he was now packaging his pecans and was selling them commercially. With an ego now balanced, Dutch finally entered the real world. It actually became him.

But some things never change, and Paul Hornung is one of the constants. The four thousand a week was only "walk around" money to him. He had always done well in business, whatever he did, and his life continued on as one big scholarship. The happy-go-lucky Golden Boy went right on in his boyish fashion, and the fun we had after the show is still talked about in Atlanta today.

Everything was going well with "Football Saturday" as Wussler continued to expand it. Furman Bisher and Pepper Rogers were now making regular appearances, and special guests were dropping by as favors to Wussler. Fred Dryer and Lindsey Nelson came by, along with other former players and personalities. In fact, a potential problem was that Paul, Norm, and I were getting less camera time. I voiced my concern to Wussler, and he casually dispelled this notion with, "Less is more, Alex; less is more."

Then late in the season a real problem developed. Wussler called me in to discuss his new brainstorm.

"Alex, we're going to establish a Special Teams Player of the Year Award. Since you were the first Special Teams Captain, we're going to name it after you. This year's winner is Hank Bauer of the Chargers. We want you to fly to San Diego on Wednesday, shoot some footage of him at practice and in his home and be back by Friday."

"That's a good idea," I said.

"I know," he answered.

"I'll do it for two thousand dollars."

"No, no, Alex, it's part of your job," he answered.

"Come on, Bob, that's four thousand travel miles and three days of my time. Pay me something."

"It's part of your job, Alex."

"Give me a thousand then, I need the money," I pleaded. "I'm not going to do it for nothing."

"Then you're fired," he said coolly.

"O.K., I'm fired then," I said resolutely. I stormed out of his office and headed for the nearest bar. I spent the next seven hours drinking tequila, cursing Wussler, and feeling very sorry for myself.

Terry Hanson and Bob Neal spent their next three hours pouring drinks into Wussler trying to get him to soften his stance.

"He's an Appalachian," they argued. "He's stubborn and proud. Give him five hundred to cover his pride."

"Not a dime," said Wussler. "It's part of his job."

"Then cancel the award," they pleaded. "We've only got three more shows."

Then reason prevailed over obstinacy, he cancelled the award.

The next morning a call came through from Wussler. "Alex," he said, "can you stop by my office this morning?"

"Yes," I answered.

"I'll see you when you get here."

I was hung over and surly as I entered his office and took a seat. Wussler, as usual, was cool and composed. His feathers never ruffled.

"Alex, we've decided to cancel the Hank Bauer piece, so I guess you're *not* fired."

"All right," I said hastily, "but let's get something straight. I've already proved I'll work cheaply, but I'm not for *sale*. You can rent me or lease me, but you can't *own* me. Is that clear?" He leaned back in his chair and lit his cigar as I stormed out of his office and violently slammed the door. I obviously had left him shaking in his shoes.

Later Hanson told me that Wussler called his office and spoke but eight words: "Alex is rehired, but he's such an ass."

Everyone who worked on "Football Saturday" was certain the show would go on forever. It was informative, entertaining, and immensely popular. But cable was growing and Wussler was thinking and Turner was ambitious. Later that spring, the NCAA took bids for a two-year prime-time football package. Turner nearly doubled the nearest competitor's bid and was awarded the games. It was cable's first football package.

The NCAA had final approval of announcers. Bob Neal was

nominated to do the play-by-play and Paul Hornung the color. The NCAA approved Neal but balked at the choice of Hornung. They stated rather undiplomatically that Paul's reputation was not good for college football. They refused to give their approval.

Once again, someone was looking out for Paul. He took exception to this denunciation and sued the NCAA for defamation of character. He won the judgment and was awarded three and a half million dollars.

Norm went back to his pecan farm in Social Circle. He died of a heart attack less than a year later.

Once again, I was unemployed.

34

So here I was nearly forty-five years old, putting on weight, losing energy, broke, second mortgaged, no job, and no prospects of one. Nevertheless, I was planning a trip to Wyoming to the Cheyenne Frontier Days. I had become a fool for rodeo.

I was about to head out to Country Lee Cummings' place in Rockmart, and I knew what to expect because Country Lee gets into the same state whenever we go anywhere.

"Journey proud," he calls it, his term for the condition he finds himself in every time he leaves home. Lee doesn't leave Rockmart often, and when he does, he gets so excited the night before the trip that he can't sleep. So he stays awake all that night, and the first night he arrives he drinks too many cold beers, meets too many people, and stays up all that night, too. Then he's so ashamed of himself for being human that he does penance by being Will Rogers for the remainder of the trip.

"People just expect more of me than they do of you," he tells me, and he means it. I really don't know why I travel with him. Maybe it's because he's the best *man* I know and the best friend a man will ever find.

I first met Lee at the Peachtree Town Apartments in the spring of 1967. A customary party was in progress, and I and my entourage were going from door to door when I saw this tall slender figure walking in my direction. He wore boots and jeans and a cowboy belt and shirt. He had long hair, for the time, which would probably be considered short today. His posture was perfect.

"Look at that hippie," I boasted. "I ought to whip his ass."

He walked straight up to me and looked me dead in the eye.

"You're Alex Hawkins," he said, "And I've been wanting to meet you. I'm Lee Cummings from Rockmart, Georgia," he said as he offered his hand. I did not accept it.

"I ain't no hippie, but if you're thinking about whipping my ass, then we'd better get after it right now. On the other hand," he continued, "I've got some cold beer in the truck. If you'd like, you can join me."

His hand was still extended so I took it. "I've been outclassed, haven't I?" I said meekly.

"Badly," he answered, and we smiled, shook hands and headed for his truck.

Lee was born in Rockmart in 1935. He's the youngest of four children born unto Clo and David Lawrence Cummings, better known as "Punch." Punch was born in Rockmart and grew up in the Great Depression days with a "Depression" mentality. "Waste not, want not," was his motto, and he both lived by it and reared his children accordingly. "Before you throw anything away, keep it seven years," he told them, "and when the seven years are up, keep it another seven."

The Depression hit hard in this northwest Georgia town, and jobs were where you found them. Even with hard work and frugality, it was tough getting by. Punch, like most men of that time, never attended college. After high school he found work with the railroad in Chester, South Carolina, where he married Clo. After six years, the Depression deepened and he was laid off.

With the money he had saved he returned to Rockmart and opened a furniture store. Watching every penny, he then opened a pool room, then a shoe shop, then a clothing store, grocery store, dry cleaners, and more furniture stores in neighboring towns. Then he farmed and bought real estate.

At six-one, 240 pounds, and with the nickname "Punch," he collected every debt. The times had made him hard, but he was more than fair, and he reared his children in his likeness. Punch had been raised by his brothers, giving him a deep respect for family and community. This, also, he passed on to his children. Punch had not attended college, but he was dead set that his children would.

His three oldest children went off to college, graduated, married and returned to Rockmart. And then there was Lee. Some people just mature faster than others. Some people know early in life what they want and who they are, and they go after it. Lee was not one of these people. He played football in high school and graduated in the lower half of his class. Fifteen minutes after graduation, he set out for Leaksville, North Carolina, to sell women's shoes.

He enrolled at Jacksonville State in the fall of 1953. He played football and partied for a year and was asked not to return in the fall. Instead, he joined the Army and volunteered for the paratroopers. Ironically, he was asked to jump out of the first airplane he ever boarded. After two years of service football and jumping out of planes, he enrolled at West Georgia. His visit there ended when he headed for Florida to lifeguard at Silver Springs.

Next, he hitchhiked to Alaska where he worked as a surveyor. He returned to West Georgia in the fall and stayed there long enough to finish the football season. Once again, he was not invited back, so he returned to Rockmart to face Punch. He worked in one of the furniture stores by day and went to night school in the evenings.

He enrolled at the University of Georgia in the spring of '58, but grew restless again and headed out . . . hitchhiking to Nova Scotia. He got as far as our nation's capital, where he stopped to say hello to legendary Congressman Carl Vinson. Vinson took a shine to Lee and talked him into staying on as a member of his staff.

Then he was back at Georgia for the spring term of '59 and, when summer came, it was on to Texas and Mexico just to see what was happening down there. That fall he was back at Georgia when his yearning for football was rekindled. He cornered head coach Wally Butts and talked him into a tryout. The six-one 160-pound safetyman and running back not only made the team but was good enough to play on the 9-1 Bulldog team that also won the Orange Bowl.

Out of eligibility, Lee spent the next two years hunting and fishing and attending just enough classes to stay in school. He spent one summer in Hawaii as a construction worker and the next in Clovis, New Mexico, farming wheat and maize. He rode his thumb wherever he went.

There just wasn't very much Lee couldn't or wouldn't do. But he was having some problems pleasing the increasingly impatient Punch. When asked what Lee was going to be when he finally graduated, Punch declared, "An old man."

Finally, in 1962, Lee graduated from Georgia and returned to Rockmart. He ran one of the furniture stores and took care of the rental property. It had taken Lee nine years and four colleges to graduate, two years of service and nearly thirty years of life to mature, but he finally convinced Punch that he was "responsible."

Lee took a run-down cinder-block-and-concrete dairy barn, sheetrocked it, slapped on a tin roof, and called it home. It was referred to as the "bunkhouse."

The first stall was turned into a kitchen and bathroom. The next stall was his living room and bedroom. The next stall was a bedroom with a sign that read "The Hawk's Nest." On the other side of that stall was another bedroom with a sign that read "Mr. Davees' Suite." And the last remaining stall was the poolroom.

The bunkhouse was located in the middle of a pasture. The winter nights are cold in the bunkhouse since the lone fireplace in Lee's bedroom provides the only heat. I've had my last drink of bourbon, from the night before, freeze in the glass on the concrete floor.

The summer days are not much more comfortable. There are no trees to shade the house and only two large fans to cool it. It is year-round Spartan living in the bunkhouse, so maybe it's not surprising that Lee has never dated steady, gotten engaged, or married. Jeramiah Johnson's wife would have left him for less.

There is *absolutely* nothing new in the bunkhouse. Lee furnished it with old or broken things that somebody else had given up on. He didn't give up on anything, especially clothes. His wardrobe consisted of two sport coats (God knows how old), a dozen pairs of jeans and western shirts (which he purchased wholesale), and two pairs of cowboy boots a friend had thrown away. He's never owned a pair of dress slacks, and he still has the dress shoes he graduated in from high school. Suffice it to say, he is no slave to fashion.

He claims to be neither a redneck nor a good ole boy. Instead he refers to himself as a gentleman. The difference, he claims, is a redneck is cheap and a gentleman is conservative. If that's true, Lee gives a new dimension to the word conservative. He does not throw away the outside leaves of lettuce, and he washes his paper plates. The last movie he paid to see was the original screening of *Gone With The Wind*.

Lee was slow settling down, and even then it wasn't easy. He's got a streak of mischief in him, and he can be a bad little boy if he'll let himself. He's more than a little human, and he has to resist temptation every now and then. In fact, he could be downright sorry. But he made his decision when he returned to Rockmart. There aren't many secrets in a town of three thousand, and everything you do gets talked about.

Lee has been a lot of places and seen a lot of things, but he finally decided who he was and what was important to him. And Clo and Punch's genes and values finally tipped the scales. His love of family and community was too strong to ignore, and he had too much pride and self-respect to run from it. So he settled down in Rockmart and, like Punch, turned family, work, and community service into a religion. Little by little he became the best *Lee Cummings* he could be.

There are two things I admire about small town people. One is that they can do things, and the other is that they will. And if Lee tells you he'll do something, you can consider it done. He's got the persistence of a spider and the work habits of an ant. You can leave your billfold with him, and you couldn't get him to lie with a loaded gun. He's thoughtful, considerate, polite, and painfully punctual. He doesn't have an enemy and he's well known in the Southeast. If he doesn't know *you*, he'll know someone who does.

He's Clancey of *The Man From Snowy River*, Gregory Peck in *To Kill A Mockingbird*, Jimmy Stewart in *It's A Wonderful Life*, and Ben Johnson in *The Last Picture Show*. He's the man his friends would like to be, but either won't or can't.

But he's got one weakness, and I'd like to point it out. He likes young women. By young, I don't mean fourteen or fifteen, but when they reach college age, look out! They're fair game! The reason he gives for his preference for younger women is simply that "their skin fits." He dated on Georgia's college campuses until he was close to fifty.

Basically, Lee's a cowboy—independent, headstrong, and proud. He was even a real rodeo cowboy until a bull named Cherry Bomb damn near killed him. From then on he was a spectator, and he got me interested in rodeo in 1975. We've been going to them ever since.

35

Although football had been such a big part of my life for so many years, I was no longer in love with it. After the collapse of the World Football League, it was never quite the same. The loyalty between teams and cities was disappearing. It was all about money. But turning my back on football created a void in my weekend life, and when Country Lee took me to my first rodeo, I fell head over heels in love with it.

All rodeos are different, and this was just a local event outside of Rockmart, but I liked everything I saw. To begin with, the price of the ticket is affordable. But it was much more than that; I noticed the neatness and politeness of the audience as they arrived in their trucks, their attention to one another as they took their seats in the grandstands, the patriotism and sincerity of the opening ceremony, the obedience and respect of the children as they covered their hearts with their straw cowboy hats at the sound of the National Anthem, the absence of booing and drinking in the stands, and the dignity and humility of the contestants, whether they've failed or succeeded. Everything about it is Americana, and what makes it so special is that it is man against *animal*.

Then, too, there's the determined look on the barrel racers' eyes as they enter the arena; the fear and confidence in the eyes of a bull rider as he pulls down his hat just before the gate opens; the daring and talent of the clowns as they rescue a fallen rider; the exquisite balance of a bronc rider trying to make that eight seconds; the timing and strength of the steer wrestler as he races against the clock; and the accuracy and quickness of the calf roper and the skill and training of his horse. Yes sir, these men are athletes, and, no, Bo don't know rodeo.

The contestants are not the big men you see in other sports. The average cowboy stands five-eight and weighs 150 pounds. He contracts with no one, and the average salary for a PRCA cowboy is under ten thousand dollars a year. He doesn't arrive on a chartered plane, but drives his own truck, maybe sharing it with another cowboy to defray expenses. They may travel as much as eighty thousand miles a year.

He doesn't stay in fine hotels; instead, he sleeps in the cheapest motels available, often sharing the room with three to four other cowboys. His training table and pregame meal is a hot dog or hamburger stand. He doesn't have a trainer, so he acts as his own. He doesn't get paid if he doesn't win, and excuses don't count.

He puts up his own money for a chance to make the ride, and nothing is refunded if he doesn't. It's on to the next rodeo and try it again. He may make four rodeos in as many days in four different states. It's rope, ride, and drive and rope, ride, and drive. "On down the road," as they put it, and likely as not, his expenses will exceed his prize money, and he's right back where he started.

So why does he do it? Because he's free, independent, and proud, and he believes in himself. It just becomes a way of life. Cowboys are like that, and I guess that's why I'm so fond of Country Lee.

I never will forget our first trip to the rodeo extravaganza supreme, the Houston Livestock Show and Rodeo—in 1976. We went to Houston at the insistence of Mr. Davees. He said we'd never seen anything like it, and he was right. Most rodeos are four-day affairs, but back then the Houston Rodeo lasted for two solid weeks. Today it goes for three weeks. It is the largest and richest rodeo in the world. Almost one quarter of a billion dollars is generated annually by this event. It dwarfs the Super Bowl and the National Democratic Convention.

It's been said that Texas is a state of mind, and Houston is the largest and most progressive city in the state. Houston will not take no for an answer. It has always been a city united. It is fifty miles inland of the Gulf of Mexico, but someone thought it would be nice to be a seaport city, so they simply channeled their way to the Gulf.

The Livestock Show and Rodeo came about in a similar fashion. Seven Texans answered a newspaper ad to organize a Fat Stock Show in Houston in 1931. A year later there were 146 entries and two thousand spectators. A few years later, the rodeo joined in and a downtown parade assembled.

From that modest beginning, it started to grow. "Go, Texan!" became the cry in the '50s, and all of Texas got behind it. These people are proud of their heritage and want it preserved, so jeans, cowboy hats, and boots are all you see in the streets of Houston during the last two weeks of February and the first week of March.

One story goes that a rancher who was grounded by fog in the Miami airport vowed he would never again go anywhere that he couldn't ride his horse home. So when rodeo time rolled around, he and three other riders left Breham, some seventy miles away, and followed the route used by the cattlemen of the 1870s on into Houston in time for the parade. That became known as the Salt Grass Trail Ride, which in turn engendered twelve more trail rides, and today over six thousand riders come from as far as Hidalgo, Texas, some 386 miles, to join the parade through downtown Houston. Go, Texan!

When Mr. Davees and Flemin Gaskins picked Country Lee and myself up at the airport, Don was wearing his 30X Beaver hat, cowboy boots, and a western-cut jacket. Lee was in boots, jeans, cowboy shirt, and a straw cowboy hat. Flemin, our driver, wore boots, jeans, hat, and a leather jacket. I was in a crew-neck sweater, green-and-brown-plaid slacks, and brown suede Gucci loafers. I wasn't dressed like anybody I saw in Houston.

"Mr. Hawkins," Don began, "we're going to have to stop by Cutter Bill's and get you properly outfitted. This is "Go, Texan!" week, and while your outfit is fashionable in Atlanta, it will not get in the Corral Club."

"What are you talking about?" I countered. "I've never counted on clothes for acceptance anywhere, and I don't plan on starting now."

"Mr. Hawkins, I understand what you're saying, but this is a little different. Everybody gets behind this "Go, Texan!" theme, and believe me when I tell you, you'll be more comfortable in boots and a hat. Just trust me; it's the right thing to do."

So we went by Cutter Bill's, and I tried on some boots and a hat, and I looked and felt like a fool.

"Mr. Davees, I'm not going to pay six hundred dollars for some boots and a hat that I'll never wear again."

"Mr. Hawkins, if it's a matter of money, I'll gladly pay for them, but it is the right thing to do."

"Mr. Davees," I insisted, "it's not a matter of money. The boots hurt my feet, and I look like an idiot in a hat. Now *you* trust *me*; I'll be all right."

All the while, Lee was looking on silently, not saying a word but now and then exchanging glances with Don.

So without changing clothes, I entered the Corral Club that evening. The Corral Club is private for members of the various committees that run the Livestock Show and Rodeo. The room itself is in the western portion of the Astrodome. It is so private that it is closed to its members forty-nine weeks out of the year.

Through its doors walk the best-looking, best-dressed men and women in Texas, if not the entire world, all of whom adorn themselves in expensive western wear. And since rodeo is all about drinking, dancing, and flirting, I couldn't resist approaching one Texas lady dressed to the nines with a, "Could I buy you a drink, Miss?"

"Where's your fuckin' boots and where's your fuckin' hat, Mister?" she snapped, then wheeled and walked away.

After a similar second encounter, I was starting to get the picture. Mr. Davees looked on with a knowing countenance. Country Lee, not fashionable but looking more like a cowboy than a cowboy, was holding court at the corner of the bar. He was surrounded by a dozen men and women who were thoroughly enjoying his company. No one seemed to care that I was an ex-pro football player and a formerly famous announcer with CBS.

Then I spotted the Yellow Rose of Texas. She was tall, thin, and handsome, and her dark eyes sparkled. Her long hair was every bit as dark and shiny as her eyes. Her leather outfit must have cost five thousand dollars and her jewelry ten times that amount. She was beautiful and regal, and she was smiling back at me. So I tried one more time: "Good evening, Miss, can I buy you a drink?"

"Where's your fuckin' boots and where's your fuckin' hat?" she inquired.

"Well, I'm not from around here," I stammered.

"That's apparent," she said as she stared down at my brown suede loafers.

"Ma'am, if you'll just have one drink with me, I'll have boots and a hat the next time you see me."

"All right," she said. "One drink, but let's go around to the back of the room. You're embarrassing to be seen with."

The next morning I was pounding on the door of Cutter Bill's a good half-hour before they opened. I bought a four-hundred-dollar pair of boots, a two-hundred-dollar hat, a six-hundred-dollar suit and three western-cut sport coats. I also purchased six shirts too western for Hopalong Cassidy, but three thousand dollars later, I was "Going Texan."

36

It's hard to single out which rodeo was the most enjoyable, but the Livestock Show of 1977 was certainly memorable. Houston's economy was booming. The city was literally growing out of its britches, and when times are good, Texans know how to spend. Mr. Davees, heavy in real estate, was reaping his share of the profits of the boom. I, with inherited money and the cash from my interest in the garbage business, was on top of my financial game.

The success of the Livestock Show and Rodeo rests squarely in the hands of some sixty different committees comprised of six thousand volunteers. Countless hours are involved, and competition develops between the various committees. While Don was not active on any of these, his girlfriend Charlie was. She was on the Chicken Committee, so that is where we found ourselves that morning . . . at the Poultry Auction.

The concept and psychology behind these auctions are elementary. They are held early in the morning before the participants are fully sober from the night before. The participants are greeted at the door by pretty little cowgirls dressed out in tight-fitting shorts, toting Bloody Marys and Brandy Milk Punches. Any sobriety achieved by five hours' sleep is quickly reversed.

The drinks never stop as the auction begins, and the bids spiral upward as the drinks go down. Now, a rich Texan bidding against another rich Texan is a sight to behold, and you've got to wonder how a man feels the next morning when he wakes up with the best turkey in Texas which cost him $52,000. Or the Grand Champion Lamb that brought $71,500. Or the Grand

Champion Barrow (a castrated male pig) that someone "stole" for only $56,000. "Red" Adair knew the feeling when he paid $150,000 for the Grand Champion Steer. But the guy who paid $62,000 for the best chicken in Texas had a lot of explaining to do to his wife.

However, after Don bought the fifth best chicken for $8,000, I felt Flemin and I should get in on the action. Flemin Gaskins had worked for the Ginther family for ten years as manager of their El Dorado Country Club. When Ginther Davis Interest was formed, he took a position with them. His title and card read, "Director of Special Services," which meant that Flemin was in charge of *whatever*.

"Flemin," I said, looking around the room and finding no other blacks, "to your knowledge, has a black man ever bid on this poultry?"

"Not to my knowledge," he answered.

"Then, on behalf of the new firm of Gaskin and Hawkins, you are authorized to bid up to four hundred dollars on the fifty-sixth and fifty-seventh turkeys in Texas."

"Yes, sir, Mr. Hawkins," he said with a smile.

"Now, keep in mind, Flemin, we don't want to *buy* these turkeys, we just want to *bid* on them."

"I understand," he said just as the auctioneer was asking, "What am I bid for the fifty-sixth and fifty-seventh best turkeys in Texas?"

"Four hundred dollars," spoke Flemin.

"Sold," said the auctioneer as I reached for Flemin's throat, but not in time to stop the sale.

"Flemin," I said, "now that we own these turkeys, we'd better do something with them. You take them home, and we'll start a turkey ranch. I know they're going to be multiplying faster than you can count, but just give me a ballpark figure on our progress from time to time."

"Yes, sir, Mr. Hawkins," he said, smiling bigger than before. "That's what we'll do with them. We'll start a turkey ranch."

It turned out that Flemin's first report was delivered a year later when Lee and I arrived for the 1978 show. When Flemin picked us up at the airport, he brought with him two cleaned Cornish hens.

"Mr. Hawkins," he said, "this is all that's left of our turkey ranch. Ain't nothing been good since Jimmy Carter took office."

We had gone to Houston early so we could ride in the downtown parade. Mr. Davees had boasted that we had never seen a parade like this one, and he was correct once again.

The parade began at 10:00 a.m. on Saturday and extended for twenty-four city blocks. It was comprised of dignitaries in pickup trucks, followed by fantastic floats, drill units, high school marching bands, and six thousand trail riders on horseback. They are known as the Salt Grass Trail Riders, and they come from all over Texas and Louisiana and gather at Memorial Park on Friday night. Imagine, six thousand mounted men, women, and children who had ridden into Houston from God knows where, some of whom had been on the trail for days and others for weeks. They had been sunned on, rained on, wind blown, and saddle chafed. They were a seedy looking group, but Don had ridden with them before, and they invited us to ride in the big parade with them the next morning.

So there we were in the back of a wagon with a group from Cat Springs, Texas, concluding their eighty-two mile drive into Houston. We were feeling very much a part of the parade, waving to the children and flirting with the ladies as we made our way down the streets of Houston. Then Don spotted a woman to his liking dressed in shorts and jogging shoes, and motioned for her to come aboard.

She very appreciatively obliged, and Don showed us *his* courting style. He pointed out buildings, historical places, gave her the history of the parade, and was otherwise very attentive to her. She was from Wisconsin, and it was her first rodeo. She had never been to Houston, but she had heard it was a "happening," so she lit out on her own to see for herself.

Some fifty cowboys trailed our wagon, riding four abreast. I first noticed this particular cowboy when he moved up from the fifth trail position to the fourth. Then to the third and then to the second. The next thing I knew he was riding alongside us with a friendly impish grin. He was all cowboy, talking with a smile and a twinkle in his eyes. He was exceptionally friendly though he never spoke a word.

Don found him so accommodating he asked if his date could ride with him for awhile. He cordially made room for her on his saddle.

As we drew nearer to the park, I noticed that our cowboy had retreated to the second position behind our wagon. Then to the third, and then the fourth, until finally he was bringing up the rear as we entered the park. Suddenly, he changed directions and galloped off with the "new" cowgirl hanging onto him with one hand and waving his cowboy hat in the other.

Mr. Davees looked on with open mouth, then collected himself and spoke: "Mr. Hawkins, let that be a lesson to us. Never give a woman an alternate means of transportation home."

While the Live Stock Show goes on for three weeks, the rodeo itself lasts but nine days. It is held in the Astrodome, and each night over forty thousand spectators are in attendance. General admission tickets sell for as little as five dollars a night, but the much sought after box seats go for as much as $1,700. Naturally, Don had a box, and we had more than enough tickets.

Each night at intermission of the rodeo, one of the top names in country and western music gives a concert. The three of us were in the upstairs Corral Club just before going to our box for the Charlie Pride show when Lee spotted a cowgirl standing at the bar. She was sucking on a long-neck Lone Star when Lee approached her about joining us for the concert.

She was a big woman, full shouldered and hipped, wearing well worn jeans tucked inside her boots. Her hat was black and creased down the front and back in a bull rider's fashion. Her skin did fit, but there was a lot of it. She was bigger than Lee. She finished off her beer, ordered a thirty-two ounce draft, and we started for our seats. It was evident she was a dirt-road sport.

We had an inside box, so we had to interrupt some patrons to get to our seats. The lights were still on and we were sliding past them when, for no particular reason that I saw, "our guest" unloaded the thirty-two ounce beer, point blank, in the face of a standing patron. The recipient nearly drowned, and about two dozen people in nearby seats were drenched by the spray. Now with both hands freed, "our guest" cocked her right arm, looking for a clean knockout, but it was intercepted by Lee before it could be landed.

The marshalls came running, and a real scene was averted only when Don produced the Harris County Deputy Constable's badge that stayed pinned inside his wallet. "Our guest" turned out to be the Southwest Motorcycle Champion two years running.

We elected to forego the rest of the concert out of consideration for the wet, nervous patrons who surrounded us.

We were back in Houston in 1980, but the mood of our group was noticeably changed. The Texas economy was still strong, but Mr. Davees was experiencing some unpleasantness. A real problem had developed at Ginther-Davis Interest.

It seems that a major Texas bank had reneged on a construction loan, so Don had no choice but to file suit against the bank—which he did, to the tune of one hundred fifty million dollars. He hired a law firm and paid them six figures cash in advance, to carry the suit through the appeal and the Supreme Court.

The magnitude and impact of a such a lawsuit prevented any further real estate activities, so Don prepared to close his offices and settled in for the fight against a billion dollar bank. With two years of law school and a totally brilliant mind, he began his study of lenders' liability law.

37

Of course, by this point in time my own financial situation had completely deteriorated, but I still refused to go to work. I couldn't stand the thought of having a boss or going to work five days a week, fifty weeks out of the year. That routine was just not for me; that was for civilians.

Also, the rodeo bug had bitten me badly, and playing cowboy is a hard habit to break. So when Lee called me in the summer of 1981 and told me to pack my bags for the Cheyenne Frontier Days, it was hard to say no.

I tried to explain that I just couldn't afford the trip, but Lee went on to tell me why I could.

"Listen," he said, "we've figured this whole trip out. There are five of us going, six counting you, and it's only going to cost three hundred and sixty-eight dollars apiece. We've figured it down to the penny . . . gas, oil, tickets, food, the works."

"Lee," I interrupted, "are you telling me we can drive three thousand miles, go to the rodeo, stay gone for six days on $368?"

"To the penny," he answered.

"Where are we going to stay?" I asked.

"That's the good part," he answered. "We've got a brand-new camper. Three people can sleep in the camper, one in the truck and two on the ground in sleeping bags. I'm telling you we've worked it out to the penny, and you're going."

"All right," I relented. "When do we leave?"

"We'll meet at the bunkhouse at seven o'clock on Tuesday."

I'd been to too many rodeos with these "Rock Martians" to

doubt their thrift. They did travel fast, light, and economically. I'd gone to the Montgomery rodeo with them earlier that spring. Seven of us slept in a single room at the Holiday Inn. Three were in the bed, one on the couch, two on the floor, and Lee, "journey proud," stayed up all night. If any crowd could make this trip for $368, they could.

All five were real cowboys, and the spring and summer weekends were devoted to rodeo. None of the five owned a wristwatch or a credit card or carried a checkbook. They never cared what time it was, and when the money in their jeans was gone, they went home.

I had never gone anywhere that it didn't cost me a hundred dollars a day, so on Tuesday, July 14, I cashed a six-hundred-dollar check, took off my watch, put away my credit cards, and headed for the bunkhouse.

At 7:05 three of us settled into our seats around a table in the back of the camper, and Lee and two others rode up front. Lee was navigating with a twenty-seven-year-old Rand-McNally Road Atlas. At the Houston rodeos I had been playing cowboy, but heading for Cheyenne I was *living* cowboy.

Those of us in the camper opened cold beers and played Go Fishing. The game ended shortly after midnight, and we went to sleep in an upright position at the card table. Lee and the boys up front were moving "on down the road." The sun was coming up in Paducah, Kentucky, when we stopped to cook breakfast. Lee, with no sleep now for two nights, did the cooking and then took the wheel, headed northwest for St. Louis and Kansas City.

We stopped, cooked dinner, and showered at a KOA campground in Henderson, Nebraska. I naturally assumed we would spend the night there, but these were cowboys. They loaded back up and rolled "on down the road."

When we arrived in Cheyenne at six-thirty Thursday morning, Lee had finally fallen asleep for an hour and a half. Financially, we were right on budget. Other than for gas and oil, nobody had spent a dollar.

Since the rodeo didn't start until Saturday, we secured tickets to the Charlie Daniels concert on Friday night and the Gatlin Brothers on Saturday. We also booked a single room with one small double bed at the Stagecoach Motel for Thursday, Friday, and Saturday. These expenses had not been budgeted, but every-one except Lee had brought along a few extra dollars in case of an emergency. Lee, hardheaded and tightfisted, had not, so on Friday he cut back to one meal a day.

We spent the next two days sightseeing. We toured the state capitol, the museum, and the Union Pacific railroad station. We drove over to Laramie and Medicine Bow State Park. Other than the Mayflower Bar and Hitching Post, we were doing very little for the local economy.

The Cheyenne Frontier Days Rodeo took place on Saturday and Sunday. Nothing like the extravaganza that takes place in Houston, this is an old-fashioned, sure enough rodeo. It is to rodeo what the Masters' is to golf and the Kentucky Derby is to horse racing. It earns the title "the granddaddy of 'em all."

We left Cheyenne about seven o'clock on Sunday evening and started our "limp" back home on our southern route. Everyone else was down to one meal a day, and Lee wasn't eating at all.

I was dog tired when we hit Denver and offered to pay for a room for the night. I wanted to see the desert in daylight. I was out-voted five to one as we continued "on down the road."

We played Crazy Eights through Colorado Springs, Pueblo, and Trinidad. I hadn't slept in a bed in nearly a week, and I was rodeoed out. I fell asleep at the card table about midnight.

The sun was already up when I awoke in Amarillo. The Red River was dry when we crossed it. I don't remember ever feeling that bad. It was hot in the camper, well into the eighties, and my tongue felt like it was wearing a sweater. The temperature rose into the middle-nineties as we pushed through Wichita Falls.

It was one hundred and four degrees when we rolled into Dallas, and the camper was a furnace. I felt like Paul Newman when they put him in the hotbox in *Cool Hand Luke*. I had been joggled about for twenty-four hours by the time we stopped to shower in Marshall, Texas. I knew how those chickens must have felt in the back of a truck on a Mexican dirt road. I was beginning to realize that I was too old to be a cowboy.

The cold beers didn't help as we hammered on through Shreveport, Louisiana, and Jackson, Mississippi. I prayed for a swift, painless death as we approached Birmingham, Alabama. I offered the boys my car and my first-born child if they would let me off in Atlanta, but they sprinted on home to Rockmart. They had to be at work in an hour or so.

By the time we reached the bunkhouse, we had been gone six days, driven thirty-four hundred miles, passed through seventeen different states, and Lee still had a dollar bill and some change.

38

The 1982 Houston Livestock and Rodeo had been somewhat anticlimactic. Oh, we had our share of fun, but Houston's economy was starting to slow and Mr. Davees, now in the third year of his lawsuit and reclusion, was not quite the same. Our post-parade luncheon was moved from Maxim's, a five-star restaurant, to Sam's, a Mexican restaurant on Richman.

Money will not make you happy, but lack of money will damn sure make you miserable. The bills were piling up, and by late spring I missed payment on my first and second mortgage. I was broke and needed a job, but the unfortunate truth was I still didn't want to look for work. Football was the only thing I actually knew, and I was now indifferent to even that. Being a middle-aged, out-of-work cowboy is tougher than you think. I was at last up against it.

I had successfully postponed growing up longer than most people. I had run the streets and bars as long and as hard as anyone I knew. I had avoided responsibility and commitment for over forty-five years, but I was at the end of my rope.

So I turned to what so many ex-jocks turn to. I opened a restaurant and bar. It had worked for Jack Dempsey, Stan Musial, John Unitas, Gino Marchetti, and many other athletes. People want to be around celebrities, and as far as I knew, I was still one of those. Sure, I had been out of the game for fourteen years, but the public still knew of me from my broadcasting days. "Build it and they will come" was my thought at the time, I suppose.

I knew a man who ran a successful steak and hamburger

place in Cobb County and was interested in opening another restaurant. He was a friend of some friends of mine, and they vouched for his honesty and work habits. I'd been involved in three previous partnerships and all three had worked out fine. So we got together and decided to go for it.

Carey Lee Dunn was his name and he ran a place on Highway 41. It was more of a truck stop than a restaurant. It only seated about twenty people, but with his limited menu of steaks and burgers and the revenue from his juke box, pinball, and video machines, he did fairly well. Carey wanted to do better than "fairly well," and he figured with my name and following and his restaurant expertise, we couldn't miss.

Carey was from Jackson, Georgia, just south of Atlanta. It's a rough, rural area where they turn off the lights at night football games so the locals can fight. Atlantans laughingly refer to Jackson as the redneck capital of the state. The differences between "rednecks" and "good ole boys" are too numerous to go into, but I figured Carey for a "good ole boy." I didn't know him that well, but he could cook a great hamburger and steak, and I needed a future.

We started looking for a location that would serve our purposes and spent several weeks looking around Atlanta for the right spot. To Carey this meant the place with the lowest rent and overhead. His place on Highway 41 was small and grimy, the roof leaked, but it did have a low overhead. One cook, one waitress, and one bartender. On slow nights, he worked it himself.

When word got back to Mr. Hunt of what I was doing, he went berserk.

"Goddamn you, Hawkins, are you ever going to learn? The fatality rate in that business is better than ninety percent. It's high time you went to work, but why that business? You and that fucking Davees are driving me crazy. Davees is sitting on his ass down in Houston when he should be here in Atlanta. Both of you can get rich in the next ten years, but not by suing banks or cooking hamburgers. Get you a real estate license and sell my Six Flags property."

And the truth was, Atlanta had recovered from the slump of the middle-seventies, and the real estate market was booming.

The city was stretching out in all directions, but mainly to the north. Carey and I were looking everywhere for that low-overhead structure, but it was nowhere to be found.

In June we stumbled onto a place in Marietta, just twenty-two miles northwest of Atlanta. Marietta, the county seat of Cobb County, at that time had a population of thirty-five thousand. It was a beautiful, sleepy little town somewhat behind the times, but it was growing. Some considered it a town with a real future. Two of Atlanta's most successful restaurant operators were of this persuasion. Between them they owned and operated a dozen of the most successful restaurants in the city of Atlanta. Surely they knew something others didn't know.

Both had opened places beside the railroad tracks just off the Marietta town square. In between the two places sat the crown jewel of the city, the old historic Kennesaw House.

The Kennesaw House was built in 1855. In 1862, Colonel James J. Andrews and twenty-three Federal soldiers were guests there when they planned the Great Train Robbery. It was head-quarters for General William Sherman during the burning of Atlanta. Sherman, so fond of the area, left eighty homes and buildings unburned. The Kennesaw House, one of the spared, was Marietta's most beloved structure.

It was a charming three-story brick building recently restored. The former hotel had been transformed into a restaurant with kitchen and dining rooms on all three floors. The cost of the renovation went well into seven figures. The Kennesaw House was available after the corporation which owned the restaurant went broke in less than a year. They were the Smith House people, who had run a successful restaurant in Dahlonega for almost one hundred years.

The Kennesaw House was but one of seven historical build-ings being restored by developer Harrison Merrill. But it was his centerpiece and showcase, and it was vital to him that the Kennesaw House be successful.

The Kennesaw House was everything we had not been look-ing for. It covered twenty-two thousand square feet, seated eight hundred people, and the rent was six thousand dollars a month. The insurance was twelve hundred, and the utilities ran three thousand more. Not only was it twenty-two miles from Atlanta;

it was five miles from I-75 and just three miles from Carey's own restaurant. There was short chance of my Buckhead friends coming out because of the strict drinking and driving laws that were rigorously enforced in Cobb County at the time. There were eight other restaurants within a quarter of a mile, not counting the numerous fast food outlets.

Still, I could not get the place out of my mind. It was charming, elegant and warm, and so terribly historic. The floors were eight-inch heart of pine, and the windows went clear to the ceiling. It had a wonderful fireplace, and fifty-two trains passed by daily. The streets outside were brick, and a wrought iron fence separated it from the railroad tracks. And while I didn't know a soul in Marietta and knew absolutely nothing about the restaurant business, I had to have this place. I had fallen in love with the *building*. Being the passionate ex-interior designer that I was, I wanted to *decorate* it!

We continued our search for a smaller, less expensive location throughout the remainder of June. But after seeing the Kennesaw House, nothing else would do, so late in the month we visited Harrison Merrill at his home in Marietta. His "estate" on Church Street was impressive. It was a 167-year-old antebellum home on six acres of lawn with two lighted tennis courts and an olympic-size pool. It had a pool house, of course, and six bedrooms. Harrison was a bachelor, a handsome young man in his mid-thirties who looked even younger. Carey and I had our lawyer with us. Harrison represented himself. It was strange talking with this man who was obviously so successful at such a young age. He was polite, but serious when it came to business. I had met my first "yuppie."

He and our lawyer were negotiating a lease for the first floor of the Kennesaw House, feeling certain nobody would be interested in the remaining two floors. From the sound of their voices, the negotiations were heated. I couldn't be sure because I had no idea what they were talking about, so I wandered through his house checking out the furnishings. Their discussions were still going on when I left for a beer.

I had full faith in our lawyer and full faith in Carey. I had no other choice; I needed to be on somebody's payroll even if it was mine. They must have had faith in me because when I returned, the first floor of the Kennesaw House was ours.

Carey took me by his bank, and they loaned me ten thousand dollars to finance my half of the partnership. The best we could figure, Carey put up four thousand and six thousand dollars worth of used kitchen equipment. That's what I was told. I never looked at the books. That was Carey's job, along with running the restaurant. My job was to decorate, promote, and handle public relations. The Atlanta newspapers labeled me the "Toots Shor of Marietta."

39

Carey's lawyer incorporated us under an existing corporation of his that was now dormant. Carey's accountant set up the books, and Carey's friends, who were handy with hammers, paint brushes, and saws, started re-renovating the place.

It was a "turn-key" operation as the Smith House people had closed in a hurry and left everything in place. We had knives, forks, spoons, plates, glasses, coffee cups, pepper, and matches. There were enough tables and chairs to seat eight hundred. Unfortunately, most of the tables were heavy pine, twelve feet long, and seated ten people. We cut them in half to seat four to six. Nothing was spent on labor. These were Carey's friends, and he traded their help off against free food and drinks. The same was true of the lawyer and accountant. Carey was thrifty . . . that's for sure.

While Carey set up the kitchen and assembled a staff, I was rummaging around the building selecting already framed pictures and miscellaneous antiques which were scattered throughout three floors. I had a sign painted to hang from the corner of the building. It read *Alex Hawkins at the Kennesaw House,* "We're on the right side of the tracks." I thought that was clever.

I had business cards printed up with the same information, and a map from Buckhead to our place was diagrammed on the back. I thought that was clever, too. I hung ferns in the windows and put plants throughout the rest of the building. I designed paper place mats with the history of the building. Over Carey's resistance, I insisted on cloth napkins. Our color was *green* . . . the color of money!

I was interviewed by the local newspapers and radio stations and arranged coverage in the Atlanta papers as well. I met the Mayor of Marietta and the City Manager. I spoke to the Kiwanis, Rotary, J.C.'s, and all the animal groups — the Lions, Moose, and Elks Clubs. A big-time celebrity had joined them, and I wanted them to know it. Opening night was Monday, July 14th. Headlines in the business section of the weekly *Cobb Extra* read: "Kennesaw House Opens!"

> The Kennesaw House reopened as a restaurant Monday night, but without much fanfare.
>
> "I had some people over to find out what we had forgotten," said the new operator, Carey Lee Dunn. Among the missing items was salt, but some seasoning was found by Tuesday when the restaurant's first lunch was offered.
>
> "We opened quietly. We hope no one was disappointed. Our frying machine wasn't working and we didn't have steaks until Tuesday night. We don't want to get more people than we can handle. Once things are under control," Dunn said, "we'll think about spreading the word."
>
> A staff of fifteen people is already on board and Dunn expects he'll need eight more after the business grows.

Actually, opening night had been rather hectic. We had an overflow crowd, but you always do when you give away drinks. In addition to a large local turnout, Bob Wussler and a crowd from Turner Broadcasting came up along with Jeff Van Note and several other Falcon players. Mr. Hunt was in attendance, along with many of my Buckhead friends.

Wussler tried to buy champagne, but we didn't have any. We didn't have steaks either, but we did have plenty of hamburgers. The hood over the grill hadn't been cleaned, and the smoke ran some people out of the bar area, but all in all, I was pleased.

Being a New Yorker, Wussler was concerned over the fact that we didn't have a coat closet.

Mr. Hunt was a little more direct.

"Hawkins, this is a beautiful place. It's a shame it's not in Buckhead. These people up here don't eat out or drink on the weekdays, and on weekends they go into Atlanta. It's too damn far to drive for your Buckhead friends, and look at those two police cars in your parking lot. The Cobb County cops are the worst in the country about drinking and driving."

But I looked around me at a full house of laughing, drinking people having a good time and thought there's nothing prettier than a crowded bar.

As we started into the day-to-day operation of the Kennesaw House, Carey and I agreed that it would be a family-like arrangement. His wife was a flight attendant, but when she wasn't flying she would do her part. His son was helping run his old business on Highway 41.

Carey divided his time between his old place and the Kennesaw House. He did all the buying, banking, and book work. I was in charge of the bar. We hired a nighttime bartender, but I tended the cash register and bar until six in the afternoon.

Every morning Libby and I arrived at nine o'clock. She swept the floors, cleaned the restrooms, and helped train the waitresses. They were all college girls who were home for the summer placating their parents by having a job. None of them had previous experience. I set up the bar, carried ice, and sliced lemons, limes, and celery that no one ever asked for. *Nobody* drank at lunch in Marietta except Charlie.

Charlie was the son of a prominent family in Marietta — OM's, as they were referred to (old Marietta money). For years Charlie had been losing his battle with the bottle. He worked awhile as a bartender, but never for any duration. He had even been discharged from Lockheed. Lockheed is a company of nine thousand employees — three thousand in the bathroom smoking and drinking, three thousand being laid off, and three thousand building airplanes.

Every morning Charlie would drink a beer, then go to his mother's house and pick up his daily fifty-dollar allowance check. He would then join me at the bar and drink lunch. He was my only regular customer. He would spend his two-hour lunch trying to talk me into hiring him as a bartender. Since he *was* my bar business, I found this self-defeating.

The locals were most supportive and tried to be helpful, but it just wasn't working out. The courthouse workers gave us their lunch business for a day or two, but they only got a forty-five minute break. It was a seven-minute walk to our building, and by the time Libby seated forty or fifty people, all arriving at the same time, they only had about ten minutes to eat and get back. Adding to the problem was the fact that all we had on our handwritten menu was a half-pound hamburger and a ribeye steak. We lost the courthouse business the first week.

Then we got the jury business, but the same problems prevailed. We lost them in the second week.

I was busy negotiating with the Rotary Club for their Monday luncheons. They had eighty to a hundred active members, but they had hard-line demands. First, they wanted to see if we were going to stay in business. Next, they wanted coffee, tea, a different meal each week, and a dessert. They needed a private room and a place to store their banners, podium, and microphone. They all had to be served at once at a price under five dollars a plate. They told me they would let me know by September.

Each day was the same. Get the ice, slice the fruit, lay out the bar and talk to Charlie. Business was not good nor getting any better. I watched people come in, look, and walk about. Some would stay, but many were leaving—little old ladies wanting a salad instead of a half-pound hamburger with greasy French fries, country people a little bit intimidated by the elegance of the place, and people who just wanted to look and share the history of the building.

The second week of August, I took Carey aside. "We've got to expand the menu. We've got to add something new." Three days later he added a foot-long hot dog and a nacho. My faith in Carey Lee wavered.

We were undercapitalized and losing money fast. Business was not picking up, and Carey was anxious. I never looked at the checkbook or made a deposit, but I knew by Carey's impatience something was wrong. He was disappointed in "my popularity" as he had counted on making money from the outset. I wasn't a draw anymore, not in Marietta. I was disappointed myself.

From 9:00 a.m. until midnight, we were there. Not many people joined us. Our attitudes changed toward one another. In Carey's eyes, I was a dumb, washed-up ex-jock and celebrity—"the dog that won't hunt." In my eyes, Carey was a low-rent redneck who could only run a truck stop for Lockheed workers. He almost fired a cook for cleaning the grill. Grease from the deep-fat fryer covered the floors. You could slide across the kitchen, and it was a *large* kitchen. Words were exchanged.

On August 18 we had *bitter* words. Carey stormed out the door screaming something about closing the place. He had abandoned the building. On August 19 I received a call from our accountant. Carey was only talking to me through him. Carey was demanding that I pay him $6,649.75, plus half the money in the cigarette machine and half of the remaining cigarettes, for his share of the business.

Well, I couldn't have done that had I wanted to; we were already late on our August rent. We had been so hurried to go into business we had not stipulated a buyout plan of any kind. Hell, we hadn't been in business but thirty-five days. I couldn't imagine how we had gone through all that money. Not knowing what to do, I turned the matter over to my lawyer and braced myself for the weekend business, which hadn't been bad. Usually we took in around three thousand dollars. I had the locks changed on the doors and prepared to carry on.

I looked forward to Sundays. After spending sixteen or seventeen hours in the restaurant from Monday through Saturday, it was a relief to have a day off. We closed on Sunday, but we still had to be there for four or five hours to get caught up on things we couldn't get around to on weekdays.

Monday morning at 8:00 a.m. I got a call from our part-time bookkeeper. She told me I'd better hurry on out there

ALEX HAWKINS

because there had been a break-in. When I arrived at the
Kennesaw House, I found a note from Carey. It read:

> Alex,
>   I picked up some of my assets . . . Sorry it had to be
> done this way. I will send you an inventory and let you
> know how much you owe me. Call my attorney if you
> have any questions.
>
> Carey

Missing were the books, one microwave oven, six bar
stools, one flat grill, half of the beer, liquor and meat, eight
burners from the charbroiler, and *all* the cigarettes and the
machine.

I called our accountant and he rushed over to take a
complete inventory. The replacement cost totaled $5,353.75.

Sometime Sunday night Carey and a helper had entered
the restaurant through the basement door, which I had
forgotten to change. I could understand him taking the
meat and booze. I could forgive him for the cigarette
machine and even the bar stools. But taking the burners
from the charbroiler, which were of no value to him, was
downright malicious. That was redneck.

40

Any half-thinking businessman would have cut his losses right there. Not me, not Alex Hawkins. I had never really been successful in the business world, but I had never had a *loser*. It was not in my makeup to accept a loss.

There was no evidence that the Kennesaw House could possibly make it. With so many restaurants in the area, even the two Atlanta restaurateurs were losing money on either side of me. The restaurants and bars that circled the square were constantly waging food and drink wars. Buy-a-meal-and-get-one-free deals were everywhere. Two-for-one drinks had given way to three-for-one.

But how I loved that building. And while the Smith House people will tell you that it hadn't been kind to anyone since Sherman, I wouldn't let it go. I had put it off long enough. It was time I became responsible, so I committed. But then came brain damage.

I called Charlie.

"Charlie, I'll hire you right now if you'll let me borrow your truck." While Charlie was getting there, I had located new burners and a flat grill. I drove to Atlanta, loaded the truck, hired an electrician, and was open for lunch. Charlie became the new bartender.

Monday was our slowest day of the week. If it happened to rain, you wouldn't get a handful of people. This day I was glad it rained. At twelve o'clock sharp, a courier hand-delivered an envelope to me. Carey was suing *me* for fraud.

Upon leaving, the first courier almost ran into the second

courier who was there delivering papers from the C & S Bank. They were garnishing Carey's wages for default on a $29,000 note.

He hadn't been gone five minutes when in walked a man from the state liquor board. He notified me that Carey had cancelled our liquor license. I wasn't a resident of Cobb County, so the license had been registered in Carey's name.

I borrowed some money from a friend of mine, called my younger brother Jimmy, a resident of Cobb County, and headed downtown to apply for another license. We were fingerprinted and filled out application forms for the city, state, and revenue department. We scurried from building to building and returned to Marietta before five o'clock. I was two thousand dollars lighter, but I was still in business.

I borrowed another ten thousand, got caught up on the rent, formed a new corporation, signed a new lease with the landlord, and cleaned up the kitchen, and then Libby and I put our heads together and tried to expand the menu. Due to the unavailability of equipment and the layout of the kitchen, it was not all that easy. We added a chef's salad, a soup of the day, some quiche, and desserts.

There is a difference between a cook and a fry cook. Carey, paying minimum wages, had hired fry cooks. Hamburgers and steaks were all they could handle, so Libby did the rest.

Charlie was my new daytime bartender. I knew he was going to be drinking, so I put him on the honor system. He kept his own count, but I charged him a dollar a drink. He remained my best customer.

Now free of this responsibility, I was ready to solicit new business. I visited Southern Tech, Kennesaw College, and Life Chiropractic College with discounts for students. I started calling my Buckhead friends, but the blue lights in my parking lot kept them away in droves. I managed another couple of newspaper interviews and was on local radio shows.

Business picked up a little, but then came the roaches. The Kennesaw House had been shut down for over six months, and without extermination it was a glorious breeding ground for pests and vermin. Roaches were everywhere, crawling along the walls, across tables and up customers' legs. Women do not care for roaches. It could have been worse, I suppose, if they had been snakes.

I called an exterminator and he came out and sprayed the basement and the first floor. The spray didn't kill the varments; it only made them faster. Our young waitresses were screaming aloud when they spotted one, and there were thousands of them. After three days, they made peace with us and disappeared.

Libby and I were working seventeen hours a day. She was helping the cooks and waitresses, and I was meeting, greeting, and seating the few people who were stopping by. Before and after lunch, I was dealing with whiskey, beer, wine, meat and produce salesmen. After that came the advertising peddlers from radio, newspapers, magazines, and coupon companies. All of whom had the answer to my problems. "You've got to let the people know you're here."

"Oh, yeah, well how did the people who filled this place on opening night find out that we were giving away free drinks? Where did they go?" Everybody had the answer but me.

Many of our would-be customers were coming in, admiring the place, glancing at the menu, and leaving. I knew it wasn't our prices; they were very reasonable. I concluded that the menu had to be further expanded, but we didn't know how. We added an omelet!

As the days wore on, Libby was wearing out. We were arriving at 9:00 a.m. and not getting out of there until two or three in the morning six days a week. She had to look after our house, too, so she started going home after the dinner "crowd" left, which was never later than nine o'clock in Marietta.

I started losing weight from work and worry. I was now under two hundred pounds. There wasn't a day that something didn't go wrong. Our air conditioning went down on the two hottest days in August. One of our two walk-in coolers broke, and several hundred dollars worth of meat spoiled. Try finding an electrician at nine o'clock at night. And where do you keep meat when you can't? I needed a manager who "knew," but I couldn't afford one. I borrowed another ten thousand.

Then the daytime cook disappeared, and the night cook had to work both shifts. I put out the word I was looking for a cook and a manager, but this time they had to know what they were doing. My weight continued to fall. Libby was starting to look gaunt. Every day was the same; only the problems changed. I was a meeter, greeter, buyer, and problem solver.

"Mr. Hawkins, Mr. Hawkins, we're out of toilet paper in the men's room."

"Then put some in there," I ordered.

"Mr. Hawkins, Mr. Hawkins, there's a light out in the ladies' room."

"Then change the bulb."

"Oh, okay," they would reply. They were nice, sweet school-girls, but I thought if I heard one more "Mr. Hawkins," I'd go out of my mind. Why did they have to be told? God, how I hated responsibility.

But I didn't have to worry about that for long. Labor Day came and they all went back to school, leaving me with only three waitresses. I lucked up on two good ones who agreed to work both days and nights. Our bar business was so bad I only needed one cocktail waitress, and I finally talked the Tall Lady into coming with us.

The Tall Lady was an artist whose studio sat right on the square behind us. She painted during the day and sometimes waitressed at night. She was good and she was fast, and she allegedly carried a following. She was tall (over six feet) and lean, she had long black hair that hung down her back. She was interesting and intelligent and honest to the core. She was exot-ically handsome and animalistically sexual. I had been trying to hire her since I opened.

That was our weekday staff, and on weekends we had friends help out. Libby and my daughter, Elizabeth, would act as wait-resses. I became the busboy. It was pure madness, but I was stubborn and proud and determined to make this place go. We were losing money every day and our fate was clearly sealed, but somehow I could not see it. I loved that building blindly, and besides, I hadn't quite finished decorating it. I borrowed some more.

Every day I would sit at the bar and look out over the railroad tracks. I've always loved trains and we had fifty-two a day. But, a train can make you lonely when the only person with you is Charlie. Charlie was, without question, the most optimistic person I've ever known. Although our meager business remained the same, Charlie imagined it was growing.

"Just give it time," he would say. "The word is getting out that we're here." It didn't bother Charlie that he wasn't making money on tips. He had his fifty-dollar-a-day allowance, and at two dollars and ten cents an hour, he was breaking even on his drinks.

Then on Friday after Labor Day, it happened. It was raining that day and we had served only two lunches, half of our normal trade. I was sitting at my desk with my face in my hands praying when in the door came a well-dressed, elderly man.

I think I should point out that I am not normally a religious person. I only pray when I'm in trouble or need help, both of which applied at the time. I was praying for guidance and/or a person who would give me fifty thousand dollars for my lease on the Kennesaw House.

"Alex," he began, "I've heard you need help. I'm Chef White. You may not remember me, but I knew you during the old days on Peachtree Street. I heard you were having trouble, and I'm here to take care of you. I was the chef at the Lion's Head. I built that business and I'm going to do the same for you."

He handed me a typed resume. There must have been forty restaurants and hotels where he had worked, and I was familiar with many of them. He was well qualified, but then I noticed his residence and age. He lived in Fayetteville, some fifty miles south of Marietta, and he was sixty-eight years old. I let that slide.

"You're obviously over-qualified," I told him, "but I don't know if I can afford you."

"We'll talk about that later," he said. "Let me see the kitchen."

He wandered around in the kitchen for awhile, taking notes, and finally he turned to me.

"There are a couple of things I'm going to need," he said, "but they're not going to cost much. Now here are my rules. You stay out of the kitchen," he said firmly. "I'm the boss here. You spend your time building up the bar business. That's where you've always been comfortable, and that's where you belong. Now get out of here and let me get started."

I smiled, shook his hand, and headed for the bar to confer with Charlie. It was time to launch an offensive. It was time for the Kennesaw House to make its move. We finally had a leader. "Chef White" was here.

41

Charlie was working on his fourth drink when I joined him. "Charlie," I said, "what can we do to build up the bar business?"

"I don't know," he answered. "I'm drinking as much as I can."

"That's not the answer," I said. "We need some women in here. From now on, all women's drinks are one dollar. Now, what else can we do?"

"Well," said Charlie, "the people in Marietta hate Howard Cosell. Why don't we rent a big screen and microphones, turn off the sound on Monday Night Football, and you do the commentary. That way nobody can fire you."

Charlie was a genius! Not only did I think it would work, I would also have a pulpit to preach from. I could get Bob Neal and Skip Caray to do the play-by-play, and I could drink and say anything I wanted. It was totally my show!

"How much will it cost us?" I asked.

"You can rent a big screen for about a hundred a night, and the amplifier, mixer, speakers, and two microphones will cost about the same. You can rent the sound system right down the road from here."

The idea was too perfect not to act on. We could have Monday Night Football live in Marietta. I jumped in the car and rushed to the rental store. Charlie was right. The whole thing could be done for two hundred dollars.

When I returned to the Kennesaw House, it was buzzing. Chef White was in charge. He had hired a new daytime cook and a salad girl. He had already fired our old meat and produce suppliers and was meeting with the new ones. They were his old friends he had always dealt with. Large orders were being placed. I didn't disturb him. He knew what he was doing. This man meant business.

Besides, I didn't have time to question him. I had fliers to print up notifying the city that Monday Night Football was coming to the Kennesaw House.

When Libby and I arrived Saturday morning, Chef White, the salad girl, and the new cook were already busy. The new cook, dressed out in a white uniform with a tall white chef's hat, was already at work. Chef White was barking orders and they were dancing to his beat. The new cook looked and acted like Don Knotts anyway, but especially the way he jumped and skittered under Chef White's command.

Chef White wore a white shirt and slacks covered by a white apron. He had a white towel across his left shoulder and carried two large knives about two feet long. They were razor sharp, shiny, and vicious. He was a very direct man and he took us aside.

"I am a chef," he announced, "not a cook. That moron in the kitchen is a cook, *if* I can teach him to boil water. I *do not* cook; I teach, taste, and instruct. The only things I cook are the sauces and soups, and these are *never* to be tampered with. Not by you or any imbecile that might work in the kitchen. Cooks are a dime a dozen, and we might go through that many before we find the right ones. I orchestrate in the kitchen, and before long you'll think I am a conductor. A symphony can only function with one conductor and that is me. I'm changing the menu rather slowly. Tonight we're adding fried shrimp, chicken teriyaki, chicken moutarde, chicken parmesan, and my famous London Broil on French bread with Chef White sauce. When those lame brains in the kitchen learn these, we'll go on from there."

I looked at Libby and she looked at me. She seemed satisfied.

"What are we charging for these items?" I asked.

"The prices range from $5.95 to $12.25," he said. "They've all been costed out and they're accurate. When our business grows, we'll gradually increase the price, but this will do for now. I've built up dozens of businesses this way."

"What do you have planned for our lunch menu?" I asked.

"That will have to wait until Monday," he answered. "But, we'll add chicken salad, shrimp salad, *my* special soups, and a smaller portion of *my* famous London Broil. Don't worry about that. Inside of a month, everybody in the city will be eating London Broil."

"What's all this going to cost me?" I asked.

"You didn't have any of the right seasonings, staples, or meats, so to take advantage of quantity discounts, the initial orders will run about five thousand dollars. That might sound high, but it's really not bad for starting up fresh."

"Okay," I said reluctantly, "but what kind of salary do you command?"

"I don't even want to discuss that right now. I've come here to help *you*," he said. "We'll talk about that later."

"But I want to have some idea," I pleaded.

"Pay me whatever you can afford," he replied. "It's not that important."

And with that, towel across his shoulder and knives in his hand, he disappeared into the kitchen.

The man was heaven sent, an angel with brass knuckles. I was walking on clouds with a man with white wings. My prayers had been answered. I was not going to be defeated. I was going to own a *real restaurant*.

I stayed at home all day Sunday watching the opening day of professional football, familiarizing myself with what was happening in the NFL. There was a lot going on. There were three new head coaches in the league, including Mike Ditka with the Bears. A new five-year television contract had been signed for 2.1 *billion* dollars. But perhaps the biggest news was the Oakland Raiders had won an anti-trust case against the NFL and moved the franchise to Los Angeles.

On Monday the phone stayed busy with inquiries as to our Monday Night Football party. The word was out on the square, and the Lockheed crowd was most interested—and interesting. We had a full house that evening as Bob Neal had joined me for the play-by-play. Financially it was a bonanza for our slowest night of the week. We took in almost two thousand dollars. A local semi-pro team vowed to make the Kennesaw House its hangout. A good time was had by nearly all. Two of our customers were arrested for drunken driving on their way home.

Chef White had stayed until halftime. He peeked at the big screen from behind the bar. He seemed ill at ease outside of the kitchen. But in the kitchen he was a commander. The cooks and waiters were toeing the mark.

A friend of ours had done our new menu in calligraphy. And as forecasted, the London Broil was being well received. The lunch business was picking up, but the evenings were still slow. Libby and I were still getting there at 9:00 a.m. but Chef White was always there ahead of us. Libby was working twelve hours a day, and I was working fifteen to seventeen. There was always something to do, and I wasn't quite finished decorating the place.

With Chef White running the kitchen, I had a little more leisure time between lunch and dinner. I visited Kennesaw Mountain and a Civil War cemetery. I walked around the square and got to meet some of the local merchants. They were friendly and apologetic about not having visited me. They were small-town people who didn't go out often. Sometimes I wouldn't go anywhere. I'd just sit outside and stare at the beautiful and historic Kennesaw House and watch the trains go by. God, that was a beautiful building.

Skip Caray came up for the second Monday Night Football game, and it too was standing room only. Drinking and working with Skip is more fun than just working with him. It was another big night, and we again took in over two thousand dollars. But at the conclusion of the Monday Night game, the NFL Players' Association, wanting its share of the 2.1 billion dollar television contract, called a strike. I was disturbed by the greed of these players. They were costing *me* my biggest night of the week.

I was paying Chef White $400 a week and getting my money's worth. He was always there before we were in the mornings, and we had to run him off at night. At almost seventy years old, driving over a hundred miles a day to and from work was killing him, but he kept right on at it.

Still try as he would, things were no better. Business remained slow. Chef White was a high-strung man with a hair-trigger temper. The slightest thing would send him into a rage. He had already quit three or four times, but Libby always talked him into coming back. He'd storm out of the restaurant with his white towel and knives, go to the nearest pay phone, and call Libby to tell her he'd quit. She would always charm him back with "Come on, Cheffie Pooh; you know we can't do without you." He would always return.

He had already tried to fire the two new waiters and the Tall Lady, but Libby had smoothed that out too. He finally did manage to run off the daytime cook, and that is when I got the worst idea thus far. I asked my son, Steele, to drop out of school and come to work with me. Steele was in school at the University of South Carolina and was working nights in a hotel restaurant. He is one of the hardest working young men you'll ever find *when* you keep him busy. When he's not covered up with work, he gets bored, and, well . . . he's a lot like his father.

Steele and I were not always close. I was a typical macho, jock father when he was growing up. I was hard and strict with him and demanded a lot. I guess I wanted him to be the superstar athlete that I never was. I would come screaming out of the stands at little league games, criticizing him loudly for anything less than a perfect performance. My Great Santini routine, of course, prompted him to withdraw from first basketball, then wrestling, and finally football. Baseball was his love, so he put up with my tirades.

Steele was the foot soldier. I was the general and he never talked back. Throughout high school I never asked his opinion or ever had a talk with him. His job was to listen. You would have thought this kind of relationship would turn him against me and make him bitter. It didn't, as he was content to despise me silently.

The night he graduated from high school, we had our first talk.

"Boy," I said, "you don't like me and I don't like you. Now there is no rule that says a father has to like his son or a son has to like his father. But I think we ought to get to know each other well enough to know why. I have no plans for the next eight days. Why don't we get in the car in the morning and drive to the Keys and fish. If at any time you've had enough of me, I'll fly you back home." He thought for a moment, looked at me oddly, and said, "All right." That night Libby prayed.

The next morning we loaded up the Checker Marathon, but before we left the carport, I asked him one last question. "Do you want this to be one of those bullshit father and son trips, or do you want to be totally honest?"

Once again he thought for a second before he said, "Totally honest."

"Then reach in that cooler in the back and crack us a beer."

We started south on I-75 and we didn't say a word to one another until we crossed over into Florida. Then we started laughing and talking and we haven't stopped yet. We returned to Atlanta ten days later, best friends.

The first thing I discovered on that trip was that Steele was a great deal smarter than I and just about as goofy. And that's why I thought it would be a good idea for him to come learn to cook under Chef White at the Kennesaw House. When I called him and made the suggestion, he once again thought for a minute and said, "I'll do it."

42

So Steele uprooted, withdrew from college, and moved back home with us. Elizabeth was coming up in the evenings after her regular job. Libby was working twelve hours in the restaurant along with taking care of the house. Now with Steele with us, it was time to circle the wagons. The battle was now being waged by the family unit.

The week that Carey had come back and "reclaimed his share of the assets," I had called some friends of mine who owned Spartan Foods and asked for their assistance and advice. They operated the Hardee's restaurants in seven states. If anyone knew what to do with the Kennesaw House, they would.

One of the partners flew down the next day to look the place over. He spent the day looking around the square at our competition. Then he flew back to Spartanburg and sent back his two best operational advisers. After considerable study, they concluded that the Kennesaw House was of no value to anyone and further advised me to get out of my lease if at all possible. Not wanting to ruin my perfect record, I ignored their advice.

Instead, I sent Steele to Spartanburg for a three-day cram course on operating a restaurant. He then returned and resumed his studies under Chef White. The two of them got along well. Chef White was stern and gruff, but Steele was used to that. He thought he was funny.

Then we got the Rotary Club's Monday lunch business, but not without concessions. They guaranteed us seventy-five lunches, but we had to give them the main dining room, and everyone had to be served at the same time. Ice tea, one meat, two vegetables, a salad, and dessert for under five dollars. The five dollars also included the tip.

There wasn't much profit in it, and it was a real headache, so I turned it over to Libby. My figuring was that the exposure would be great, and they would all come back with their wives for evening meals. And, I was right . . . one of them did!

In early October my landlord informed me that he had leased the third floor of the Kennesaw House. The new tenant was opening a magic bar.

The Smith House had gone under, I was going under, and now some nitwit was going to open a *magic bar!* Had everyone gone crazy?

The name of the new place was Merlin's, and the new owner was as naive as I was. He honestly believed that Marietta would support a magic bar—a place where people sat around and watched magicians perform. And he started putting his money where his mouth was. He brought in a team of carpenters, electricians, and painters and began yet another restoration of the Kennesaw House. I started *actively* looking for a buyer.

But then came the roaches again. When Merlin's exterminated the third floor, I discovered where my roaches had gone. But this time there were even more of them. So I, in turn, exterminated and drove them back upstairs. Merlin's sprayed again and sent them back down. We were playing ping pong with roaches, and it was getting expensive.

After a week or so and several thousand dollars, the game ended. The roaches were too tired of running up and down, so they either died or hid on the second floor. Either way, they were gone.

Merlin's was costing a fortune to open, but that was not my concern. I had troubles of my own. My financial picture looked bleaker by the day. It was now clear, even to me, that the Kennesaw House was nearing its end. I had to find a buyer for my failing restaurant in Marietta.

The long hours were taking their toll. My weight was down to 185 pounds, and my clothes were hanging on me. Then I discovered I had arthritis in both hips. I was worried, tired, and disagreeable. The same thing was happening to Chef White. I never saw a man try harder, but nothing seemed to work. The food was not great, but it was better than the rest of the places. The truth was, everybody on the square was losing money. The business just wasn't there. One of the Atlanta restaurateurs closed his doors and the other was getting ready to. Totally frustrated, Chef White stormed out one last time and called from the pay phone to tell us he'd quit. This time I let him. Steele was now running the kitchen . . . without pay.

For the first time in my life, I was not having fun. But the thing I missed most was people. The few new friends I had made in Marietta all went home early and seven o'clock is late there. Then I was left with Charlie and the Tall Lady. So I fired the night bartender, who wouldn't talk to anyone, and hired Charlie's best friend, David. David was a modest drinker, a good family man, and honest. But more importantly, he was someone I could talk to. Charlie always left around eight, and the Tall Lady liked to do stretching exercises. At these times, she didn't want to be disturbed.

So along about nine I'd belly up to the bar and David would pour me a bourbon, and we'd sit there and talk and listen to the trains go by. How lonely the sound of a train whistle at night in a near-empty bar. I was learning to loathe the sound I had once loved. Each clickety-clack was another nail in my heart. I was miserable.

Then out of the blue came a call from Bob Wussler.

"Alex," he spoke, "how are things in Marietta?"

"Slow," I answered. "Real slow."

"I'm sorry," he said. "I was afraid of that. Can you get away this weekend to broadcast a football game in Washington?"

"Who's playing?" I asked, not caring.

"The Players' Association is hosting an All-Star Game. Actually, they're playing two games. One in Washington on Sunday and another in Los Angeles on Monday."

"Sure," I said. "How much does it pay?"

"Fifteen hundred," he said calmly.

"Three thousand?" I countered.

"The job pays fifteen hundred. I thought maybe you needed to get away, and I know you need the money. Be there on Friday." And with that, he was gone.

Captain Outrageous was at it again. Ted Turner, with his

foresight and daring, had sensed that the appetite for pro football had not yet been quenched. He had tried to package some games with the NFL, but Pete Rozelle would not even return his calls.

But now with the strike going on, it was a new ballgame. Ed Garvey, President of the Players' Association, wanted to put on an All-Star Game to upstage the owners. Putting on a football game is no problem *if* you have the players. Neither of the three major networks would dare touch this game. Their contracts were with the owners, not the players.

Enter Ted Turner, fractious, bold, and irreverant, but locked out of the bidding. Scoffed at by the networks, not recognized by the Big Boys. Calls un-returned.

Keep in mind now, it was Turner who signed Andy Messerschmidt, baseball's first free agent, and this same dichotomous Ted Turner, who owned the Atlanta Braves and Hawks, and was the majority stockholder of Turner Broadcasting, a *non-union* company. Now he was siding with *labor*. But then, that's Ted Turner. At any rate, when Shelly Saltman, agent and packager acting on behalf of Ed Garvey, contacted Turner, through Wussler, the deal was quickly put together.

That evening I was in my office talking on the phone to a Baltimore sportswriter about the strike and the upcoming games when I was frantically interrupted by Steele. One of the convection ovens had been left open, and the heat from it had set off the sprinkler system and flooded the kitchen. Nobody knew how to get the damn thing stopped, and the water was cascading out into the main dining room.

I ran to the kitchen doors and looked in. If you don't think those sprinkler systems will put out a fire, you're real wrong. I've never seen so much water. Noah never had it so good. You couldn't see across the room. Steele and I grabbed a couple of brooms and started sweeping the water back into the kitchen and out of the dining room. The dozen or so customers looked on in total bewilderment. Finally, we found the controls and turned it off. Just another leisurely evening of pleasant dining at the Kennesaw House. I didn't know any of the people who dined there that night, but I never saw any of them again.

Nevertheless, on Friday, October 15, I was a new man. For the first time in months I was excited. I was going somewhere and doing something I knew about. On the plane ride up to Washington, nobody ran up to me in a panic with, "Mr. Hawkins, Mr. Hawkins, we're running out of gas and the wings are falling off." That was someone else's worry. I was free of responsibility. I was *free*.

It was wonderful being in a fine hotel, being with *people* again. I was happy . . . damn, I was happy! But then I noticed a change in me. I had always enjoyed having dinner in Washington. Duke Ziebert's and The Prime Rib were two of my favorite restaurants, and I ate at Ziebert's on Friday and The Prime Rib on Saturday. Both places were packed, and both meals were excellent, but I couldn't enjoy them. I found myself watching the waiters and bartenders throughout the meal. These were real restaurants. These people knew what they were doing. It made me feel like an idiot. My heroes were no longer movie stars or athletes. My new heroes were people who could run successful restaurants.

As for the "All-Star Game," well, it wasn't an All-Star Game at all. The players who did show up were, for the most part, lesser-knowns, now on strike for almost a month, needing the twenty-five hundred dollars it paid. And the real reason the game was played was to embarrass the owners and let them know that the *players* were the game and without *them,* there was no game.

Since football is a labor-intensive business, they had a point. But the owners were not about to blink. They had strike insurance and all the major stadiums tied up. More importantly, they had all three networks in their corner.

But I was working for Ted Turner, and he paid one million dollars for the two games. I knew where my bread was buttered, and just like the participating players, I, too, needed the money.

I had always sided with the owners in labor disputes, but my attitude had changed. I no longer knew many of the owners. These were not the same people who had built the game. They were Johnny-come-latelies who were profiting from it. I didn't owe them anything and they didn't owe me anything, or so I had been thinking. But now that I was forty-five years old, I was thinking differently. I was, for the first time, frantic about my future.

Under the Bert Bell Pension Plan which was started in 1959, I could take an early retirement at age forty-five. It didn't amount to much, about $300 a month, but that was only one-third of what baseball players received. In 1959 the owners were getting only $1,000,000 a year from television. Now the owners were receiving $420,000,000 a year from television alone, and our pension remained the same. There was something wrong here. This didn't seem fair. Where was my piece of the pie?

Also, I didn't have arthritis in 1959, nor did my teammates. But between the ages of forty-five and fifty, things catch up with you. Two out of three of us have permanent injuries, and there are no major medical plans for the retired. Hundreds of Jim Otto's swell our ranks, and suddenly you realize what you were being paid for—the condition of your body for the remainder of your life. That is your payback for all the applause you received as a player. But the owners controlled the press and the media, and while they were hurting their own game, they were winning the war against the players.

Well, the game was played before an unenthusiastic audience of twelve thousand. Louie Giamona returned the opening kickoff for a touchdown, but that was the only eventful moment of the day. The players were all afraid of getting hurt, so little intensity was displayed.

But Ted Turner was pleased and so was Wussler, and they were off to Los Angeles for the Monday Night Game. I flew back to Atlanta to watch it on TV. Paul Hornung did the color as, once again, Louie Giamona returned the opening kickoff for a touchdown. David, the Tall Lady, and I were the only ones watching it at the Kennesaw House bar.

43

The players' strike continued, and so did my search for a buyer. Both of us were fighting a losing battle, but I liked their chances better than mine. The players were forfeiting *their* game checks, but they in turn were costing the owners money. Nobody was winning. I was costing myself and my friends money. I had already lost $50,000, so I borrowed even more money to keep it going.

My blind, stubborn pride and determination, which had always sustained me, was now devouring me. I had nothing to sell but a lease, which I was delinquent on; my good name, which was now worth little; and good will, which had vanished with the water and roaches.

Then out of the blue came some visitors from Atlanta. They were with an advertising firm who handled the Southern Bell Yellow Pages account. They wanted Paul Hornung and me to do a television commercial right there in the Kennesaw House. They offered us $10,000 each for the spot, which would be viewed in North Carolina, South Carolina, Georgia, and Florida. It would be aired for a year starting in February.

The theme, of course, was how I had built up my business by advertising in the Yellow Pages. If that wasn't funny enough, the tag line was: "Big Winners Come On Strong With Southern Bell Yellow Pages." In addition to the $10,000 and the millions of dollars worth of free advertising, they threw in a half-page ad in the Atlanta Yellow Pages.

It was timely and perfect. Finally, I had something to sell. Surely I could get $100,000 for my name plus millions of dollars worth of publicity. It was the hook, the gizmo, the answer. Paul came down from Louisville, and we shot the commercial. The ad agency started its editing, and I started *aggressively* searching for a buyer.

Paul had been in the restaurant business himself. Before he went back he asked me this question: "Alex, when you decided to open a restaurant, why did you choose Marietta over Buckhead?"

I told him the Kennesaw House wasn't in Buckhead. He wasn't altogether satisfied with the answer, but he loaned me $15,000 before he left town.

I got on the phone and called everyone I knew in the restaurant business. Surely with all this publicity someone would be interested in buying me out. In addition, I told all the whiskey salesmen. There is no better way to get the word around than to tell a whiskey salesman, especially if you tell him it's a secret. Oddly enough, no one was interested.

Mr. Hunt was particularly outspoken and deflating.

"Hawkins, you dumb shit, that commercial ain't going to help you one bit. *Nobody* in Atlanta is going to Marietta to eat, and even fewer people are going to come from the Carolinas or Florida."

My weight was down to 180 pounds, so I lowered my asking price to $50,000.

My business remained off, but after forty days the players' strike was still on. On Halloween night I was attending Ted Turner's party when up to me walked a very excited Ted Turner.

"You're just the man I want to see. You know those players, don't you? Will they listen to you?"

"I don't know," I answered. "Listen to what?"

"I want you to call them and tell them if they'll stay out on strike I'll continue to televise their games. If they want to own their own teams, they can. I'll give them all of the gate and twenty percent of the TV money. Tell them they can hire the coaches of their choice. They can't fire them, but they can hire whoever they want. What the hell," he said, "we'll still make a hundred million dollars and we'll have a lot of fun." He then turned and disappeared into the crowd.

Later that evening, I ran into Wussler and related what Ted had said to me. "Was he kidding?" I asked.

"Ted does not kid," Wussler answered matter-of-factly.

"Should I contact someone?" I asked.

"Why not," said Wussler.

The next day I called Jeff Van Note, vice president of the Players' Association, who was in Washington in a strike strategy meeting and related Ted's proposal. Jeff said it was very interesting and he would pass this information on to Ed Garvey. Meanwhile, Ted and Wussler were in contact with Brig Owens, a former player who was now working full-time for the Players' Association. Even though Ted had lost a million dollars on each of the All-Star Games, he still wanted the action.

Brig told Ted the players would need twice as much money as before, or one million a game. Ted thought for only a moment before replying, "It takes money to finance a revolution. You've got a deal." He had learned that from Castro.

Whatever the reason, Brig never got back with Ted, and the strike ended two weeks later. But it would have been interesting to see what could have happened to the face of professional football if the players had remained on strike. Ted Turner does not kid, and cable television had arrived. The big boys were getting smaller, and a United States Football League was going to start play in March of 1983. Without the greed of Donald Trump and with the help of Ted Turner, who knows what might have happened.

Meanwhile big things were happening at the Kennesaw House. After weeks of renovation and I don't know how much money, the moment had finally arrived. Merlin's was having its grand opening. Marietta had a Magic Bar!

The owner and his wife were nice people. They had been down for dinner and drinks on a number of occasions, and they couldn't have been more friendly. Since they were only serving finger food, they felt their traffic would help our business. People would come and have dinner with us and then go upstairs and be entertained by the magicians. I could see how this could work, but I was a little envious that they would get the drink business.

They reserved a table for Libby and me up front by the stage in the main magic room. The owner and his wife were the main attraction. Their act was followed by five or six other magicians, each performing for about twenty minutes. I have always hated magicians because I've never been able to detect how they did their magic and no magician has ever shown me. These were no exceptions. It frustrates me that I can never catch them.

We stayed about two hours before going back downstairs. We had no one in the restaurant or bar. But there was a line outside waiting to get into Merlin's. It's hard to sell a drink or meal when someone is giving it away upstairs. But Merlin's had spent a tremendous amount of money reworking the third floor and promoting their place. They were entitled to their opening night. Sooner or later we would get some of their overflow.

The first week they did a nice business. Merlin's was new and unique; furthermore, it provided the only entertainment around the square. But after a week the novelty wore off and Marietta returned to normal. The dozen waitresses who worked opening night were reduced to six. The six magicians were trimmed to four.

Then some problems developed that I hadn't anticipated. Merlin's didn't open until five o'clock in the afternoon. While they didn't serve much food, there was no way to get rid of their trash except to bring it down on the elevator, through our main dining room and through our kitchen. An inconvenience to both of us and an eyesore to our dinner guests. The lease clearly stipulated that the foyer in the Kennesaw House was common area, freely accessible to both tenants. We worked it out where they brought all their trash down before five o'clock.

One other thing . . . the few people who enjoyed magic were late arrivers and late stayers. Merlin's did not close until two in the morning, and had no way of closing off our bar area or the main dining room if we wanted to leave early. I had been there long enough to know we wouldn't do ten dollars worth of business after ten o'clock. So I bought wrought iron gates to close off the open area. The gates and installation cost just under two thousand dollars.

The month of November was bad for both Merlin's and me. Every morning Steele and I were getting up at eight. Libby would have breakfast ready and Steele and I would head out in the Checker Marathon for Marietta. Libby would clean up and join us by noon.

It wasn't necessarily a bad drive, just seven miles north up I-75 to the 120 Loop and then three and a half miles to the Kennesaw House. Still, we didn't talk much because we were still tired from the night before. We didn't get out of the restaurant until after twelve, and by the time we got home and settled in, it was always two or three o'clock. We were sleeping four or five hours a night and standing on our feet all day. Steele was now working both shifts as the evening cook had run off with one of the waitresses. But it wasn't the work that was getting me; it was the hours and the worry. I had to sell that place! I couldn't stand a loser.

Then I got a call from a prospective buyer. He came up from Atlanta and had lunch. Then he came back for dinner the next evening. He owned one restaurant and was interested in buying another. My asking price was $50,000. His response was "Get Serious!" I countered with $40,000 and told him all about the Yellow Pages commercial. He told me about the same thing Mr. Hunt had, but in nicer terms.

He offered me two thousand a month, but I had to be there in the evenings and run it. Two thousand a month was less than I was losing, and I probably should have taken it, but I was proud. How come poor and proud are almost always synonymous? I turned it down. I still had that wall to decorate.

The days dragged on and the nights seemed longer. I can't explain what I was doing to myself. My weight dropped to 170. Hell, I weighed more than that in high school. Every night it was David and me and two or three customers watching the Tall Lady stretch. I just couldn't figure it out. Steele was doing a hell of a job in the kitchen. He had taken Chef White's recipes, eliminated some, and improved on the rest. The food was excellent and we never got a complaint, but it just wasn't working.

The first week in December we started getting requests for private parties, but in order to handle them we had to open on Sundays. We were now working seven days a week.

And, of course, something was always going wrong. The chimney was forty feet high and wouldn't draw the smoke out if it wasn't gradually heated. This procedure took about an hour every day. On a bitter cold Monday we lost our heat, and the Rotary had their lunch in overcoats and gloves. The walk-in coolers were forever on the blink. I practically had an electrician on retainer. The electricians, plumbers, rent, insurance, utilities, payroll, and payroll taxes were eating me alive. And then I had to buy my third liquor license of the year.

The Tall Lady was always in a good mood, though. It didn't seem to matter if she made money or not. She was always up. She got into the Yuletide spirit and ornamented the door frames and the bar with green garlands and big red bows. The place was absolutely gorgeous. I got so carried away that I went to the expense of spotlighting and finishing the wall that had been bothering me so badly. Now I was done. I had finished decorating the Kennesaw House, my personal "Little Shop of Horrors."

The Sunday before Christmas we catered a private party for my Buckhead friends. They wanted and paid for a first-class party, and we gave them one. Steele was magnificent. We borrowed a lot of fine silver and did ourselves proud. Paté, shrimp, oysters, tenderloin, and champagne, along with the usual fruits and cheeses. It was so superb even the buckhead crowd was impressed. It was our only finest hour.

Most of the guests had never been there before, and they couldn't understand why we weren't doing business. We kept the bar open for two extra hours. Then just before closing Dave Black, my old partner in the garbage business, took me aside. He was still working for Waste Management Company, which had bought us out.

"I don't want to ruin your Christmas, but do you know what each of us would be worth now if we had taken stock instead of cash?"

"I have no idea," I answered.

"Twenty-three million dollars," he said with a smile.

Suddenly Merlin's went crazy. These people had put their life's savings into a magic bar that was doomed to failure. Their place was as tacky as ours was tasteful, but they had spent a fortune on it. The husband and wife were now the only magicians, and they had cut back to three waitresses. They were desperately holding on for the same reason I was. I called it pride, but it was really stupidity.

And when things go badly, we all tend to want to blame someone else. Merlin's panicked and made another mistake. They dressed up a manikin and stationed it in the foyer just inside the front door of the historic Kennesaw House. I was livid, totally beside myself. I called the landlord and objected. He told me they were absolutely within their rights. That was the common area.

"All too common!" I screamed.

"Where is my rent?" he screamed back.

I hung up. Hard times were getting to us all.

When the manikin mysteriously disappeared, they replaced it with an even gaudier one. This one also vanished, but was later found on the railroad tracks. Then they sent a third one down, along with one of their waitresses and a cardtable and chair.

She just sat there numbly watching the door. Whenever customers entered, she rushed up and greeted them with "Welcome to Merlin's" and highjacked them into the open elevator and on upstairs. She returned moments later as if nothing had happened.

At the next arrival, she beat me to the door again, but this time I wasn't going to play tug of war. Before the elevator closed, I had thrown the manikin, table, and chair in with them. The elevator went up and did not return. I was furious and needed a drink. When I stormed up the steps to the bar, the Tall Lady was doing her stretching exercises.

"Knock that off," I ordered. One does not order the Tall Lady. She looked at me strangely, took her leg off the railing, removed her garlands and ribbons, and marched out the door. She will always be remembered as the Tall Lady who tried to ruin Christmas.

The day after Christmas we were right back at it, but this time with drugs. I had been taking Ativan, a strong tranquilizer, since early in the month. I was completely exhausted and shaking, but I was forty-five years old. Now my twenty-two-year-old son was sitting beside me, and he was shaking, too.

"Take one of these," I said as I handed Steele an Ativan. "It

271

will keep your hands from shaking."

Each day got worse. We hadn't been talking to each other very much on the drive out, but now when we hit the 120 Loop it was total silence. We exchanged knowing glances, and I understood that knotted-up feeling was in the pit of his stomach, too. The hardwood floors I had once been so fond of were killing my arthritic hips. I now despised the 120 Loop, those fifty-two trains, *and* the Kennesaw House.

Finally, what was so apparent to everyone else was clear even to me. This place was a loser. I was a loser. I had run out of time, money, bullshit, and hope. I had no more fight in me.

It was like standing on the sidelines with your team trailing 16-7, with twenty-nine seconds remaining on the clock, out of time-outs and the other team's got the ball. You're beat, mister, and that sick feeling of resignation comes with it.

But this was not a game. This was the real world, and these were real debts to real friends who had financed my folly. I had finally hit the bottom. A washed-up jock, broadcaster, and celebrity. A goddamn civilian. How was I going to live with that?

I was broke, deeply in debt, behind on the rent, insurance, and utilities. I'd lost $75,000, thirty-seven pounds, a damn good attitude, and *almost* all of my sense of humor.

Wednesday after lunch I went back in the kitchen and talked to Steele. "Son," I said, "I've got a damn good idea."

"What's that?" he said with a sarcastic smile.

"Let's close this damn place."

"Are you serious?" he asked, hoping I was.

"There's nothing left to do. Let's take what we can on Friday night and have a Grand Closing party on Saturday. We've fought the good fight and lost, and now let's salvage what we can. Don't buy any more food if we can get by without it. We'll auction off what's left on Saturday night. We should be able to take in enough to get you back in school."

I notified the ad agency that they were going to have to scrap the Yellow Pages commercial, and, oh, how I hated to forfeit that money! I called Jerry Blum at WQXI and asked him for a favor. I told him I was closing the restaurant, owed some money, couldn't pay it, but didn't want my creditors to think I was sneaking out of town. I asked for a free commercial that went something like this: "I'm Alex Hawkins at the Kennesaw House. For all you hundreds of thousands of people who have never been here, we are having a Grand Closing on Saturday, starting at 12:00 noon. Everything we've got left will be $1.00. See you then."

Jerry thought it was the funniest thing he'd ever heard of and ran the spot hourly for three days.

Saturday I dressed out in a tuxedo with a black boutineer and headed for the Kennesaw House. Steele and I laughed all the way up there. The Grand Closing started out modestly and picked up from there. Then a steady stream of people swelled to a torrent as the evening progressed. Some of the other radio stations joined in since no one had ever heard of a Grand Closing. I hate to guess how much free publicity we were given. Wussler came up with a camera crew, and I was interviewed by CNN and TBS.

Since many of my friends in Atlanta were coming for the first time, I helped direct them by renting two beacon spotlights. It may have been the biggest event that ever took place in Marietta. The mayor was there, the city manager, the chief of police, my landlord, all the other restaurant owners, and yes, even the Tall Lady.

Country Lee Cummings and six of the Rockmartians came down. Mr. Hunt was there with H. M., and I got a telegram from Mr. Davees, who was now in the fifth year of his lawsuit. I got flowers and telegrams from friends with CBS and all over the country.

The Grand Closing was far and away my biggest night ever. We took in $4,000, enough to get Steele back in school. It ended around midnight when I hugged Libby, shook hands with Steele, danced the last dance with Elizabeth, and pondered what the hell I would do next. . . .

EPILOGUE

The Kennesaw House—Since I closed the doors, it has taken down two more tenants. The scoreboard now reads: Kennesaw House 4, Visitors 0. It sits vacant and empty beside the tracks in Marietta.

Bob Wussler—Bob left Turner Broadcasting in 1990 to join Comsat Video Enterprises. He is president and CEO of this Washington-based firm and one of the most powerful and oft-quoted men in the media today.

Paul Hornung—When the $3\frac{1}{2}$ million dollar judgment against the NCAA was reversed in a higher court, Paul just shrugged and went on with his businesses. He is currently in radio, television, manufacturing, printing, real estate, night clubs, and a soybean refinery. As always, he is doing quite well.

Country Lee Cummings—He closed his dry goods store and with undisclosed assets and zero liabilities was instrumental in raising $4\frac{1}{2}$ million dollars to open the United Bank and Trust in Rockmart. In just a year and a half it has deposits of $18,000,000. He is on the board of directors of the bank, the Aragon Hospital, Polk County Chamber of Commerce and is a trustee of the Floyd College Foundation. He still does not own a suit, a credit card, a touch-tone phone, or a wife.

Mr. Davees—After favorably concluding a multi-million dollar settlement of a ten year lawsuit against the billion dollar bank, he remains single and is doing splendidly as a Houston millionaire in oil and real estate.

Mr. Hunt—After holding his Six Flags property for fifteen years, he finally sold it back to them and actually became the millionaire he always featured himself to be. Nothing much else has changed.

And I am still broke and unemployed.